RIDING SKY HIGH

RIDING SKY HIGH

A BICYCLE ADVENTURE
AROUND THE WORLD

Pierre-Yves Tremblay

Foreword by
Bernard Voyer

Skyhorse Publishing

Skyhorse Publishing books may be purchased in bulk at special discounts for sales promotion, corporate gifts, fund-raising, or educational purposes. Special editions can also be created to specifications. For details, contact the Special Sales Department, Skyhorse Publishing, 307 West 36th Street, 11th Floor, New York, NY 10018 or info@skyhorsepublishing.com.

Skyhorse® and Skyhorse Publishing® are registered trademarks of Skyhorse Publishing, Inc.®, a Delaware corporation.

Visit our website at www.skyhorsepublishing.com.

10 9 8 7 6 5 4 3 2 1

Library of Congress Cataloging-in-Publication Data is available on file.

Jacket design by Anna Christian
Front jacket photo: Thinkstock
Back jacket photo: Jean Denis Cantin

Print ISBN: 978-1-62914-799-4
Ebook ISBN: 978-1-63220-108-9

Printed in the United States of America

To Lili and Victor

"Waiting for exactly the right moment to make your move usually means inaction." —Jean Rostand

Acknowledgments

In moments of deep loneliness as well as those of intense happiness, my journal, which I scribbled in day after day, filling every inch of the page, has been my most faithful companion. Thanks to Lili, who meticulously transcribed and edited all my letters and writings and made them the basis of this book. Without her, it simply wouldn't exist. Thanks to Caroline, my sweetheart, who understood my need for challenges and faced them with me. To Victor, for being the light in the shadow. To Jean-Pierre Doré and Jean-Denis Cantin, who were my partners in this crazy dream. To François Gouin for his suggestions. To Stéphanie Wells, Jean-Marie Talbot, and André Leclerc for their objective insights. To Christian Beaulieu and Nicole Fradette for proofreading the manuscript and for their timely comments. To my Uncle Antoine, for his moral support. To France Fillion, one of my teachers, who introduced me to the joy of reading. And finally, a special "thank you" to those who welcomed me into their homes during my travels.

Translator's Note

....

August 16, 2011

Recently, I caught up with Pierre-Yves in Chicoutimi, Quebec. This is his hometown and where he ended his epic journey on Day 863—November 23, 1996. Chicoutimi is also the place where I married a local girl in 1981.

Unlike Pierre-Yves and my wife, Sylvie, I am not a "bleuet" (blueberry), an affectionate term for those who live in the Saguenay region, north of Quebec City. But as a fellow world traveler (born in Adelaide, South Australia) I know that our journey through life can take us on many an unexpected turn. Such twists of fate are so well described in this book.

Pierre-Yves is exactly as you imagine him to be: a good-humored, fairminded, go-getter who knows how to enjoy life. Looking through a shoebox containing his original journal and the letters sent home, I could see that his passion and sense of accomplishment was still a beacon of inspiration some fifteen years later.

Translating this book was quite the trip all by itself.

Enjoy the ride.

Peter Dare Mystic, Quebec

Contents

Foreword

....

Just taking off. Going around the world. It's a dream we all share. But on a bike! . . .

Besides the sheer physical effort, this epic adventure is about a person confronting himself, alone, with his bike; encountering life, its possibililities and limits; dealing with his emotions and everything that compels him to keep going, to persevere. It means exchanging glances and sharing a slice of life with people from so many different cultures. It also means overcoming the many pitfalls: too cold, too hot, too windy, too high . . . such is life on the road. Pierre-Yves had to draw deep within himself to overcome such constant challenges.

Perhaps this heartfelt account will help us understand the mysterious and irresistible passion that fuels such an adventure. The satisfaction that comes with successfully circumventing the globe is not short-lived . . . indeed, it deepens with time.

So we'll join you, Pierre-Yves. Take us along, and tell us all about it.

Bernard Voyer
Explorer

Chapter 1

....

Past
Memories
Resurface

Arrival in Paris—July 15, 1994

After an uneventful flight, our plane lands firmly on the Charles de Gaulle tarmac. Passengers unfasten their seatbelts, get up, and gather their belongings as the plane taxis toward the terminal. Having been cooped up in a cramped space for the past seven hours, they are in a hurry to leave. But, inevitably, they still have more waiting before they claim their checked luggage and clear customs.

I just sit and watch the disembarking passengers. I've got plenty of time. I'm just about to start an epic cycling trip that will take me and my traveling companions, Jean-Pierre and Jean-Denis, all the way from Paris to Hong Kong.

Weighing in at 306 pounds, our personal gear, plus bikes, make heads swivel. The customs officers are more interested in our itinerary than the contents of our luggage. After some chitchat, our passports score their first travel stamp: Charles de Gaulle, Paris, France, July 15, 1994. We exchange looks. A great adventure is about to begin.

Simply hopping on our bikes is out of the question. Each has been dismantled and carefully packed, with re-assembly requiring at least two hours' work. The downtown shuttle for the city center is already waiting. We're the first in line.

Fortunately, the driver is nowhere to be seen. With no luggage compartment on the mini-bus, it takes us ages to stash our gear . . . twenty-odd saddlebags, plus our disassembled bikes in three huge boxes! On his return, the shuttle driver, obviously annoyed by the sheer quantity of our gear—which means lots of passengers will have to wait for the next shuttle—leaves the terminal swearing under his breath.

I chat with a friendly lady in her sixties sitting next to me while Jean-Pierre and Jean-Denis keep an eye on our pile of bags. She happens to be a nun and is surely moved by the trip we're about to embark on, because she digs deep into her bag and pulls out a medal of the Virgin Mary. She hands it to me with a smile and urges me to wear it, so that Our Lady will protect me throughout my travels. "God bless you!" she adds. I mull these words over in my head. The nun gets off at the next stop, leaving me in a thoughtful state. What just happened here? A message? A warning?

The bus stops abruptly, jolting me out of my reverie. Here we are in Paris. The driver, now a little more relaxed and obviously keen to leave, helps us unload. On this particular morning (the day after Bastille Day, France's national holiday), the city seems to be sleeping in. Some city workers are dolefully cleaning up after the previous day's festivities. They look wryly at us three naive tourists, buried under an avalanche of equipment, who somehow hope to hail a cab.

For two long hours, we put up with one taxi after another passing us by. Then one wily driver finally stops for us. Any concerns about saving money have now been forgotten thanks to jet lag, lack of sleep, and the endless waiting around. He could have asked for the moon, and we would have given it to him. Soon enough, we find ourselves at Denise's apartment. She's a family friend who gave me somewhere to crash in Switzerland six years earlier. We are taking advantage of her place in Paris while she is at her parent's home in Lausanne. Denise lives in a small, back lane in the 7th Arrondissement area. As agreed, the key is under the doormat. Hardly having set foot inside, Jean-Pierre and Jean-Denis collapse onto our pile of bags and promptly fall into a deep sleep.

Sure, I'm just as tired as they are, but I can't sleep: I'm more in the mood for daydreaming and reflection.

Distant memories come flooding back to me: camping trips, Florida, the Caribbean, the French Alps, British Columbia, Germany, Switzerland, Austria, Italy, cycling tours, Canada, college, and university. I enjoyed so many glorious family vacations over the years. Ahhh . . . the pure magic of camping! After a long road trip or a day full of activities followed by a campfire feast, all six of us—Dad, Mom, François, Maryse, Bruno, and me—would pile into our small tent. I felt the warm camaraderie and family togetherness. I felt so close to those I loved the most. Thanks to these trips, I had an inkling I was moving toward some distant purpose, always learning and making new discoveries, getting closer to what's really essential. . . .

On one of these trips, when I was just six years old, I happened to make friends with a young American during a stay in Florida.

While we played baseball, he taught me some words in English. I was so proud to repeat them. I'm bilingual now! With just a few expressions, we managed to understand each other.

And how could I forget the Christmas holidays (three years in a row!) we spent in the West Indies, where steel band music filled the evenings. My mother let me stay up, alone, to listen late into the night. The joyous sounds flowing from these huge metal pans transported me, making me deliriously happy. I was fascinated, enchanted, and completely won over by this new culture and these inspired musicians. I imagined what might happen next: they invite me into their homes, as a friend. I share their meals, and they tell me about their lives as artists, about their hardships and troubles, but also of their love for this sunny, holiday music that brings them so much enjoyment.

Music . . . how many times have I woken to the sounds of music, marking the start of yet another family ski day. Two long hours on the road before daylight to reach Grand-Fonds in Quebec's Charlevoix region, where I spent most of the time carving out new ski trails in the forest's underbrush. Even at this young age, I wanted to go beyond the beaten track. The quick-and-easy path was not for me. Habit and routine, even less so. Already, my instincts were pushing me to go further.

At twelve years old, I left for two weeks in the summer to stay with a host family in British Columbia—the first trip on my own.

Despite my naiveté, I quickly realized that a few words of English do not make of me a language expert! I had to take the plunge. This immersion was my first step toward independence and self-reliance.

A little later, a trip to the French Alps organized by my mother hit me like a revelation. We arrived in the middle of a blizzard. It was a complete whiteout. In the morning, opening my curtains, I was awestruck by the immense crags and rock faces jagging aggressively toward the summit, set against a brilliant, blue sky. That day, before anyone else, I set out on this majestic terrain to tackle the trails awaiting me. Indeed, I made so many discoveries that I became the appointed guide of our group. I was practically levitating. From that moment on, my love for mountains has never stopped growing, and my desire to go always further, always higher, has become ever more deep-rooted.

At fifteen, with my friend, Patrick, I set out on my first bike tour—a 600 km (370 miles) round trip between Chicoutimi and Quebec City, via Malbaie, mountain country. Such a venture involved both planning and improvisation. For example, toward the end of our first day, we were tired, and, with twilight setting in, we still hadn't found a place to pitch our tent. The edge of a lake seemed attractive, but it was so windy, we couldn't start a fire for our supper. Famished, we knocked on a few doors until a Good Samaritan let us use his barbecue. The food was atrocious, but we were still happy to share this meal together. We knew how to go with the flow.

Next year, and again by bike of course, I undertook a 1,200 km (750 miles) trek from Chicoutimi to Montreal, by way of La Tuque. This was much to the chagrin of my mother, who found every conceivable reason to dissuade me. South of Lake Saint Jean, I rode through an area where there was just me, trees, and bears. A relentless heat wave went on for four days, hitting highs of 42°C (108°F) . . . I needed to keep exhaustion at bay. Traffic was nonexistent. Alone in the middle of this terrifying forest, I set up my tent for the night. At dawn, for the first time, I began to understand just how important self-reliance is and how much strength you can derive from it.

Five days later, I was pushing through a torrential downpour. It was the very same shower that caused the floods in the summer of 1987. Soaked to the bone, I knocked at the door of a nearby residence to ask if I could pitch my tent there. However, the proprietor wouldn't allow it—not on his property. Dejected and disappointed, I was back out into the rain. I eventually settled down in a vacant lot, away from the road. Taking shelter in my tent, I became aware of a basic truth: if I'm in a jam, it's solely up to me to get out of it.

Barely back at home, I was off again for a year-long stay in Bonn, Germany, where I was to be housed with a host family, as part of an intercultural exchange program. The first three months were extremely difficult. Not only was I in a class where I didn't understand a single word, but worse, the host father had no desire whatsoever to take in a foreign student to begin with— that was all his wife's idea. He berated me every chance he got. Meanwhile, I lived in the attic in a poorly heated room. I felt extremely isolated.

One evening, at supper, the father started yelling at me . . . in German. The family looked at me, noticeably ill-at-ease. If only I understood, maybe I could have explained, made it right somehow. All wrongs were attributed to me; I was a vulnerable target. I was under the impression that I was at my own trial. I remained stoically impassive . . . until I burst into tears. That evening, I took refuge in my room, and I cried. I felt I must get tougher and learn how not to be discouraged. I had to convince myself that there's always a solution, a happy outcome eventually.

And sure enough, just before Christmas, I moved in with some very nice people. Since their holiday vacation had already been planned, I had to take care of myself until they returned. This gave me the chance to travel through Switzerland, Austria, and Italy. I had fun, simply feeling like a kid again, as I traveled through this part of Europe. Better yet, the anguish of the last three months gradually dissipated. With a $5-a-day budget, I played the hobo, sleeping in train stations, in parks, or under the stars. Fellow vagrants adopted me. I really wanted to experience this parallel life that is uniquely theirs. I saw the fun side of this kind of adventure and not merely as a cheaper way to travel.

The rest of the school year unfolded wonderfully. I met some amazing people, and I quickly learned more German, quite beyond my expectations. I returned to Quebec with a joyful heart and a head full of adventure stories yet to be told.

But going back to school was difficult. Since I didn't finish high school in Quebec, I was accepted on probation for college. At the start of the semester, I met my chemistry professor and mentioned that I was having some difficulty following his class. He said he was not surprised and even doubted whether I could actually catch up. Now the challenge was squarely on my shoulders. As the youngest of four kids, the academic bar had been set high. François, Maryse, and Bruno always got excellent grades at school. My parents didn't pressure me, necessarily, but my studies took precedence over everything. In our home, the ones who studied were masters of their own time and free of domestic chores. Sporting achievements never super- seded good marks. I was stung by the comments of the professor, who more or less gave up on me and left me to my own fate. I vowed to prove him wrong. My studies became my top priority, and my efforts were rewarded accordingly—by the end of the semester, my grades were a full nineteen points above average.

After college, I was accepted for the engineering program at McGill University in Montreal. I doggedly applied myself to my studies while getting summer work as a tree planter on reforestation projects in the far north of Ontario. After the long months of intellectual endeavor, this physically demanding job revitalized me. Besides getting me into shape, the job helped pay for my school fees and my annual expenses. I even had enough money left over to finance yet another project—a bike ride across Canada—5,205 kilo- meters (3,200 miles) in twenty-nine days, at the rate of 180 km (110 miles) a day. I raced through as fast as I could, so I wouldn't miss the start of the school year. Looking back, all I remember is the scenery flashing by.

* * *

I had a wonderful upbringing. I traveled far and wide and had lots of fun. Now's the time to get serious: studies, diploma, work, family . . . I've always been fascinated by engineering, construction, anything mechanical. But with hardly one year gone by, I feel an increasingly persistent need to live new experiences. I am happy, apparently satisfied. Apparently, because deep within myself lurks a burning desire, stubborn and single-minded, to go beyond myself at any cost. Consciously or not, am I seeking out hardships and challenges that I have yet to live through? In my heart, I know I'm ready for another project, longer and more difficult than all the others. Asia comes to mind. Maybe by bike? Whatever the trip, it would not be like my mad dash across Canada. Cycling is a superb means of transportation if you know how to adapt to it, to master it. It leads you off the beaten path, to where people really live their lives. By bike, villages and mountains appear little by little, starting off as a few blobs of shape and color, as if you were painting your own landscape. Then there's the pure satisfaction of reaching the goal, the euphoria of getting to the mountaintop and discovering the other side. On a bike, you have the time to feel the very pulse of nature.

But cycling also means following a ribbon of asphalt that sometimes goes on forever. Some scenes are so similar, flat, and endless that you wonder if you're actually going anywhere. You lose touch with reality. You think that maybe life has forgotten you, leaving you pinned down somewhere unknown on a motionless and lost landscape. You're often face to face with the unrelenting wrath of the elements: rain, wind, heat, cold, and even snow. Biking, most of all, makes you confront your limits.

My curiosity is unabated and remains unrequited. I yearn to discover what lies beyond my sheltered world. But such an expedition contains far too many risks—I must find the right partner. I need to share the fear and know that I am not alone. I muse over the ideal candidate who would be willing to share my folly. He has to be in good physical shape, mentally tough, a winner, able to control his fears, and willing to face adversity. He has to be decisive. This description makes me smile. I'm asking so much of this person . . . can I offer the same?

I have Jean-Pierre in mind, an old school buddy from way back when and former Canadian judo champion. He, too, has a hankering to take off. Plus, his physical and mental capabilities more than make up for his lack of bicycle touring experience. And best of all, he has a lot of faith in me.

In January 1993, we make a firm decision that in the summer of 1994 we'll begin our one-year odyssey that will take us from Paris to Hong Kong. A handshake and a confident look seals the deal, which will henceforth make us inseparable partners. In June, our duo becomes a trio with Jean-Denis, also an old classmate, joining in on our adventure. Athletic and with energy to spare, he's a major asset in planning our trip.

I already know a bit about Europe, but everywhere else is uncharted territory for me. I have no real knowledge about the Paris–Hong Kong route, except that all the maps show that there is indeed a road that leads to the Far East! We'll modify our route as we go along. First stretch, roughly: France, Switzerland, Italy, Greece, Turkey, Iran, Pakistan, India, and China—via Tibet.

I must admit, I'm somewhat afraid of the unknown. I assess the risks, hoping for some sort of reassurance. I find none. When I look back on my past experiences, all the various pitfalls are the first events that spring to mind. Even so, I realize that we've already been through the conception, birthing pains, and delivery of our plan. Our project has been born—now it's time to make it happen. . . .

My fears are justified. During my cross-Canada tour, an Australian, unaccustomed to driving on the left-hand side of the road, clipped the rear-view mirror attached to my handlebars. A family friend, less fortunate, lost a leg in a similar situation. How often do drivers overtake cyclists on narrow roads, knowing full well the danger they put them in? And it's hard to imagine that drivers will improve the further we go east! I already know that our bags on both front and back wheels will result in a parachute effect, causing wind drag. The bike, with its three-hundred-pound. load, becomes a lot less maneuverable. When a truck passes me, it pushes me toward the outside, but immediately after, its suction pulls me back toward the center of the road. If I'm too closely followed by another vehicle, I can't rely on the driver's reflexes. I can only count on my own reaction time. And when one truck overtakes another, I have to be fully aware of the road width, because I know for them I'm pretty insignificant.

These are just a few of the dangers we face on the road, not to mention the political, linguistic, or religious uncertainties. In fact, there are more reasons not to go. If I believed all the stories, movies, and news, I'd be well advised to stay "in my own backyard." My determination, however, is unshakeable.

* * *

We begin to take steps to finance the project. Potential backers bombard us with questions: Are we going to write a book? Make a short film? Will we take part in information sessions on countries visited? Will we conduct regular interviews by phone? Will we be available for newspaper stories? Of course, there are no answers—we hadn't even put foot to pedal yet. 'You want a bearskin? What type of bear? We've still got to kill it. In fact, we haven't even spotted a bear yet!'

Despite this, our bikes are fully sponsored, and we're offered a reduced price on our saddlebags: a total savings of $6,000 for our group as a whole. The sale of T-shirts bearing our team image brings in a further $5,000, and the rest of the financing (about $8,000 each) comes out of our personal savings. I put a good part of my tree-planting money toward this sum.

Preparing our gear takes up an entire year. We start with assessing what type of equipment we'll need, focusing on weight, resistance, reliability, compatibility, and adaptability as well as figuring out how this will all fit together. As for clothing, I'm thinking the onion look: layers of clothing that I can easily peel off and put back on, as I need to. Then there's purchasing the necessities: mess tins; multi-fuel camp stoves; utensils; tent; sleeping bag; ground pad; medicine; first-aid kit; clothes for hot, cold, and rainy weather; footwear; road maps; waterproof bags; raincoats; tools; spare parts; and personal items. We have to know exactly how the bags are to be organized, filled, and positioned on the bikes. There's no sense in needlessly repacking our bags each day. On this issue, I've learned a lot from my previous experience.

The sheer amount (and cost!) of the vaccines required is enough to makes us feel sick. Japanese encephalitis, rabies, hepatitis A and B, cholera, diphtheria, whooping cough, tetanus, and typhoid: all this rings up to a healthy sum of $600, and that's not counting what we spend on anti-malaria pills and medical insurance.

To celebrate our departure, our friends throw us a going-away party. My equipment is all laid out in the basement. The guests are curious to see what I'm taking with me. Their questions surprise me—aren't I worried about not having enough shaving cream?! I feel privileged. Many would have liked to be in my place, minus the effort. They repeat the warnings that I've heard so often before . . . dangerous strangers . . . strange dangers . . . sure, sure. . . . But that's precisely why I'm hitting the road—to meet and interact with the unknown. To learn, to know, to experience. Everybody hears what I'm saying, but nobody really understands.

* * *

Behind the chain-link fence bordering the tarmac of Quebec City's small airport, our close friends and family gather to see us off. Caroline, Jean-Pierre's sister and my girlfriend for the past few years, smiles at me, but I know her heart is about to break. She would have rather that I stayed, but it doesn't show. She hides her pain and sorrow well. One year seems such a long time when you're just twenty-two years old. My mind is in a whirl as I peek out of the tiny porthole of the plane, now barrelling down the runway. One last, parting look at my loved ones, and already I can't wait to see them again.

Chapter 2

....

Learning As
We Go

As clueless tourists, we brave the frenzied swarm of Parisian drivers, making our way to the Champs-Élysées. In this hectic rush, where common courtesy has no place, we quickly learn to handle our loaded bikes. What a sight! And I'm not talking about seeing the Eiffel Tower. How ridiculous we must look, hoping to cross Europe and Asia, when we can barely make it through the streets of Paris.

The three of us all squat at the foot of the iconic tower for our "official" departure photo. Our bikes gleam in the sun. The equipment is so bright that it's blinding. Our bike wear has yet to absorb a single bead of sweat. We are as pure as the driven snow, still oblivious to the adventures and misadventures that lie ahead. Curious passersby ask us about our destination. The answer is short, shy, and shifty: Hong Kong. We're confident and ready to roll but, at the same time, intimidated by the enormity of the challenge ahead. Combed, clean-shaven, and with shiny, sunscreened faces, we look like young recruits marching off to war, roses in our lapels.

Glancing one last time at the Eiffel Tower as it recedes in my rearview mirror, my fears and worries rise up again. I touch the medallion the nun gave me, now dangling from the handlebars. A shiver runs through me. I'm afraid of death. I have the impression that by setting out on this crazy adventure, I'm tempting fate by taunting the Grim Reaper. I love life, even if I am a little reckless. I reassure myself yet again that Lady Luck will smile upon me. If only we could know what awaits us and stop at the edge of the abyss. When you ride, each passing vehicle is like an "abyss." I hate having to admit we are, ultimately, at the mercy of each driver we come across. But if I'm on the road right now, it's because I need to see everything and live it all. This need is just as great as my fear of death. No . . . make that greater.

We ride until dusk and then stop in a quiet, randomly chosen park, away from prying eyes. Our first campsite meal is not exactly French haute cuisine de rigueur, but a good bottle of red makes up for it.

DAY 5, and following
French countryside—July 19, 1994

Already five flat tires . . . and it's just week one. Our "miracle" inner tubes seem to have a valve defect, so we fall back on the good-old, "gut" type—less sophisticated but more reliable. My trusty odometer, the same one I used when I crossed Canada, has just given up the ghost. And since it never rains but pours, our gear has all been completely drenched. We realize much too late that we haven't sealed our waterproof bags properly! Despite the damp outcome, we find a way to laugh it off. We're hardly at the end of the world yet and certainly not at the end of our troubles. These small setbacks are easy to fix on friendly ground, but what happens if we're stuck on a mountain or in the middle of a desert?

During this first week, we start to notice all the little annoyances that bug us. We divided up the common equipment equally among the group, but each remains responsible for carrying his own personal stuff. After our first real climb, we watch Jean-Denis attend to some spring cleaning. With his head buried deep in his saddlebag, the short-fused Jean-Denis tosses out anything superfluous. Jean-Pierre follows suit, offering his coffeepot to a local farmer—sure to make his mornings a little harder to bear.

We accept and carry out these minor adjustments with good humor. Even a momentary flash of anger from one of us quickly succumbs to the stifled laughter of the others. We become more complicit. This is shaping up to be one beautiful adventure.

DAY 12
Dijon, France—July 26, 1994

My journey is in jeopardy as of today. I may have strained or even torn the lateral ligament in my right knee while playing soccer. Jean-Pierre warned me not to play, but, being pigheaded, I did it anyway. In the heat of the moment, somebody accidentally tripped me, and my knee gave way. Now I can't walk, let alone ride. Jean-Pierre, a physiotherapist by profession, deems that we must wait a few days before knowing the full consequences of this mishap.

I am lying on my bed in the youth hostel, staring at the ceiling. The only thing I can do is apply ice to my knee every half hour or so to prevent the swelling. I'm upset with myself. It was an intense game between French and Italian nationals, and I should never have joined in. I didn't cross the Atlantic to play soccer, after all. I raise my eyes heavenward. I just want a second chance. Please, dear saints and angels. . . .

DAY 17
Arbois, France—July 31, 1994

While I'm bedridden, Jean-Pierre and Jean-Denis get to play tourist under the bright sun. They visit the city, taking in relics from the past and, of course, checking out the wineries!

After a five-day layup, it's time to leave. I still can't walk, but, miraculously, the movement required to push the pedal causes me only a slight pain. But any stops verge on the agonizing. Fortunately, I have two amazing teammates who lend me a hand by dismantling my tent and loading up my bike.

DAY 18
Jura Mountains, French-Swiss border—August 1, 1994

Today is the true litmus test. We're in the valley at the foot of the Jura mountain range, which separates France and Switzerland. Barely into the first few miles, we hit a wall. Except for a few goats and some stubborn cyclists, nobody else ventures there, other than by car. We pitch camp three quarters of the way up the mountain. Still a way to go, but my knee holds up.

I follow my physiotherapist's instructions to a tee. My diligence is rewarded. The saints seem to have been listening. Phew. . . .

DAY 23
Lausanne, Switzerland—August 6, 1994

I have arrived at Denise's parents' home in Lausanne, Switzerland, and for the past four days, they have been treating us like royalty. They have a charming house just a few steps from Lake Geneva. A real paradise. I spend my days admiring the mountain peaks across the lake, dominated by the biggest of them all, Mont Blanc, which tops out at 15,770 feet. I'm now able to walk . . . in fact, I'm itching to get going. The sheer beauty of these mountains gives me the courage and inspiration to face them head on.

Today, I bought Caroline a braided bracelet at the market. I'll wear it while we cross the Nufenen Pass and send it to her afterwards. I think of her, how she accepted this separation, how she is letting me live my dream. And keeping me closer by setting me free. . . .

DAY 30
Nufenen Pass, Switzerland—August 13, 1994

After this much appreciated rest, we head back up the Rhône Valley. A narrow road leads us to the foot of Nufenen. At 8,130 feet, this road is the highest in all the Swiss Alps.

Our 3,600-foot ascent is gradually spread over eight miles or so. The road is just like Switzerland itself, impeccable. On the other hand, the road users are annoying. It's a long weekend, and buses full of sightseers inch along at tortoise speed, obliging impatient drivers to make risky attempts at overtaking them. The hairpin bends are protected from steep drops only by a low concrete wall. As the apt Swiss saying goes, "Natural selection takes care of bad drivers!"

The first three miles have us believing that the climb would be child's play. Suddenly, and as sharply as a line drawn in pencil, bare rocks replace the thick undergrowth. Without any shade or cover, we are at the mercy of the sun's dry heat. We see very clearly where we're headed . . . a little too clearly! Just an endless road rising abruptly in front of us. Our stops become more and more frequent as we need to constantly catch our breath. Our water supply is almost dry. Discouragement mounts as we spot the sharper bends ahead leading to the summit. Our odometer shows we still have four-and-a-half miles to go. The road becomes steeper and steeper, and the summit is far from being conquered. My hundred pounds of luggage seems more like two hundred. I've been climbing for more than three hours, and every push forward feels like a knife stabbing into my thighs. My legs just can't do it anymore, although my stubborn pride begs to differ as it wills them to push on.

Approaching the last bend, we're out of both water and energy. I choke up as I near the sign marking the summit: "Nufenen Pass, height 2,478 meters." Less than three weeks ago, I was laid low on a bed, unable to walk, and here I am now, on the highest pass in Switzerland, and with breathtaking views I have to say! The whitest of snow caps contrasts sharply with the bluest of skies. The air is crisp and fresh, but the intense sun continues to beat down on us. I take in a sweeping bird's-eye view of the Rhône Valley, as well as all the neighboring valleys. As if by chance, my exhaustion evaporates.

DAY 35 and after
Italy—August 18, 1994

As I cracked the eggs for our usual omelet this morning, I should have been wary of the streaks of blood in the yolks. The absence of trouble and strife, the cheerfulness, the clement weather, and the steady rhythm that we've so readily adopted has blinded me to this bloody detail. Unfortunately for us, our innards don't fail to notice. Cycling and bellyaches don't sit well together. This episode gets me thinking about the Far East.

DAY 53
Cerignola, Italy—September 5, 1994

Yesterday, a kindly Italian farming family received us with open arms to spend a relaxing night on their farm, complete with a delicious meal washed down with ample local vino. Today, after a seventy-five–mile day and a quick shower and wash in a public-park sprinkler, we can't find anywhere better to stay than in a muddy tobacco field, far away from the road. Although very humid, the night looks like it'll be warm, so we'll chance sleeping without our double tent covers. The sky is mostly clear, and I would be surprised if it rains. Our bikes are padlocked to the chain-link fence that surrounds the field, and our saddlebags are well stashed under our tents. All that's left to do is sprawl out on top of our soft and downy sleeping bags. After a hard day's ride, such a splendid bed is a real gift.

Each morning, with the rising of the sun, we've grown accustomed to hearing from our wake-up rooster, Jean-Denis, first and foremost. His running "Are you awake, yet?" commentary usually intensifies until we groggily answer him in turn. But this time, in the middle of the night no less, it's Jean-Pierre who wakes us up instead. He claims to have felt some raindrops. He installs his double cover as a precaution. We begrudgingly do the same, even if it means converting our tents into veritable saunas.

Jean-Pierre was right. The rain begins falling, and its constant pitter-patter on the tent beats like a gentle lullaby. We drop off to sleep again . . .

that is, until flashes of lightning and thunder join the party. This time, it's impossible to get some shut-eye with the thunderstorm now in full fury. Fortunately, both the tent floor and sides are waterproof. But for how long? My tent literally floats . . . it's like I'm lying on a waterbed! Jean-Pierre freaks: his is a swimming pool. He goes out into the pouring rain to try to figure out some sort of water run-off. That's when he discovers that we've been sleeping in the field's drainage channel.

The tobacco field is made up of a succession of parallel undulations on which the plants grow. The low parts of the rows serve as run-off canals that eventually join a much wider and deeper channel. This main channel is exactly where we've so cleverly pitched our tents. It's all belly laughs as Jean-Pierre plods toward my tent, both feet caked in mud, with this astute observation: "I know we're having a field day, here, but don't you think this is another great reason to ban smoking?" His tent is unusable, and he gratefully moves into mine, "a five-star resort," as he puts it. Meanwhile, Jean-Denis stacks saddlebags one atop the other, so as to sacrifice only the bottom one to the rain gods.

Consolation prize: never in my life have I seen such an extraordinary light show. As a wild succession of lightning bolts strike every other second, a kaleidoscope of electric flashes transform the night.

Albeit with two of us in a one-person tent and one semi-dry sleeping bag, we still manage to doze off again. The number of miles we've swallowed during the day makes for pretty powerful sleeping pills at night.

DAY 61
Piraeus, Greece—September 13, 1994

My odometer hits the 1,800-mile mark as we near the limits of the harbor city, Piraeus, in the South of Athens. From here, boats leave for the Cyclades, an idyllic island group set like sunlit jewels in the Aegean Sea. After cycling through twelve consecutive days where temperatures exceeded 95°F, we are ready to drop. Island living pops up at just the right time. A two-week break surrounded by open sea is just the ticket before tackling the Middle East.

Dozens of boats, all crammed with passengers, plus cars and trucks, are jammed up against each other. Total anarchy. It's complete chaos at the ticket counters as well. They're organized in such a ragtag fashion that you couldn't possibly know the right line unless you were a regular passenger. After two failed attempts and an hour-long wait under the blazing sun, we finally score three tickets to Paros. We're advised to put our bikes on board the boat and return fifteen minutes before departure. Excellent idea: it's practically impossible to bike with the congested traffic and a ridiculous number of cars per square foot.

As light-footed and hungry pedestrians, we choose a cheap little restaurant where I ate a few years earlier. Mercifully, we have two hours to kill in this air-conditioned oasis. The restaurant is full, and if we eat too quickly, we'll be pressured to free up our table for other restless customers. No way are we going back outside, as hot as an oven, until we absolutely must.

Satisfied and satiated, we return to the dock a good half an hour before we had planned. Yikes! Disaster! Our boat is nowhere in sight! I run around feverishly to find an official, who informs me that the boat has already left . . . on time. Furious, I go back to the ticket office, where I get a terse response to my queries. "Sorry. Not responsible for late passengers!" the clerk replies. I snap back, exasperated. "But we're early!" The guy looks at his watch. "One hour late, you mean." Convinced that he's taking the mickey and utterly certain that we're on time, I ask the next person I see for the time. The answer floors me. Arriving in Greece, we forgot all about the time-zone change . . . none of us had adjusted our watches accordingly.

We stand there, with just the clothes on our back—cycling shorts drenched in sweat, T-shirts stinking to high heaven—but also, thankfully, with our papers. The rest of our unguarded gear is blissfully sailing across the deep blue sea.

An express boat goes to Paros, but, according to our new time, it has already left. Inexplicably, a sympathetic local, who seemingly came out of nowhere, offers to help us. He's the only one who speaks English among all those we've accosted. Bending over backward, as if it were his own property, he manages to radio the captain of the boat, who informs him that he won't be returning to Piraeus until next week. He will tell his crew to off-load our bikes when they reach the port of Paros. There'll be no guarantee that our gear will still be there when we arrive, but it's the only choice we have. Aware that our Samaritan has done his best, we thank him a thousand times for his precious help. Twelve hours later, finally on the boat heading for Paros, I anxiously go over all possible scenarios in my head. I'm slightly desperate. We simply don't have the financial resources to replace everything anew. We're paying for our carelessness. At the restaurant, we took our own sweet time, got a little too comfortable. Now we're paying the price!

We arrive at the quay at dusk. No bikes. My heart is pounding. Then I spot another landing pier farther along. Jean-Denis rushes ahead into the darkness; Jean-Pierre and I follow him slowly, far behind, to prolong hope, to delay the hour of the execution.

Jean-Denis waits for us dumbstruck and incredulous: stacked up, one against the other, sit our precious bikes . . . fully intact and in full view of any passerby who cares to look.

Now I begin to believe in miracles. Fate is telling me something: not only can I but, indeed, I must continue on.

Chapter 3

·····································

Always a Roller Coaster Ride

DAY 78

Lindos, Rhodes, Greece—September 30, 1994

What best describes Paros, Santorini, and Rhodes? For these three Greek isles we visit, it's best summed up by sleep, sun, and sand. We swap our bikes for mopeds and join the happy, holiday crowd. We wile away the days strolling on sandy and pebbled paths in search of treasures: a quiet little bistro, a deserted beach, ancient ruins, a small fishing port.

We find Santorini particularly fascinating. Once a major center of civilization, it was ravaged by a volcanic eruption around 1500 BC. After millennia of erosion by the Aegean Sea, the only reminder of this catastrophic event is the crescent-shaped half crater on which the resourceful inhabitants have ingeniously built numerous small, white houses with vibrant, multicolored doors and windows. On the crater's inner face, where the slope is the steepest, you can follow paths carved from stone, on foot or by donkey, all the way up to the town center, perched on the side of a cliff.

Seventeen days have already gone by at this leisurely pace. Standing on the top wall of the Lindos fortress, we can see Turkey's coastline. We're troubled by disquieting rumors of a countrywide cholera epidemic. As nobody seems to know the real story, we decide to stick to our schedule. It's imperative that we get across Turkey before the winter sets in. We simply can't hang around to find out if there's any truth to the rumors.

Yet another challenge awaits us. . . .

DAY 78 and following
Marmaris, Turkey—September 30, 1994

Just a forty-five-minute hydrofoil ride is enough to transport us to a whole-new world. We receive a warm welcome from the customs officers, who immediately dispel the worrying rumors we've heard. We've made the right decision.

If Europe is a trip, the East is an odyssey! How did two neighbors, so close to each other, manage to keep their distinct characters so well? Endless thoroughfares of bazaars and street merchants shape my first impressions of Turkey, along with the tantalizing aromas wafting from curbside food stalls. *Pide,* the Turkish version of pizza, is very popular and quite delicious. Better yet, we can stuff ourselves for less than three bucks!

To escape the stifling heat of our small room, we spend our first night on the inn's rooftop. At dawn, we're awoken by the call to prayer, ringing from the surrounding minarets and echoing throughout the city.

The morale of the troops couldn't be better, but each of us is acutely aware of the challenges ahead.

And for myself, I spend some quiet moments, silently musing about a certain trip around the world . . . but all in good time.

DAY 80 and after
Nearing Kemer, Turkey—October 2, 1994

On our first night camping out, a garage mechanic not only welcomes us into his home but also offers up his roof as a campsite for the night. The man explains the house has never been fully renovated. And that suits him just fine because as long as the house stays in this state, he benefits from favorable mortgage payments. With steel rods jutting up from the edge of the roof, we feel like birds in a cage. In fact, we're happy with this set-up. After a day of anyone and everyone bombarding us with questions, we like the idea of being in our own tent, our own bubble and refuge, where we can float above the frenetic street life below.

Everywhere we look, up and down the streets, we come across high, elevated taps from which water can be pumped using a long, metal rod. We assumed they were for believers to purify themselves before prayers, as is the custom in other Muslim countries. Not so. They provide a more mundane cleansing ritual . . . washing dirty cars! And to think we were using these surreptitiously, so as not to offend the locals. To be sure, the idea of rotting away in a Turkish jail leaves nobody indifferent. Such is the nerve-wracking power of the movie, *Midnight Express*, which has left a deep impression on us, whether we like it or not.

Since leaving Marmaris, we've been riding like abused pack mules on a sinewy, mountainous road, with the mercury edging close to 100°F. On top of this, there's another complication: finding food. We're well off the tourist track, and gas stations, which cater primarily to truck drivers, are few and far between. The impoverished villages we come across offer us little in the way of food, and what there is available is barely edible.

Faced with the prospect of a lengthy period without food, we stop in some godforsaken place, where there appear to be just two paltry shops. Noticing the sketchy hygiene of what apparently passes for a restaurant,

Jean-Pierre and Jean-Denis prefer to buy a jar of honey and some bread from the neighboring store, the only other business in town. Since I hate riding without fuel and more substantial sustenance, I decide to put my not-exactly unwavering trust in the "restaurant" cook. Because I can't understand a single word he's saying, he leads me to the kitchen. I would have preferred not to have seen what was back there. He opens a non-refrigerated cupboard in which sit a few slabs of meat, piled one atop the other. He gestures that he won't be taking the top slab, where a myriad of flies are dining, but rather the one below. Incredibly, I agree to this. Despite my let's-do-it enthusiasm, I don't have the heart to tell him that the meat really looks like roadkill. So I'm not so sure I've made the right decision, but I'm so hungry that I'll take a slice from whatever he serves, top or bottom. . . .

With the cheesiest smile he can muster, he serves up the meat with a small cucumber-and-tomato salad on the side, probably as a ploy to distract me from the rest of my meal. Jean-Denis is almost jealous, until he spots several hairs, like fresh parsley garnishing the dish! Desperate times call for desperate measures: I take off my glasses so that, in blurry, blissful ignorance, I don't have to see what I'm eating, while a smirking Jean-Denis digs back into his honey pot.

I digest this course of events and take it all in, I must say. My fellow itinerants, on the other hand, are sick as dogs. Not exactly comparable to roadkill, but definitely not a pretty sight either: cramps, nausea, vomiting, and diarrhea. Bad choice. Was the honey more lethal than the meat? We'll never know . . . I guess I can thank my iron stomach, although I know it offers little sure-proof protection against my reckless culinary capers.

After a harrowing night, Jean-Pierre wisely decides to take the bus to Kemer. Jean-Denis declines to accompany him, despite his pitiful state. He too, simply can't eat or keep anything down. The road is no picnic either, and every conquered mountain merely hides a bigger one behind it.

Jean-Pierre had a rough ride, as it turned out. Aware that diarrhea causes dehydration, he drank half a gallon of water before getting on the bus. This bus didn't have a toilet, and, worse, there were no stops along the way. All the while fruitlessly wishing for the bus to break down, run out of gas, or maybe blow a tire, he still wonders to this day how his bladder held up during those six long hours. When we finally join him two days later, he has yet to see the funny side, despite our relentless teasing.

Kemer, located on the Mediterranean coast, is a vacation getaway, mainly frequented by German tourists. It's the off season, and Jean-Denis, our savvy negotiator, finds us an incredible deal: living room, kitchen, bathroom, and three bedrooms for just six bucks a night. We'll spend two days there, the time it takes my two ailing road warriors to fully recuperate. At the market, a farmer advises me that you should never consume an egg that floats. Preparing an omelet, I try this out, and, bingo, the egg floats like a beach ball.

DAY 87 and after
Nearing Goreme, Turkey—October 9, 1994

We leave Kemer, apparently hale and healthy. I don't want to jinx it, but I suspect there's more hiccups in store for us. We are making our way across very uneven terrain that is constantly pushing our physical limits: scaling a thousand feet—times three—daily is exactly like tackling the Nufenen Pass every day.

Why can't we just switch off gravity? "Paris to Hong Kong by bike" is a very short way to describe such a Herculean effort. I'm starting to see that there's nothing short about this venture at all! Before we set off, I listed the various countries and ascribed an incentive focus for each one: crossing France will be a quick race, Switzerland will offer us breathtaking views, Italy will be our last country before taking a break on the Greek islands, Turkey will mark the cusp of the Middle East, in Iran we'll delve into the heart of the unknown. And after that? Pakistan, India. I've already been swept up by the dream even before finishing the list. Up until now, this simple mantra, Paris–Hong Kong, had revived my spirits and filled me with pride. But today, I hardly dare say the phrase for fear that my resolve should collapse in a pitiful heap.

Tonight, I'm huddled in my tent, practically dying of hunger. We pedaled until dusk only to land in the middle of nowhere. Inaccurate road-maps and our lack of vigilance have cost us dearly. We have nothing to eat or drink, and we're still twenty-five miles from the nearest village. Since leaving Kemer, we've always had emergency supplies on hand: water, rice, canned tuna, and chocolate bars. Tired of carrying this added weight, which we stupidly considered useless, we ditched it. We must have been in the same frame of mind that inspired our "wacky tobaccy" field day in Italy. Jean-Pierre is furious. I share his frustration, but I'd rather not say anything—it'll only make me hungrier! Our self-imposed fast will last a not-so-fast twenty-six hours. . . .

Two days later, the health of Jean-Denis deteriorates further, and we're forced to take him to a private clinic in Aydincik. The doctor on duty speaks neither English nor French, but, much to our surprise, he gets by with a bit of German. In any case, he cannot make a quick diagnosis without doing the necessary tests. The doc recommends that Jean-Denis sticks to a diet of rice and bananas only and prescribes more Imodium. He's taken five Imodium pills in the last twenty-four hours, already! We make the decision for him. He must go on ahead by bus to Goreme. But, adding to his woes, he's not allowed to board the bus because of all his gear. At the end of his rope, he wearily mounts his bike and switches to autopilot. Poor Jean-Denis, fading fast, right under our noses, and we're clueless as to what we should do about it. He's not going to die on us, is he?

For his part (and for the first time), Jean-Pierre mentions his overall fatigue and the pain he's feeling in his knees. His punishing years of judo are now taking a toll on his body. The team's morale has never been so low.

* * *

DAY 95
Goreme, Turkey—October 17, 1994

We reach Goreme in Cappadocia, and I take stock of the physical effort needed to make it this far. In the end, taming the Turkish coast was just as amazing a feat as it was a painful one. Of the twelve days on the road, eight of them required climbing at least 3,300 feet per day in 95°F-plus heat.

The contrast was particularly stark when we left the coastal plain and climbed a torturous 5,500 feet to reach the Anatolian plateau. The temperature fell to the freezing point at night and hardly rose to 50°F during the day. It was like landing at Montreal's frigid Mirabel Airport in mid-January after a two-week vacation in sunny Florida. Summer clothes were cast aside to make way for gloves, toques, and scarves. And to think I used to complain about the heat.

I never anticipated such cold spells so early in the fall. They say air temperature drops one degree for every 300 feet we climb. I can attest to that. We thought we thought of everything. Mother Nature always finds a way to put know-it-alls in their place.

DAY 100
Goreme, Turkey—October 22, 1994

Although grappling with heat, cold, wind, mountains, sickness, and injury has been a major pain, applying for an Iranian visa opens up a whole new can of worms.

If the shortest route between two points is a straight line, the bureaucratic path is unquestionably the longest! Iran has no embassy in Canada, so we couldn't get our visas before we left home. In Rome, we moved heaven and earth to collect photos, passport confirmation, and letters of introduction from the Canadian embassy, to be then finally referred to the Iranian embassy in Athens. In Athens, we slogged through fifty miles in this overcrowded, polluted, and noisy city, only to be casually told to have a little faith and put our trust in the Iranian border guards.

Wary of the welcome mat that awaits us at the Turkish–Iranian border, we decide to take the 200-mile bus ride to Ankara, the capital, to try for that precious passport stamp one last time. Just as in Rome and Athens, we go through the same charade all over again in Ankara. Naturally, the different departments are located at opposite sides of the city, the transport system is inadequate, and the language is comprehensively incomprehensible. Two days of legwork results in four days of waiting around, twiddling our thumbs. An act of faith, indeed. Not kidding.

I stay in Ankara on my own while Jean-Pierre and Jean-Denis return to Goreme to tune up our bikes and get them ready to roll. Ankara is a major urban center that has nevertheless kept its rustic roots. The pace is slow, much slower than that of similar-sized European cities. I spend hours sitting on walls, lost in the background, just watching everyday life: the shoeshine boy engrossed in his job of shining leather until it gleams for just pennies a pop, the storekeeper who sweeps his front entrance between customers, a laborer carefully refitting cobblestones.

Because of the poor heating in my room, the cheap hotel where I'm holed up provides thick, wool-felt blankets for guests. Since my sleeping bag doesn't do the job for the winter months, I ask the innkeeper if he will sell me one of the blankets. His answer is a categorical "NO." I wave a wad of Turkish bills under his nose. He remains indifferent and unwavering. As a last resort, I take out a $10 greenback, which I carefully place on the glass counter. He snatches it up, holds it up to the light and says without missing a beat, "How many you want?"

After a long and tedious procedure, I finally receive our passports stamped with the official seal that will grant us entry into Iran. It took a full nine days to get the green light, but I consider us fortunate nevertheless, because the two Brits and the American who preceded me had no such luck. They will have to backtrack or divert around the country.

On returning to Goreme, I rejoin my buddies, and we take full advantage of Cappadocia before we set our sights on Iran. Located on the Anatolian plateau, this region of Turkey is known for its fairy chimneys. These impressive, cone-shaped rock formations rise up one next to the other in a lunar-like setting. Even more startling, the inhabitants have carved their homes out of the rock base and created religious sanctuaries decorated with wonderful frescoes. Among these stony, lacework monuments, each more surprising than the next, nestle hidden gardens, vineyards, and orchards. The brittle rock, which hardens in contact with air, made it possible for inhabitants to dig underground cities, with dwellings several stories high, where they could take refuge from marauders.

We cut short our stay in this paradise, because we don't want the snow to take us by surprise. Five mountain passes lie in store for us, three of which top

6,500 feet. Then we trail the foot of the famous Mt. Ararat, before entering the Republic of Iran. We have no idea what's ahead. No idea, that is, except for the fact that temperatures will be very cold in the Elbourz mountain range in the northwest, although the weather should improve as we get closer to Tehran.

People keep telling us that Kurdistan, just east of Turkey, is very dangerous for travelers. And as for Iran, we must be completely "bonkers" to set foot in that revolutionary hotbed, period. These comments are a carbon copy of those I've already heard back home, but my mind is made up: I'll judge for myself when I get there. Nothing will deter me. I'm up for it. More than a simple bike ride, the challenge we face in the coming days will be a question of survival.

Before leaving, I mail Caroline the bracelet I picked up in the Swiss market as well as a tiny glass vial containing a single grain of rice on which my name has been engraved. For the past month, phone lines have been particularly bad, and we're having trouble staying in touch. Using the mail is the most reliable way of passing on news.

DAY 101 and after
Nearing Sivas, Turkey—October 23, 1994

Pervasive and bone-chilling cold await us when we depart Goreme. This scares me. By nighttime, I'm completely drained. I shiver when I put up my tent, I shiver when I cook, and I shiver when I lie down to go to bed. I'm grateful for my new felt blanket, and I readily accept this additional load if it means greater comfort. Nights are damp and drizzly, and the mercury now drops below freezing. I stare straight ahead into the distance, resolutely focused on keeping my spirits up.

DAY 107
Sivas, Turkey—October 29, 1994

Much to our distress, Jean-Denis has decided to return to Quebec. In spite of his Nydazol treatment, the virus continues to wreak havoc on his system. He's been repeatedly sick since we entered Turkey, but we always hoped that he would eventually be OK. He has never thrown in the towel. His big heart would have carried him to the end of the world, but his body, weakened by chronic diarrhea, simply cannot go on. His immune system has become so weak that the slightest morsel of food makes him sick. This morning, after an indescribably difficult night, Jean-Pierre accompanies our brother in arms to the hospital. It's the end of his journey. With a heavy heart, he gives us any equipment we may need to continue en route.

Chapter 4

....

Anatolian Winters Pack Quite a Punch

DAY 107 and after
Sivas, nearing Agri, Turkey—October 29, 1994

And then there were two . . . the trio is no more. Jean-Pierre and I leave three days before Jean-Denis returns home. We're wary of what November may bring. I'm getting a few sniffles, so I abide by the onion principle: namely, to wear the bare minimum during a climb so that sweat doesn't freeze to my skin when I go downhill. Newspaper around my torso under my clothes absorbs any excess humidity while also serving as an extra barrier against the biting wind. This same newspaper trick also proves to be an effective way of keeping my feet warm.

Villages are a rare sight, so the idea is to reach Agri as soon as we possibly can. We can't afford the luxury of being tourists anymore. Our chances of success rest squarely on making a fast exit from this wintry hinterland. Our race against the cold unites us more than ever.

DAY 114

Agri, Turkey—November 5, 1994

We endure the glacial cold for a grueling seven straight days in order to rack up the 400 miles separating us from Agri. Seven days without a wash . . . seven days of eating and sleeping outdoors.

The cold is utterly exhausting, but we have no choice but to keep pedaling on. Very early in the morning, the cold stirs us out of our bed—ample incentive to get going, for sure. With icicles forming on the tips of our noses, with numb, frozen hands, and with hunched shoulders and chilled bodies shivering uncontrollably, we briskly pack up our bags and hop on our bikes. We have to ride along for five or six miles just to get warmed up to eventually pull over and prepare breakfast: bread, honey, and eggs, all washed down with lots of water.

If we're lucky enough to have a sunny day, the temperature becomes tolerable around noon. Most of the time, however, we must battle the cold. Since the days are getting shorter, we ride until dusk before choosing a camp away from the road—if possible, near a creek. We pitch our tents, and, after putting on all of our clothes, we prepare supper, which more often than not means rice and tuna mixed in with a packet of soup. All that's left to do is take shelter in our tents and hope for a few hours of rest.

On the fifth day of this mad dash, Jean-Pierre is surprised to have to wrest me from my sleep. I vomited and had diarrhea all night long, barely getting two winks. Bloated bellyaches and excruciating cramps twist my stomach in knots. Should I continue or take a day's rest? Jean-Pierre takes down the tents while being very careful not to step on one of the many "land mines" I have planted through the night. I leave my fate in his hands and trudge along like the living dead to the next village—a twenty-mile zombie ride, indeed.

Today's outcome verges on the miraculous. After a substantial lunch, I've regained my strength, and my stomach pains have completely disappeared. We covered about seventy miles in all, and, according to my watch, which records changes in altitude, that included a total climb of 4,250 feet, a new record for a single day. It's getting late, so we stop at a gas station to eat. Jean-Pierre sits in front of me; it's colder than an Inuit's freezer. In the final two-mile climb, he neglected to peel off a layer of clothes, and the merciless cold got to him during the descent. His woolen toque firmly pulled down over his brow, back and shoulders stooped forward, staring at the floor, teeth rattling nonstop, he vacantly sips the steaming cup of tea between his mitts. He's exhausted. Admittedly, we went well beyond our limits, but I try to reassure him by pointing out that now we're just two days from Agri, and soon we'll be out of the cold. He says nothing. He doesn't have the strength to believe in what I'm saying or even to return a smile.

Nevertheless, the last night spent on top of a 7,600-foot-high ridge at a frigid 14°F did little to cool our hot streak of enthusiasm. The next day, slowed down by a vicious headwind, we tackle the seemingly endless miles to our last Turkish stop at a snail's pace. There, we'll be rewarded by a well-deserved rest. During this last push, we became dehydrated because our water supply froze up. Finally, resting on the bed of a small, dirty room in Agri, we each guzzle down one and a half gallons of slightly salted water to rebalance our electrolytes.

I feel warm for the first time in ages. Jean-Pierre takes a nap next to me while I stay wide awake to relish this blissful moment.

DAY 116
Agri, Turkey—November 7, 1994

I've been in Agri for a couple of days now, but my apparent joy and relief belies a slight nervousness. The peace and quiet is hard to bear, especially after the previous days inching along an interminable tightrope. I'm worried this respite will just turn into inertia, and we'll never want to leave again. The obstacles I've surmounted so far required extreme amounts of physical and mental energy, and I'm practically crushed by the idea of stepping back into the ring for yet another round. It's as if I'm presently living a future directly lifted from the past. For example, although cozy inside my sleeping bag, I catch myself tensing my fingers and toes as if I'm still in my tent, still feeling the cold. From previous experience, I know that this state is caused by excessive fatigue. In order to give body and soul a rest, you must detach yourself from reality, or rather, from the stress of the past that you still carry with you. Otherwise, it's pretty useless to even begin to think about restarting again.

DAY 120
Agri, Turkey—November 11, 1994

We've already been here six days, since November 5, and we're still waiting for our care package from Canada. A precious parcel indeed, filled with letters from close friends and relatives and, hopefully, very warm clothes. Otherwise, we would have long since departed Agri. Winter is nipping at our heels, and another flurry of snow would add to the two inches already covering the ground.

I rely on brief phone calls to let people know my current location and general state of health. Plus, I regularly mail off my personal diary entries along the way. Fortunately, to receive mail, we are using the "poste restante" system (general delivery), established in post offices world-wide. To get mail to us, the sender simply writes our name on the letter or package addressed to Poste Restante with the name of the city and country on our route. To claim the package, we just show up at the city's main post office with two pieces of ID, one of which must be a passport. Letters and parcels unclaimed within three months of delivery are returned free of charge to the sender.

Not surprisingly, my mom and dad prove to be my most faithful correspondents on this epic adventure, taking charge to include any letters gathered from my friends. They also make the most of this opportunity by slipping in vitamins, rolls of film, extra pairs of thermal underwear, and some recent photos. For her part, Caroline pours her heart out in her letters—an ongoing conversation of sorts, one that has fueled our relationship since my departure.

Agri is a grimy, poor, and boring city of some 50,000 inhabitants. Thankfully, after meeting a young guy in the street, we befriend a group of Turkish school teachers. We communicate in English or German. I say "Turkish" teachers, because since we left Sivas, we are in the Kurdistan region, mainly inhabited by Kurds, a people with their own distinct language and culture. For centuries they have lived east of the Anatolian plateau, hemmed in by the bordering countries of Armenia, Iran, Iraq, and Syria. The cause of the chronic conflicts originated when General Mustafa Kemal, known today as Ataturk (Father of the Turks), drew up the borders of Turkey while annexing the Kurdish homeland. When the Ottoman Empire collapsed in 1923, he oversaw the birth of modern Turkey by appropriating all the lands to the Aegean Sea in the West, to the Black Sea in the North, to the Mediterranean Sea in the South, and to Mount Ararat in the East.

Much of this territory is settled by the Kurds, but they don't have full rights. Today, they're rebelling against Turkish state authorities because they have been denied the sovereign state promised to them by the Treaty of Sèvres, a pact signed on August 10, 1920, at the end of World War I, between the Allied Powers and the Ottoman government. This arbitrary redrawing of borders made them a people without a country. Furthermore, the Turkish government now bans them from speaking their own language and mandates that Kurdish children attend Turkish schools, specially designed to assimilate them. The Kurds founded the Kurdistan Workers Party (PKK) to ensure protection of their fundamental human rights. From this political party sprung rebel groups who use force to achieve their goals.

Since 1984, fighting between the army and rebels has claimed more than 17,000 lives. Even if I am in the line of fire, I have to say that the conflict is not so easily discernible. We're more scared of what we've been told rather than what we actually see. There's a chance that we might find ourselves at the wrong place at the wrong time, and a bomb might go off at any moment. Yet it seems to us that the cities and towns are relatively quiet. Terrorist attacks were staged recently in Erzurum, but we saw nothing of this when we passed through, two weeks after it happened. War is in the air, but nobody knows when and where. We're reassured that, so far at least, no tourist has fallen victim to a fatal attack. On the other hand, three Swiss nationals have already been taken hostage recently, forcing the Turkish government to negotiate.

The situation is very different for our Turkish teacher friends. The government sends them to teach in a Turkish school in Kurdish territory for one year, a mandatory condition for receiving their diplomas. These hapless primary-school teachers, who embody the destruction of Kurdish culture in the eyes of the rebels, are choice civilian targets. Worse still, three teachers have recently been killed in a village in the South. It goes without saying that they are terrified and counting the days before the end of their contract, so they can head back West.

DAY 122
Agri, Turkey—November 13, 1994

No tourist has ever stayed as long in this city as we have. Why on earth would they? It boasts the lowest recorded temperatures in Turkey: -65°F (that's right, minus sixty-five degrees Farenheit!). We're becoming so well-known that enthusiastic cries of "bicyklet" follow us wherever we go. At the post office, which we drop by religiously every day, employees fussing over their work find time to offer us a daily cup of tea.

We make the most of our spare time by visiting our friends in the small village where they teach. Ten miles outside of Agri, this impoverished hamlet shows us what real hardship is. Surrounding fields barely produce enough food to feed the villagers, who live in dilapidated shanties made from stones and dried earth and scattered willy-nilly along muddy roads. Just two wells provide drinking water for the 800 inhabitants. But what makes it more insufferable is the never-ending bitter cold, which permeates the community at this 6,000-feet altitude. Not a single home is insulated, and even the schoolhouse is unheated. No wonder the kids lack motivation! Sitting on a frozen bench, the ability to concentrate and the desire to learn are drummed out of them by their own clattering teeth. . . . It simply breaks my heart. When I return to my grotty boarding room, I feel like I'm entering a palace.

DAY 124
Agri, Turkey—November 15, 1994

Ten days have come and gone, and we're still in Agri, waiting for our parcel. The cold intensifies. We no longer have a choice; we must leave tomorrow.

These long stopovers give me pause for reflection. When planning this journey, I was acutely aware that mental preparation was going to be just as important as physical readiness. It would be crucial to stock up on what I call "do-or-die energy." And in the most testing moments, I will draw on this energy. It compels me to keep on keeping on, the main fuel that drives me to the end of my dream. After seven taxing days in Agri, my do-or-die energy quota was seriously low. This temporary deficit triggered an alarm sent by my body to my subconscious that total exhaustion was imminent. With the adrenaline flowing, we don't feel fatigue, and without a clear message from the subconscious, we risk crashing the system. This message thus acts as a circuit breaker that prevents us from blowing a fuse, if I can put it that way. From now on, I should take care of my fatigue before it becomes extreme and overwhelms me. But how can I avoid taking the easy road and not become complacent? Any reason to stop and recuperate would be good enough, since each and every day is exhausting!

Do-or-die energy is almost inexhaustible for anyone who has had a long time to prepare and who can replenish it as needed. But how? Here's the way I do it. I refuse to feel sorry for myself after a relentless day of rain, wind, heat, or cold. Instead, I'm proud of the fact that I've overcome everything nature throws at me. Plus, I'm grateful for the enriching encounters brought about by oftentimes chance meetings. I relish spectacular scenery and savor new flavors. Most importantly, I tap into my boundless capacity for wonderment and my ability to be surprised and delighted by all and sundry. I spent a good part of two years building up my stock of do-or-die energy, knowing that it will take me wherever I want to go. With this approach, I see light at the end of the tunnel, find comfort in hardship, and take account of results rather than difficulties, always focusing on the road to victory. I know every ounce of my being is ready to face the test. I am fired up with adventure, and I remind myself that my guardian angel will protect me as long as this passionate flame burns within me.

It seems to me that the more I go eastward, the further away "the East" actually is! Distance is only quantifiable if there's a fixed reference point. Iran may be far, but far from what? This country is quite a stretch from my hometown of Chicoutimi, Quebec, but in my present reality, it's just 125 miles away. Similarly, for an Iranian living in Tabriz, Quebec is the end of the world. So finally everything's relative. Maybe it's Quebec that's the remote, far-flung land!

My spirit fills with images of Turkey: majestic mountains, lofty passes, rushing rivers, deserted and idyllic beaches set against cliffs that jut out to meet the azure blue sea. Turkey means a warm welcome from country folk, a privileged contact forged from the uniqueness of our adventure. We didn't see any crowds gather around packed tourist buses. On the other hand, our humble bicycles have such a magnetic effect on the locals that, come nightfall, we need to find sanctuary away from the hubbub we cause for some quiet solitude on our own.

Iran seems more approachable now. We're still being advised not to go there, but our slow progress toward this so-called danger zone makes me less afraid of it. Good luck, ol' buddy!

* * *

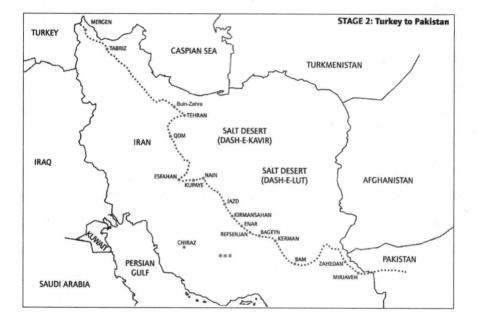

Chapter 5

· ·

One Day at a Time

To get to the Iranian border, we have to bike along the foot of the famous Mount Ararat, where, as legend would have it, Noah's Ark landed after the flood. From its lofty peak of 17,000 feet, this giant mountain majestically dominates the region, and although we're seventy-five miles away, its presence completely fills the horizon. What an incredible sight Mount Everest must be at 29,000 feet! I catch myself smiling at the comparison—higher, bigger, farther, harder? Maybe later. . . .

Iran's Customs Enforcement proves to be very strict: there's an official ban on bringing in magazines, foreign music, photos of women not wearing the chador, alcohol, and cigarettes—in fact, everything that symbolizes the West. Rows and rows of trucks filled with goods wait to be checked, while buses and cars are inspected with a fine-tooth comb. A truck driver tells me he's already been here a whole week waiting to get his entry permit. Traveling as groups, the long-distance truckers accept this situation, because it is an integral part of their work, and they're duly compensated. Plus, the trucks themselves are well equipped for long layovers. In fact, the border looks more like a vast campsite, complete with all the basic amenities: toilets, non-potable water, and a general store. It's an eclectic gathering of all nationalities, where English serves as the common language.

We already have our one-week transit visa, but if I had listened to the lackadaisical advice given by the embassy staff in Greece, I would be joining the ranks of the truck drivers. Having spent more than an hour just getting the stamp allowing us to leave Turkey, we decide to work our way through the line up in the direction of the Iranian checkpoint. A gauntlet of people, toting their immense suitcases, are everywhere in our path, but, incredibly and without so much as a grumble, each steps aside to let us pass. At the head of the line, customs officers, their heads buried inside luggage, systematically scrutinize every item they come across. It's finally Jean-Pierre's turn, and he follows suit, opening one of his saddlebags; the officer immediately makes a sign to motion him through. Jean-Pierre looks at me, somewhat bewildered. Instinctively, I give him a nudge with my front wheel so that he gets going before the officer changes his mind. I stick right behind him like his shadow. We're home free. Nobody sneaks past the Iranian border, except us! Very odd.

A snow-capped mountain range topping 13,000 feet serves as our welcome mat, extending for the next twenty miles. It's icy-cold weather, but I'm in seventh heaven. Small, makeshift shops line the village streets. Old cars, similar to those I saw in Russia, whizz by. Once again, I'm in another world.

The harried scenarios that I had imagined simply don't play out. On the contrary, people smile at us and even wave, tentatively. My fears dissipate little by little. Our fears, ultimately, are conjured up by what we don't know. When you're finally confronted with the unknown, you start to get a grip on it and learn to see things for what they really are. I can truly expand my limits and horizons by seeing how people actually live and by understanding their culture. In fact, these life lessons are the real purpose of my journey, and today, I'm reaping the rewards.

Except for some villages that we pass through, the road is lined on both sides by a rocky plain that extends over several miles before it stumbles onto the foothills of snowy summits. Sparse vegetation nevertheless provides sustenance for a few wandering sheep, watched over by their shepherd. The evening comes, and without really knowing whether we have the right to camp wherever we like, we hunker down behind a lean-to shelter for any stray herd animals (like us!). On the horizon, as if they were changing the guard, the sun yields its place to the full moon. Nature breathes softly. Otherwise, there's not a sound to be heard.

In a hushed voice, Jean-Pierre reluctantly confesses that his knee pain is becoming unbearable. He's almost at the end of his tether. He suffers from patellofemoral trauma brought on by all the years of judo. The misaligned kneecaps have abnormally worn down surrounding cartilage, thereby causing swelling and inflammation in both knees. Movement is both restricted and punishing.

On the following days he rides at a devilish pace, a candidate for exorcism. I feel like he's pulling me along, so far as his knees will allow, giving me his all, so I can save up on my strength. He leads the way, acting as the windbreak, and won't allow me to do the same for him. Little by little, it's starting to get me down. I can feel that he's withdrawing from the journey, withdrawing into his own bubble. While leaving his last ounces of energy on Iranian asphalt, he realizes there's no way out, no possible cure. On the contrary, there will be repercussions, and he will likely suffer from them later on.

DAY 131
Tabriz, Iran—November 22, 1994

When we ride into a village, our "traveling circus" brings out the mob, and someone who speaks English usually steps forward to volunteer as our guide and interpreter. We're looking for affordable accommodation in Tabriz when Reza approaches us. In impeccable English he tells us that he is the owner of a factory specializing in rubber parts. He offers to help us. Our instincts, always on shark alert, warn us to be wary. The proverbial Good

Samaritan in a city like Tabriz? Maybe too good to be true. He leaves us at a hotel and announces to us that he'll drop by tomorrow morning. We still have our guard up.

Reza comes back exactly when he said he would. He treats us to a tour of the city and then invites us back to his place, where he lives with his parents. The home has bare white-washed walls, Persian rugs on the floor, some basic furniture, a TV, and a few cushions. Subdued lighting brightens the room's white walls. We eat with Reza and his father only. His mother, who prepared the meal, disappears into another room. She will only eat the leftovers . . . when the men are done.

Four days have passed. Reza is a true gentleman. He unabashedly takes care of our every need, including renewing our transit visa, which was due to expire in a few days. Because we're traveling by bike, it's an easy matter to renew our visas for an extra month. We have a more serious problem to deal with, however. My back wheel is just about to kick the bucket. For two weeks, I've been spending about an hour every evening straightening it out, with no lasting results. Today, Reza brings the best "go-to" repair guy in town. How about that—it all works out for the better!

In Iran, international relations are at a low point, which means, among other things, that no bank will accept our credit cards. We're in a bind: we've run out of Iranian cash and have no legal means of accessing more. Reza helps us convert our Turkish liras to Iranian rials on the black market. This transaction causes an unbearable amount of stress. If we're caught, it'll mean jail time, because in Iran, laws are there to be respected! To minimize the chances of getting busted, Reza leaves us alone with the money dealer who drags us toward dark corners further and further away from the main part of the bazaar. We're the only foreigners in this sleazier part of town, and our presence causes heads to swivel. An accomplice pokes his nose out from behind a stack of Persian carpets and motions us to join him. He hands over a wad of bills and then disappears in a flash. Without even checking to see if he's given us the right amount, we scurry back to Reza so he can get us safely out of here.

We had never imagined playing such a dangerous game. I have no appetite to repeat such intrigues, and I vow to be thrifty. With a hearty meal of chicken, rice, salad, and yogurt, readily available for just $1 (drink included), I'm sure I'll manage.

Before leaving, Reza reminds us that the Great Salt Desert (Dasht-e-Kavir) begins just south of Tehran and that it will be followed by a sand desert (Dasht-e-Lut). To encourage us, he mentions that we've only got another 450 miles to go before we hit warmer weather! In any event, we would really love to spend Christmas and New Year's under the hot sun, like lizards on a rock, somewhere in Pakistan.

Reza has helped us so much that I ask him flat out why he has been so kind and generous, a typical reaction from a Westerner. He says it gives him a good opportunity to not only practice his English but also gives him a rare chance of hearing unfiltered news about the outside world. When I persist, he asks me a favor. Would I invite him to Canada if I were ever to write him? It's the only way for an Iranian to be able to leave the country. He hastens to add that, unfortunately, his current financial situation makes it impossible for such a trip. But you never know, perhaps some day.

DAY 137
Buin-Zahra, Iran—November 28, 1994

Jean-Pierre's knees are getting worse day by day. Chronic pain never eases up, even after a day of rest. Anything that involves bending his kness is done at a very slow pace while he very gingerly tries to support himself.

Yesterday, we rode under sleeting, icy rain, and this morning, I don't have the energy to argue anymore. The cold sticks to our asses like parasites in the gut! We've been perched on this plateau for forty-one long days and nights. The mountains no longer hold any charm for me. Not today, anyway. Tomorrow, we arrive in Tehran. Finally.

DAY 138 and following
Tehran, Iran—November 29, 1994

We meet up with another Reza in Tehran. He spent seventeen years in England, speaks flawless English, and takes us under his wing to show us around this very populous city of seventeen million. To my great relief, I'm now able to use my credit card to stock up on rials. Although the cost of the hotel room blows our budget, meals are copious and delicious . . . and still less than a dollar a pop.

To reduce congestion, only a limited number of vehicles are allowed into the downtown core. Public transportation, however, is scant. So to get around, pedestrians stand by the side of the road and wave an arm, as you do to signal a motorist to slow down. Drivers slowly cruise by with windows rolled down and pick up passengers headed for the same place, all for a fixed price. It's a mix of hitchhiking, carpooling, and hailing cabs, where everybody wins.

At six o'clock this morning, Reza and his buddies treat us to a typical breakfast in a suburban restaurant. In the entryway, four large pots sit on gas stoves, bubbling away with a sheep stew, made up of every single part of the animal, hooves included—ewe had to be there! It is served according to a time-honored ritual. Since our arrival in the Middle East, we've developed a keen sense of what's BS and what's not, which serves us well this morning. So now I get the joke our hosts find so amusing. We're to eat the part of the animal exclusively reserved for guests—it's tasty testicles! As there are only two, we can't even share them. Refusing food in Iran is very rude, showing a distinct lack of politeness. Out of the corner of his eye, the cook has noticed our poorly disguised disgust, knowing full well that we were resigned to doing the right thing. Thankfully, he burst out laughing.

DAY 142
Tehran, Iran—December 3, 1994

Today is decision day—a day of import, courage, and sadness.

Jean-Pierre will return to Quebec. He cannot take it any more. Turkey's mountainous terrain, coupled with the severe cold, is the last straw. The acute pain makes him feel nauseous, clouds his thinking, and deprives him of any fleeting pleasures we might come across. The dream turns into nothing but pain and suffering. Of course, he would like nothing better than to continue. He's worried that his departure will prompt me to give up. I reassure him that it won't happen, that he was the best possible traveling companion, and that I'm glad we made it so far together. But today, as fate would have it, we must part. He's relieved that I'm not holding it against him. How could I?

He packs his luggage, making sure to leave me his best gear, including a sleeping bag a whole lot warmer than mine. I hand him a silver pendant, set with gemstones, to give Caroline on Christmas Eve. "Maybe I could keep going a bit . . . at least until Pakistan?" He gets up but immediately has to sit right back down again. He can barely stand. He cradles his head in his hands. "At first, we were three, today we're down to two. Tomorrow, you'll be on your own. Ready to take on everything coming your way. Don't give up. I want you to reach your dream. Do it for yourself, but also for me, OK?"

As he flies off with British Airways, I will leave Tehran on the wings of my guardian angel. I have a heavy heart, heavy with sadness at his departure, heavy with the loneliness seeping through me, heavy with anxiety regarding the challenges in store for me, heavy with the weight of my own ambitions. The decision is made: I will leave in two days.

DAY 144
Tehran, Iran—December 5, 1994

My mother listens to what I have to say to her without flinching. She agreed with my project, provided that I didn't go it alone. Today, she is forced to reconsider her original terms. She insists that she still has total confidence in me and that I have her full support, but I know deep down she's worried sick. She could cope with everything about the trip, except the idea that I was out there alone. At the same time, she would feel guilty forcing me to abandon the saga. Her already-light sleep will be further disrupted, but she will live with this added anxiety for the sake of a successful trip. My father barely conceals his own anguish. Caroline is beside herself.

My decision is taken, and they know it. There's nothing to add except to promise them that I'll stay prudent. Always.

After six days in Tehran, I leave, just as a snowfall blankets the city. Viaducts are coated in ice. Vehicles and motorcycles are slipping and sliding all over the road, and my narrow tires don't make life much easier for me.

I'm barely on my way, and already two motorcycles have careened into the cars immediately in front of them. On the outskirts of the town, road conditions stabilize, but a strong north wind plummets the temperature down to 5°F. My hands and face are frozen stiff as I hurl downhill after a 1,000-foot climb. I've had enough, so I stop for lunch. My only consolation is the much-improved sleeping bag that Jean-Pierre left me, and my one and only motivation is to bring my first solo day to a close. Heading directly south, I dream of laying on a bed of flowers in a beautiful, pastoral valley, any day now. Dreaming makes you forget.

After lunch, the wind changes direction. I come to a fork in the road, and, more misery, I'm denied access to the new route. There's nothing for it but to take the old, abandoned road instead. Then, I make one mistake after the other. My first mistake was thinking I could make it to the next town before nightfall. My second, to think that the distance to the town, as shown on the map, referred to the new road and not to the old one. My third, not having any emergency food on hand. And my fourth, having no info whatsoever on any rest stops before the next town. When there were two of us, we could live with a few slip-ups . . . but alone?

I find myself on a deserted road. The wind is killer, and the ridge much higher than I expected. I have no clue whether there's a town at the end of this desolate road. Fatigue creeps over me. My errors weigh on me heavily. The day is zipping by, and I still have no plan B. I dare not believe that anybody lives in this godforsaken place, on this dirt-poor road. All I see is an occasional, stone dwelling, practically in ruins. Panic sets in. I kick it up a notch, despite being pummeled by the elements. I start to sweat hard, so I stop for a break. The wind immediately freezes the sweat to my skin. I have nothing warmer that what I'm wearing. If the cold gets the better of me, I'll have to stop here and camp without supper. Then I'll have to restart tomorrow morning without breakfast. I dry off and anxiously get back in the saddle to face the road again. The landscape offers little comfort. Always the desert, only the desert, and then more desert. To top it off, this wicked wind slows me down and taunts me like the devil himself, roaring wildly in this woebegone wilderness.

The setting sun vanishes and leaves me all alone, in a cold sweat. The night air is frigid and permeates everything. I don't want to sleep outdoors. I'll get hypothermia, guaranteed. I'm having trouble controlling the dark thoughts that cross my mind. Despite my efforts, I'm inching along like a slug. My fingers have turned into cocktail sausages, and my right wrist is chilblained. I have a searing pain in the left knee. It's pitch black.

After having given up all hope of a miracle, I spot a twinkling light off in the distance. I approach it with tears in my eyes and realize that yes, it is, truly and unmistakenly, a rest stop for travelers. Seeing the state I was in, the store keeper quickly lights up the kerosene stove, which he will have to turn off before leaving. He throws together a meal for me and invites me to sleep inside. The smell of kerosene snaps me out of my stupor. I feel as though I've gambled with my life in just a few short hours. I must recoup for tomorrow. Is that even possible before sunrise? I pedaled more than six hours at a steady 5°F. It's 7 PM, and the wind is still howling.

I feel extremely alone, and it's only Day One without Jean-Pierre.

DAY 145
Isfahan, Iran—December 6, 1994

Twenty-four hours is all it takes to feel this horrible burden: I'm no longer part of a team. I can't count on the physical and moral support of a traveling companion any more.

I don't know what to think. I have no real physical excuse to stop. My knees and my stomach hold up fine, but it's hard to stay motivated. I had convinced myself that it would be warmer after Tehran, and I was wrong. Right now, I'm smack dab in the middle of an exceptional cold spell that lowers the temperature to -4°F at night.

Today, it's my misfortune to run straight into a snowstorm, in a part of the world where you usually find sandstorms. Quite the "special" day for a Quebec cyclist who ought to be homesick for some snow. What a nice surprise, but you really shouldn't have! GORE-TEX® socks on my feet, newspaper pages around my shoulders (odd but effective), scarf wrapped around my neck, and two layers of plastic bags swaddling my hands: I'm fully geared up to face forty miles of the white stuff coming at me.

I'm humming along at a nice clip when a car flags me down in this snowy escapade. In broken English, the driver, accompanied by another man, offers to give me a lift to Esfahan, an ancient Persian city. I decline, knowing this would mean a forty-five–mile detour. But they insist, one even offers me the chance to stay with his family. My yearning to want to meet new people and see how they live their lives finally wins me over, and I accept.

Foolishly, I thought I'd be invited into his own home as he had me believe. Instead, I find myself in a decrepit room where he's stowed away his elderly father. The poor old soul is bored to death, nervously fingering his worry beads, staring blankly at the light of the gas stove, and waiting for god knows what. Death, presumably. I'm offered the opportunity to take a shower in the doorless wooden hut . . . outside! The thermometer says it's just 12°F. No problem. I simply have to light up the water-tank heater and wait thirty minutes. Having followed his instructions to the letter, I make a dash for the steaming shower. Cold air wafts in and forms a freezing cloud around my ankles. In spite of this minor inconvenience, the room is transformed into a real sauna. What a thrill! I take full advantage of this unlikely luxury to savor the present moment. I lather up like a madman and manage to wash my hair a bit when the water turns from hot to cold before you could say "Jack Frost." My Finnish sauna turns into a polar bear dip. In shock, head, hair, and body covered in soapsuds, I fiddle with the faucet hoping to save the day. It's a waste of time. Breathlessly, and with billowing, cold air filling the whole room, I try to wash off the soapy lather sticking to my body as fast as I possibly can. I'm frozen solid. Without even toweling off, I rush outside, bolt directly to the room and dive into my sleeping bag. Screw supper, I'm not hungry anymore. I'm lying near grandpa, who patiently waits for the Grim Reaper's imminent arrival. I can keep him company for one more night in this world, at least.

DAY 146
Esfahan, Iran—December 7, 1994

When we traveled as a pair or a trio, I could talk about my moods. Now, I can only talk to a mirror. I can't tell if it's just my imagination or whether

I'm really suffering. I no longer know my limits; I've lost perspective. I must be able to detach myself, forget what's going on, and dream of finding a certain inner peace. I have to fight every inch of the way, and that's not easy.

All things considered, I spend a quiet, pleasant day in Esfahan strolling through this remarkable old city. The river, slowly flowing through the city center, provides a genteel atmosphere of peace and quiet in spite of the hustle and bustle of the nearby traffic. In contrast to other Iranian cities, this one seems more conscious of its self-image. Everything is clean and well laid out. Shaded pedestrian pathways meander along the river banks for several miles. Esfahan is the jewel of Iran, and its inhabitants are well aware of it. After lunch, I sit on a bench to enjoy some local pastries, and, bundled up in my jacket, I doze off. I wake up feeling rested, as if the river's flow had taken away some of my solitude.

I'm 190 miles from Jazd, 410 miles from Kerman, 740 miles from Zahedan, and 790 miles from the Pakistani border. Why am I keeping count? Because reveries about the southern warmth reassure me. I can't understand where this reluctance to get going again comes from. My mother would surely tell me to take the bus instead of torturing myself, but it's not so easy, because once you get to a destination, you're faced with other challenges. What to do then? Go by bus? That would mean I would end up not spending a single day on my bike. Problems and pitfalls spring up every day, regardless. Be that as it may, I opt for the bike. It gives me certain advantages, so I'll live with the inconveniences.

I'm shaken up a bit, and I can't seem to muster the energy to tackle everything in front of me. Since getting to the Anatolian plateau in Turkey forty-five days ago, and especially after talking to Reza, I was sure the cold would stop as soon as I arrived at the Great Salt Desert, just south of Tehran. I don't feel like fighting anymore. The last couple of days, even the last few weeks, have been so demanding that I feel like an empty shell. I can't see the end. Just the cold alone was enough to drain so much energy out of me that precious little remains to replenish my morale and keep my spirits up.

I feel like I'm facing a wall, a wall so high that I get dizzy just looking at it. I'm a prisoner of my most absurd dreams. My own rampant ambition

Chapter 6

· ·

Captive to a Dream

DAY 147
Kupayeh, Iran—December 8, 1994

Believe me, I'll never forget the distress, torment, and misery that festers inside me on the eighth day of December 1994. I feel brutally alone in this wretchedly bleak abyss. Engulfed in this deathly cold, each minute feels like an eternity. I have ridden a whole sixty miles with plastic bags as gloves, newspaper around my head, my socks pulled up to my knees, and my vest zipped up to my chin. And a nagging throb in my right knee keeps reminding me I'm not invincible. On the contrary, I've never felt so vulnerable. The cold battering my body now targets the very depths of my being. It attacks my innermost spirit and my soul.

I am attracted to danger like a moth to a flame. I cannot resist it. I am forced to push my machine to the limit, to the fire. It's just short of madness.

There's no longer any rhyme or reason to my behavior. I've reached the point of no return.

I feel such a deep pain that I'm having trouble describing it. It's as if someone was poking around in my head with a scalpel. I can't think logically any more. Ideas are no longer my own; they float adrift in their own universe, a world of wide-open space just like the empty expanse that surrounds me: the desert. The absence of any distinguishable landmarks just reinforces the paranoia. I'm in my own deformed time-and-space continuum. Nothing is out there to convince me of my present reality. The very last moment is all that exists, in the present and in the future. There is no past. Front or back, everything looks the same. East is the direction of the rising sun, and west is where the sun sets. But when the sun is directly overhead, north, south, east, and west become one. What I see today is what I saw yesterday and what I'll see tomorrow. My thoughts seem to be burned on a record that is spinning ever faster and faster. I can't stop the gears from turning, so I get sucked deeper into the vortex. Where will I land when I come back up? I'm worried, because I feel like I'm losing my grip. My aim now is not to reach the end of the world but rather to reach the end of my sanity.

By every means possible, I try to blank out the 750 miles of unforgiving, cold wasteland I have yet to cross. I simply try to put in six hours of cycling every day. Again tonight, I wonder how I've come this far already.

My arrival is usually expected everywhere I go. In these parts, news travels like the wind. Townsfolk are friendly and, for the most part, intrigued by my adventure. They ply me with questions: Where do I come from? Where am I going? Am I married? And always the same questions, so much so that I'm on the brink of understanding Farsi! Caroline's photo, front and center on my handlebars, is of particular interest. "Your wife? Want picture!" At a checkpoint, a military officer asks me to hand it over to him on the pretext that it's illegal. Why illegal?

"Hair no good, no chador!"

He wants it badly. So do I! That's why I demote Caroline to the bottom of my saddlebag. From now on, medals and photos will be out of sight and out of everybody's mind, except mine.

Questions about Canada are both numerous and difficult, because very few speak English in these isolated villages. "Canada cold?" accompanied by a shivering gesture is easy to understand, but explaining my religion is a more complicated matter. Our conversations look more like nonverbal sign language than a cultural exchange. Be that as it may, the language barrier sometimes presents a wall that I cannot surmount.

Two of my questioners, with some vigorous gesticulation, make it understood that they would like to invite me back to their home. I accept without a second thought. We place my bike in the back of the pick up and we're off. I soon realize that I'm doing some back tracking, but riding the extra miles tomorrow will be well worth it for the chance to sleep in a warm bed tonight. The drive is a long one. As we leave the village, we abruptly veer off onto a dirt road, apparently leading to nowhere. A sign shows we've already driven twenty-five miles. That means dedicating a whole day to retracing this route. I suddenly feel like I'm in a trap. I slink down in the backseat. I have to find a solution quickly, because every minute leads me further and further away from my primary objective: namely, to get out of this wretched desert and to the Pakistani border as soon as possible. Not to mention, my entrance visa is about to expire.

Another worry crops up. I'm a little nervous about their sexual orientation, and I don't want any misunderstandings. I ask them to stop and explain to me exactly where they live. I try to make them understand that they live too far off my route, and ask if they would be so kind as to take me back where they first picked me up? After a solid five minutes explaining my quandary (which seem to me more like fifty), they accept.

So, I'm dropped off right where I began . . . but damn! Another blow. Now the restaurant is closed. All I can do is jump on my bike and head for the next rest stop. The sun will soon go down. I have to act fast. I ask where the next road stop is. "About a mile," I'm told. Pleasantly surprised, I nevertheless double-check with another group who tell me it's about two miles down the road, maybe three! I'm used to these "guesstimates" where you need to multiply the stated number by two. I should know—I've been keeping tabs on this. Why worry about an extra one or two miles after having ridden sixty already? The reason is quite simple: when I'm asking, "how far to go?" I'm exhausted and at the end of my rope. However strange it might appear, it's during these last few miles that I begin to sweat profusely, to freeze, and to get nagging knee pains. Obviously, from their vague answers, distances don't have the same importance for them as they do for me. How could they? At first, this bothered me. Now I enjoy figuring out the actual distance, based on local estimates and my own stats. This time, I turned out to be right, after pedaling another five miles before reaching the next restaurant. There, I'm asked all the same questions, the same ones as before, and the time before. I repeat the same answers as patiently as Job himself. It's well worth it, because the restaurant owner extends an invitation to stay indoors overnight, cozy and warm, in a back room. The Iranians are an unlimited source of grace and kindness. Nobody in these parts would hear of me sleeping outside in such cold temperatures.

DAY 148

Yazd, Iran—December 9, 1994

After cordial goodbyes with the usual exchange of addresses, I leave the restaurant. To cheer me on, the locals swear that the road leading to Nain is relatively flat, except for a mountain that is nothing much more than a hill. Yeah, yeah, naturally I believed them hook, line, and sinker. Sitting pretty behind the wheel of a 150-horsepower truck, all mountains are molehills, but on a bicycle loaded up like a camel, it's a different matter.

Later that morning, as I hurtle down from the other side of their "hill" at top speed, I hit a pebble in the wrong place and blow the inner tube of my front wheel. As I'm fixing it, a magnificent motorcycle roars past me then comes to a halt. Such a machine can only mean a European. It might be blarney, but he says he's Irish, and he's going around the world on his hog. He's followed the same route as me and says the section between Agri and Tehran is covered with two feet of snow. He was even forced to take the train. Somehow, I managed to avoid a snowstorm like the Irish biker experienced.

For the first time, I'm riding without wearing anything GORE-TEX®. The pure joy of sunrays beaming down on me does wonders for my body and soul. I feel reborn. My knee is fine, and I suspect the cold was the problem. At least, I'd like to think so.

The day is skipping by and still no sign of life anywhere. A trucker tells me there's a restaurant between Nain and the next town. Truckers are the only ones I can rely on for this type of information. I'm riding hard, when suddenly a swirling wind whips up. At long last, I spot a restaurant, just as the sun sinks below the horizon. I lean my bike against the wall, take in the beauty of the dimming sky, and then try to open the restaurant door. Closed. Fuming with disbelief, I look all around. Maybe I'm being spied on. I leave in a furious mood, still in shock. At this moment, the road is bumper-to-bumper full of trucks, buses, and cars, all competing like they're part of a Formula 1 Grand Prix race. More alarming, not a single vehicle has headlights on.

After seventy-five miles, I'm still pedaling. My problem is not a lack of energy but the rather the danger of cycling blind. It is now completely dark. My bike has very few fluorescent reflectors stuck to it. Vehicles whiz past without their headlights on, real but invisible missiles, which can torpedo me into oblivion at any time. Every time I hear a truck approaching, I pull over and stop well off the road. I didn't hear a bus coming, however, and it passed so close by that it made my blood curdle. I have to stop . . . this is way too dangerous.

But I've got no food left. So be it, I'll have to hitchhike. Since I'm not visible, I take out my flashlight and flash it at the passing vehicles. Ten minutes go by until a car finally stops. A teeny-weeny car. A man jumps out to offer me a lift in broken English. This is wonderful, too wonderful. His son also gets out to help. I cannot believe that we managed to jam everything into such a confined space! But we did. The bike and the saddlebags hang by the skin of their teeth on the outside of the trunk.

The twelve-year-old son is learning English at school. In spite of his father's coaxing, he keeps mum. The father carries on the conversation as best he can. As we become more at ease, I take this opportunity to ask a burning question of mine:

"Why no lights when drive?"

He looks at me with a half-smile and answers me, straight up: "Because better for battery!"

We arrive at his place in Yazd, just in time for supper. I'm surrounded by the whole family . . . except, as per usual, for the women and girls. They will take their meals in another room, once we have finished ours. I'm treated not merely as a casual drop-in, but rather as a distinguished guest. I certainly didn't ask for so much, but I accept it gladly. A cousin comes to join us. He spent four years in the United States, where he got married. In 1978, upon his return for a two-week vacation, he was intercepted by customs officers and forced to live once more in Iran. Meanwhile, back in the States, he left behind his wife and a child that he hasn't seen since. He is an engineer-designer and worked for Bell Helicopter in the United States. His genius inventions include a type of bolt used on NASA's space shuttle, which now bears his name: the "Kamal Bolt." During the war with Iraq, he also developed a system to divert and destroy Iraqi missiles aimed at Tehran. He's not exactly my image of a braniac: disheveled hair, huge thick glasses, and only two teeth evident . . . two buck teeth, at that. In a nutshell, it's all happening inside his head.

The father sends away his son, and we're now between adults. Their faces light up. There's mystery in the air. The son returns with a small portable stove and disappears again.

"You smoke?" The father asks me.

"Occasionally, with friends," I reply.

"I mean opium, you try?"

And here's me thinking we would be roasting marshmallows! Instead, he pulls out a pipe: long stem with a bowl at the end. He lights up the burner and heats some small, sticky lumps. Using a needle, he transfers the melted opium into the bowl of the pipe. It's my turn now. They look at me, eager to see my reaction. Really, it would have made no difference to me if I were smoking opium or the living room carpet. The real joy for me is to find myself in a lost town in Iran, right in the heart of the desert, with an ex-cop and an engineer who I've hardly just met and who already consider me part of the family. It's in these moments that I find the true meaning of my journey.

I don't indulge in my opium trip beyond the first puff. I'm indifferent to legal or moral issues, but my body simply says, "No." A day of cycling is much too demanding, so I can't take any risks that would jeopardize my progress.

My new friends succumb to their own enjoyment and don't pressure me after my second refusal. While I'm busy writing in my journal, the father notices the word "opium" at the top of the page. He asks me not to mention anything about this evening, because the government often opens the mail. This could come back to bite them and cause them grave problems. I'm inclined to take these comments with a grain of salt, but their somber attitude is warning enough. The atmosphere noticeably relaxes when they see me erasing the word "opium."

As I leave the room to "point Percy at the porcelain," I come face-to-face with the women of the house. They quickly cover up their heads. I'm surprised and apologize immediately. The father tells me it's a good idea to knock before entering a room where women might be present. In Tehran, I had been told that the wearing of the veil was optional inside the home, but it seems that religious rules apply differently from one family to the next. Here, they cut me off from half of the family.

One thing is certain, these people are happy. I can feel it. The key to their happiness is not based on material values, easy morals, or lax religious views. Plainly, they must find happiness deep within themselves.

DAY 149
Yazd, Iran—December 10, 1994

When I was in Tehran, I was so sick that I wonder if, instead of eating an egg, I maybe ate a chicken fetus. Again tonight, I was woken up by horrible cramps coupled with diarrhea, and I had to deliberately throw up to get some relief. Maybe it's caused by the ubiquitous ground-meat kebabs that I'm being fed day after day and that my gut refuses to digest anymore. I'm nauseated just thinking about them. Strangely enough, this morning, I still have a queasy stomach, but I do feel better.

I go sight-seeing around town and catch one of the oldest and most fabulous mosques in the whole of Iran. Its main minaret, which rises high over the city, was once a guiding landmark for the caravans coming in from the desert. The old city is a labyrinth surrounded by a very high wall. Inside, you get a strong sense of the past, thanks to the inhabitants who still faithfully follow the old ways.

As is the case for all desert towns, Yazd has a big problem when it comes to drinking water. As a safety precaution, I filter it first, then add two drops of bleach for every quart of water. The taste is not great, but a swig of public-pool water is easier to handle than full-blown gastric warfare.

This evening, an air of sadness underlines my imminent departure. What's on the menu for supper doesn't matter to me; their company is all that counts. I leave the choice of restaurant up to them. They say we're going to the best place to eat in town.

In shock and awe, I'm instantly nauseous when I see the cook making his specialty through the window—kebabs! I haven't even set foot in the restaurant, and already I feel sick. All the same, I'm still intrigued by the preparation of this dish that I can no longer stomach. It's simple: the cook dips his (more or less) clean hand into a bowl to grab a fistful of ground meat, which is then repeatedly squeezed onto a skewer until it sticks. I always wondered how they managed to get that wavy shape on the skewer . . . now I know.

The aroma hits me as soon as I put a foot into the entranceway. All I see are platefuls of kebabs, plate after plate. The father orders as bile backs up in my throat. In Iran, politeness dictates no food offered generously by a host shall be refused. Neither shall second servings, just be sure to eat eveything on your plate. The host is satisfied only when he deems that his guest is fully sated. The hardest thing I've had to do in my life. Compared to this, crossing the desert was a piece of cake.

I must speak with the father. My mouth goes dry.

"In Turkey, I was very ill because of the kebabs, and I cannot eat them any more."

I also don't want to tell him how sick I was last night for fear of hurting his feelings.

"Yes, but Turkey bad meat, here very good!"

I couldn't find the strength to persuade him, so I flatly refuse to partake of the kebabs. The last thing I need tomorrow is a projectile-vomiting exhibition from my bike. So I stand my ground; he doesn't insist.

"If change mind, I can try!" I say.

I can't watch them eat without thinking that my resophagian gastric reflux emesis might ruin this beautiful meal.

Regardless, today, I was treated like royalty. As they say so well, and with so much conviction, "You're family, and our home is your home."

This kindly patriarch tells me how sad his children are to see me leaving.

"If you weren't traveling by bicycle, you could stay longer."

I reply that if I hadn't been on my bike, he wouldn't have stopped to give me a lift, and we would never have met. I was so close to them; I shall never forget them.

While I write, the father sits at the end of the table, taking advantage of my presence to benefit from our remaining few hours together. His son, sitting across from me, looks at me intently. My writing fascinates him; it's so different from his. He looks up words in the dictionary to share with me. His mother beams, seeing her son getting so much out of such an exotic contact. The atmosphere is magic. Peace and quiet reigns supreme in the room as if, by mutual consent, we were communicating through the voice of the heart and soul.

* * *

DAY 150
Kermanshah, Iran—December 11, 1994

With a heavy heart, I bid farewell to these generous people, who would like nothing better than keep me a few months longer. I leave behind my regal life to re-begin as a cyclist. Such encounters supercharge my spirits, as if by magic.

Following a hilly route, I can see the next ten miles stretched out in front of me.

Since Isfahan, rest stops have been more and more spaced out on these desert roads. I need to plan more. It's three in the afternoon, and I've arrived in Kerman. Even if it's still early, I bunk down for the night in a restaurant meant for truckers located along the main desert route. It's the prudent thing to do. I say "restaurant," but it's no St-Hubert chicken joint, like in Quebec. It's a plain, rectangular, concrete block, with zero ambience, empty most of the time. Some religious icons hang on the walls. On one side is a primitive toilet and, on the other, a rudimentary kitchen, in the center of which sits a red-hot kerosene stove. Oddly enough, the outside doors stay wide open, even in this cold weather. The abundance of oil and its ridiculously low cost—less than a penny a gallon—doesn't encourage anyone to save on fuel.

The menu is not very adventurous, the same old chicken and rice, but it is delicious, especially after a long day of riding. Tomorrow for breakfast, as usual, I'll take three eggs with some yogurt and honey. A mountain of rice, some bread, and a pot of tea will also appear, even though I didn't order it. A few thankful gestures and words of appreciation in their own language does the trick: this evening, I'm invited to sleep in the heated dormitory, usually reserved for road-weary truckers. It's a welcomed privilege. Finally a bed (a real one!) and a pillow.

As I read through my journal, thank goodness I had no idea what was in store for me in Iran. During an evening like this, when everything is well with the world, I'm in seventh heaven, but in the daytime, when I return to the friggingly frigid cold and when my knee starts to ache, I descend once again to the depths of Hades. I feel like the devil's puppet or, rather, a devil of my own creation that I can't seem to shake.

Through much wishful thinking, I manage to persuade myself that come tomorrow, everything will get better. Getting back to reality is cruel, because my troubles just loom larger, even as my energy level drops. Much to my great despair, my dream is starting to slowly but surely fade away.

* * *

Chapter 7

....

A Deadly Desert

The weather is just as bad as ever. No rest stop anywhere in sight, so I'm forced to eat outside, near the ruins of an ancient caravan shelter. There's only one wall left standing. The others must have been swept away by the desert's harsh winds. I stretch out on the ground, under some shade, to take advantage of a few minutes of rest—a rare break from the day's ride. The sky is clearest blue, but the air is icy. Silence reigns. I'm alone in the world. My desert angst tapers off for a moment, enough to enjoy a light snack: yogurt, walnuts, cereal, bread, local cheese, and carrot jam.

Back in the saddle again, my knee jolts me back to the painful reality, slowly killing me. The same words echo incessantly in my head: "I can't keep going, I can't go on . . . obviously, I'm going to have to quit. No, I can't give up, I have to continue. But why should I continue? I can't keep going, I can't go on . . . face it, I'm going to have to quit. . . ." I snap out of my torpor, doing my best to end my racing thoughts, but my mind's totally adrift. The evil gears churn even faster. Fear of failure is so overwhelming that I cannot chase it away.

My visa expires on December 22. Just ten days away. I could get an extension, but if I don't cross the border by December 29, my visa for Pakistan will expire. One way or another, I must put in twice the effort. Yet I desperately need to rest. My badly weakened morale has to support a badgered body. Already, I've waited much too long. I can't stop. Something is pulling me under. Unable to accept defeat, my ambition would rather see me utterly destroyed. Up to this point, it has meant my survival. Now I'm worried that it will end up killing me.

> Traveling is living
> But it's also surviving On the road, rejoicing But also, suffering
> Being faithful to your ambition Becomes quite a mission
> Especially as the wind chimes
> In with the other climes Suspending you in time
> When comes the night
> You muster your might
> To face another day
> With hopeful heart at play

DAY 152
Rafsanjan, Iran—December 13, 1994

This evening, I am alone in the desert, staring at the door of the roadside restaurant, closed till morning. I pitch my tent, hoping I'll still be here tomorrow, because I've stopped at a favored entry point for Afghani drug traffickers. This isn't what's keeping me up tonight, however. I'm having trouble digesting my food. Cramps are tearing up my guts. Suddenly, I have a bellyache so violent that it hurls me out of my tent to vomit, still barefooted and half-dressed. It's just 20°F outside. A pang shoots through my body like an electric shock. My bowels are about to explode. I squat and let loose like there's no tomorrow. The malaise continues. I can't stop shivering. I'm going to freeze on the spot.

Even curled up in my sleeping bag, I can't seem to get warm again. My teeth are chattering away, out of cold but also out of fear. Minutes creep by like hours.

Finally, the restaurant opens its doors at six in the morning. I dash in to get close to the just-lit stove. Whatever my woes, another day lies ahead. I try to force down what's on the menu. No surprise here: rice, chicken, and eggs.

DAY 153
Bagian, Iran—December 14, 1994

"I can't go on, I must face facts and give up. No, I can't give up. I must go on. No, I can't do it any more. . . ."

I'm at my breaking point.

At 1:17 AM on December 14, 1994, while I pedal against every atom of my being, I'm shaken by a spine-chilling howl. The deepest cry of release. The final push in a painful birth. Escaping the bowels of the Earth, far from society's confines, even my own servitude, shackled to my bike and my pathological desire to perform. Time and again, I longed to hitch a ride with a passing vehicle and get out of the desert. The logical thing to do, no question. But I was incapable of taking action. In fact, I wasn't ready to ride out of this nightmare. I felt a strong contradiction between the yearning to end my suffering and the desire to go even deeper to heal my soul. As I lost hope, I retreated into my bubble, the same way Jean-Pierre had done before his departure. I ceased to exist. I biked on despite myself. My body could barely continue even as my will pushed it forward, mercilessly. I felt like I was mutilating my soul, a torment I shall never forget. I even flirted with death. Now, the world is my oyster, mine for the taking. Everything is back on track. I've even ironed out all the kinks that have cropped up over the passing years. I've lost none of my ambition—rather, I've become its master. I destroyed myself so I could better rebuild myself. It's done! I reached the melting point so that I might forge a better me. I have nothing more to prove. If my trip ends here, I'll be fully satisfied. I can return home with my head held high.

Be that as it may, I nevertheless continue on, propelled forward by the sheer joy of the journey, as well as a burning desire to savor this new, hard-won freedom.

I don't know what to write anymore. I feel so good, it's making my head spin. And it's hard for me to figure out what just happened, exactly.

I camp near a cemetery where a funeral is in full swing. According to local custom, close friends and relatives of the deceased congregate around the grave, to eat together and chant prayers. Snuggled up in my sleeping bag, I am lulled to slumber by this languid lullaby, good enough to put the dead to rest. . . .

DAY 155

Bam, Iran—December 16, 1994

Upon entering the town of Bam, after a ninety-five–mile day, a young man jumps in front of my path and implores me to stop. He says he studies English at the university and absolutely wants me to meet his family. The villagers have known about my imminent arrival, and the poor guy tells me that he's been waiting for me for more than five hours. I'm tired, but how could I refuse? His mother is very happy to receive me. Out of nowhere, his three brothers, sister, cousin, and father emerge. In a concrete room furnished with a solitary Persian rug and some embroidered pillows, we sit down and talk around a kerosene lamp, which offers us both light and warmth. The student acts as our interpreter. The mother questions me about my religious customs and eventually asks if I believe that Islam is one of better world religions. She obviously expects a positive answer, which would no doubt reassure her. Why this ceaseless need to "convert" those of different faiths? Maybe it's because we're all so afraid to question our own beliefs. This generous family has welcomed me as one of their own—isn't that the best proof that you can love your fellow man unconditionally, whatever god we believe in?

DAY 158
Zahedan, Iran—December 18, 1994

My bicycle loaded with supplies, I spend two days of solitude on a road where only a nutter would bike, or so I've been told. Having thrown up twice during night, I shakily make my entrance into Zahedan, a somewhat so-so arrival, diminished by fatigue and exhaustion. What's more, I've just discovered that my back wheel is damaged: two busted spokes, leaving half-inch gaps along the wheel rim. With potholes in the road and the weight of the luggage, it's only a matter of time before it's completely kaput. I'll move some extra load to the front wheel, but that won't last long. It's impossible to find sophisticated equipment, like the new spokes and rim I need, in the countries that I'm traveling through, and if I don't get a new wheel rim soon, that'll be it. I'll keep pushing until the wheel gives out, come what may. I'm absolutely determined to finish my last fifty-seven Iranian miles in the saddle.

This evening, it's a frat house celebration with a dozen Iranian students. We're getting plastered tonight . . . on tea! They're good people, but the same old question always pops up: "Do you have sex photos?"

DAY 160
Mirjaveh, Iran—December 21, 1994

Iran kept surprising me, right up until the end. Thirty-five miles from the Pakistani border, I run into a raging sandstorm.

And I thought I'd seen everything! The wind blows ever more strongly. In an instant, the sky is covered in a dense cloud of sand. I've lost all my bearings. I try to follow the road, but it's vanishing right before my eyes. Sandy gusts restrict my vision to less than six feet. Wind aside, the sand-blasting stings my arms, thighs, and face. I keep one eye open, the other closed. My clothing, my equipment, and my bicycle chain are filled with grit. My derailer starts creaking. No traffic means less danger but also gives me trouble knowing which direction I should be heading. Finally, at the fifty-five-mile mark on my odometer, I spot the border-control checkpoint at Mirjaveh. Success! I made it across Iran.

Three Sweet Victories!

A capital "S" plus a Winston Churchill "V."

The first victory: to have become free of prejudice about this country that previously so frightened me.

The second victory: to have crossed daunting mountains and taunting deserts by bike, alone, in the dead of winter.

And the third: to have pushed my limits to the extreme.

* * *

Chapter 8

....

Another World

DAY 161
Iranian-Pakistani Border—December 22, 1994

At 9 AM sharp, the border opens. Like all cyclists leaving Iran, I must comply with the country's final-exit requirements. As the law stipulates, I must leave the country with my bike and gear, as registered in my passport. Slowly, I cross the neutral zone between Iran and Pakistan.

And so a new chapter begins: Pakistan. Each border I cross is a doorway to the unknown, a world inviting me to get to know it. The contrast is striking. Pakistan is a developing country, still in an era where oxcarts and manual labor are the rule. There are a few dilapidated shanties lining the route, I've never before passed through such a ragtag border.

I present myself to the immigration officer, who is more interested in my cycling gear than in my passport.

"Bicycle license?"

I tell him the brand name of my bike. He doesn't buy it.

"Visa no good."

My mouth goes dry, and I start to feel queasy.

"Why?"

"Because no allowed to travel by bike in Pakistan without special pass!"

I shudder to think I might have to retrace my steps. Nobody has ever spoken to me about any special bike permit, and I suspect he's just hitting me up for a bribe. My arguments fall on deaf ears. He's not even listening as he says again and again:

"No allowed . . . No allowed."

I remain patient and polite, because I realize he'll surely have the last word. Suddenly, after ten minutes of pointless discussion, he lets me pass. As simple as that. I don't even try to understand why.

Then, I get it. Leaving the border, I notice that my visa, initially valid for three months, is now good for just one month! The vindictive bastard did the dirty on me by reducing my visa stay without me realizing it. I fume and curse, but don't dare turn around in case he makes my situation even worse. I know he doesn't have the authority to pull such a stunt, but if I want to pursue my journey, I need to eat a slice of humble pie.

I pedal hard on sand and gravel for a mile or so before finding something vaguely resembling a road. Time to rock'n'roll! I change my rearview mirror from left to right, because, in Pakistan, vehicles drive on the left-hand side of the road. Barely wider than a car and full of ruts and potholes, this road is a real bitch to ride on. Comparively speaking, Iran was a cyclist's paradise. A headwind changes into side-wind gusts. But thankfully, the sand cover stays on the ground, and I manage to avoid a sandstorm, although I'm moving about as fast as a turtle. I've got nearly seventy-five miles to clock before I reach the next village, Nok Kundi. Crossing the border meant a time-zone change, so I set my watch an hour and a half ahead. It's already noon, and I have little chance of arriving at my next destination before nightfall.

My health remains questionable. My egg breakfast starts to give me some serious problems. I pedal nonstop but feel like I'm going nowhere. Nothing on the horizon. Five solid hours of cycling, and I've only come across five vehicles. It's late, and I still have twenty-eight miles to go. This time, I wisely decide to ask for help. After half an hour waiting on the side of the road, a truck finally stops and agrees to give me a lift to the Nok Kundi checkpoint. I've made the right choice, because both the wind and the road conditions aren't getting any better. In fact, in some places the road is blocked by sand drifts up to two feet high.

Arriving at the checkpoint, the policemen on duty make me an offer of tea with milk, which I cannot refuse. They tell me that a 200-mile stretch between here and Quetta is under construction. It will be impossible to ride under these conditions. My mind spins as I try to make sense of it all. Hoping for a miracle, I try to curry favor with the policemen so that they might get me out of here, but it's a waste of time. My problem is the least of their concerns.

The tea takes effect. I start having stomach cramps due to food poisoning, fatigue, or frustration—who knows? I have to leave this accursed place at all costs. A hundred yards farther along, I stop at what is supposed to be a restaurant: scruffy, shady-looking food hawkers, plates buzzing with flies, and a standard of cleanliness that would make any stomach turn. Mine is already on edge. I'm belching up rotten eggs, and the pains in my stomach turn me off any food whatsoever. Although my legs are as wonky as cotton balls, I hop back on my bike and exit the village, where the paved road ends. I've now got a better idea of what's involved in crossing this country: dubious eats, precarious health, a lack of passable roads, a wheel about to bite the big one, and a visa that expires in less than a month.

I wish I could find somebody who could get me out of here, somewhere where I could have a rest for a change. Exhausted and demoralized, I wait four long hours at the edge of the desert, alone in total darkness. With not a soul on the horizon, I return to the checkpoint to find a bus station.

With my bicycle strapped to the roof, we're off. What a relief to just sit back and enjoy the ride! Barreling along at 40 mph on a sketchy road— heaven! The bus is loaded to the rafters, people everywhere, filling both seats and aisle, while music blasts away. Inside it's a party, lit up like a Christmas tree. Outside it's a black hole . . . an infinite void. Peace of mind, finally.

Only a few hours until I reach civilization. Just one problem, which soon becomes serious: the egg I ate.

In no time at all, the stifling air inside the bus, the jarring vibrations from the bumpy road, ubiquitous cigarette smoke, and the blaring music transform my dream into a nightmare. I never felt so trapped in my entire life. I'm becoming increasingly more nauseous, and I wonder who'll be the lucky recipient of my imminent vomiting. Two hours later, they announce a thirty-minute pit stop. It's surprising what your stomach will serve up even when you think it is empty.

The next seven hours go by smoothly enough, but then we hit six road-blocks. Officers take an inordinate amount of time meticulously checking IDs and luggage, both inside the bus and on top of the roof. Other than that, no real holdups. We're in the Balochistan region, a hub for drug trafficking between Pakistan, Afghanistan, and Iran.

The bus comes to a halt, parking on the curbside of a deserted main road in Quetta. The passengers break out as if they were prison escapees. After sixteen hours in this mobile, metal cage, who could blame them? It's still dark, but I get back on my bike and leave, hard-pressed to find somewhere nice to sleep. I settle for the first cheap hotel I come across. For two dollars, I get four concrete walls, a bed, a small window, a Turkish toilet, a washing basin, and warm water between 6 AM and 8 AM. Bingo! I've hit the jackpot.

Tomorrow is Christmas Eve in Canada, but here, it's just another day. It's raining, a novelty for me because I haven't experienced anything falling from the sky since passing through the desert. I sense that a kinder, gentler nature is back on my side again, and I'm calmed by the soothing pitter-patter of raindrops drumming on my window.

DAY 164
Quetta, Pakistan—December 25, 1994

No longer able to sleep, I go for a walk on Ali Jinnah street, the main drag. Everything is quiet right now. Businesses are closed, but roadside stalls lining the streets swarm with life. Soon they will have to feed the wave of workers. The street will become a huge open-air kitchen. A few small and weatherworn wooden benches serve as seats, but most will eat on the run—fast food indeed.

My greatest joy is to sniff about and taste everything: beans in tomato sauce, chicken and rice, fried fish, hot peppers, fruits, sugar cane—a tantalizing cornucopia. There's no menu as such, but everything is in plain sight, simmering away in huge pots on small, propane burners. To avoid any bad surprises, I sneak a peek at what customers are being served, and when a dish looks appetizing, I point at it and say, "One, please." If I happen to return to the same place, I'm immediately recognized and obligingly served the same thing.

In Pakistan, as in Iran, bread is always served with meals. It's baked lightning fast and served piping hot. The breadmakers make it look like child's play: flatten a ball of dough until it becomes very thin, thin enough to spin like pizza dough. In one fell swoop it's stuck to the inner wall of a round-wood stove using a cotton pad. The part stuck to the wall becomes crusty, while the other side puffs up under the heat of the embers. The result makes for a delicious serving, crunchy on one side, chewy on the other.

Twenty-four years ago today, I was born. For my birthday, I treat myself to a space heater. Merry Christmas. Hugs and kisses to all of you. I think of you a lot.

DAY 165
Quetta, Pakistan—December 26, 1994

I've slept twenty-four of the last thirty-one hours. Where can I find a bank that accepts Visa, right in the heart of Pakistan? Two hours of fruitless searching. Bank tellers look at my card as if it was a worthless piece of plastic, and, worse still, I'm told my Iranian rials might as well be Monopoly money. I turn to the bazaar. Here, they don't turn their noses up at my rials. Pass "Go" and collect $200 . . . I'm flush with dough.

It's raining, so I decide to return to my room. Feeling expansive, I indulge in a rickshaw ride, sitting comfortably under the canvas hood of this man-powered three-wheeler, painted a thousand different colors. Here, as everywhere in the region, honking comes as naturally as breathing, which gets pretty exhausting after a while.

My back wheel has finally died. The last sixty miles did it in. Here, you only find bikes from the Jurassic Period. With Karachi in the extreme south of Pakistan under a security curfew, Lahore is the only major city in the East where I could get a new wheel. Without knowing exactly how to get the new wheel to Lahore, I'll contact my mother, who, thanks to her travel experience, resourcefulness, and necessary means, will know how to get the job done. Forced to accept this setback, I take the train for Lahore, a twenty-six-hour journey. By local word of mouth, I learn that very few tourists manage to make it across the Quetta-Lahore route without being robbed or worse. It's even been dubbed "The Alley of Thieves."

DAY 167
En route to Lahore, Pakistan—December 28, 1994

A sleepless night spent on a small bench, cold enough to freeze the nuts off a squirrel, followed by a twenty-nine-hour train ride to get 185 miles eastward. In jam-packed stations, shouting hucksters of all ages ply their wares: beans, lentils, rice, cookies, tea, and cakes. Barefooted beggars follow them in this boisterous procession. When I can't sleep, I take the opportunity to check out each station, to stretch out my legs and sample the local culinary delights.

We are now passing through the Indus Valley, a cradle of civilization dating back to the third millennium BC. People work quietly in the fields, carrying their loads on the backs of donkeys. Having done their part tilling the fields, buffaloes are resting by the side of the road. For the first time since I was near the Turkish coast, I find myself less than 3,000 feet above sea level. The weather is warmer. Everything is green. Population density has sharply increased. I've left my desert angst far behind.

DAY 168
Lahore, Pakistan—December 29, 1994

Unfortunately, I'm not spending my holidays in the best of health. All night long, I shuttle between bedroom and bathroom, always accompanied by these infamous belches with a peculiar, rotten-egg taste. A Belgian and Swiss, with whom I've just become acquainted, suffered from the same misery. They tell me it's a typical symptom of giardiasis and recommend that I take Flagyl®. Jean-Denis was prescribed Nidazol at the Turkish university hospital, and it turns out that it's basically the same medication.

Giardiasis is passed on by eating contaminated food, whereupon a batch of microscopic worms set up house in the host's bowel. After an incubation period lasting as long as twenty-four weeks, these parasites can be counted in the millions. As a defense, the digestive tract reacts by causing the bowel to empty. Regrettably, certain worms find refuge in the folds of the intestines and wait for more food to start reproducing again. Thus, a vicious cycle is created: growth, purge, regeneration, purge, and so on. Without treatment, the system cannot rid itself of the parasite.

In a living room back home who would dare mention, to friends and strangers alike, the current state of their bowel movements? Here travelers talk about their intestines even before they swap names and addresses. This long trail of tubing is often the sole determinant of a happy or hapless stay.

I stop by a private hospital run by the Salvation Army, hoping a doctor will confirm the diagnosis of my fellow travelers. But he says that I'm suffering from gastroenteritis and adds that I should refrain from eating any spicy food. I look at him as if he's advised me not to walk on sand in the middle of the desert. Here, the only food that you can get would burn the inside of a dragon's mouth. He steps out briefly and returns with a handful of antacids and red pills, which he carefully counts out, with suspiciously grubby fingers, into a "pre-owned" plastic bag. If he thinks that I'm going to pop these "tic-tacs" without knowing what they contain, he's got another thing coming! If I don't feel any better tomorrow, I'll try the red antibiotic pills (which turned out to be Flagyl) . . . start popping, stop pooping. End of story.

I've just found out that the Karakorum road, which follows the mountain range at the western extreme of the Pakistani Himalayas, has been temporarily closed because of heavy snowfalls. Since this route was not on my original biking itinerary, I'll go visit it by bus for a well-deserved break while waiting for my new wheel to arrive from Canada.

DAY 170
Lahore, Pakistan—December 31, 1994

I'm in a great mood, so I visit the Lahore zoo and enjoy a quiet walk in the old town. The bazaar looks uncannily like the one in the movie City of Joy. Everyone goes about their own business. I like sitting on the sidewalk, back against the wall, simply taking in the scene. At first, passersby stop to look at me, top to bottom, but after a while, I fade into the background and become part of the scenery. I keenly observe their practiced habits; their meticulous gestures, even while doing mundane tasks such as dicing sprigs of wilted parsley, fascinate me. The way they prepare a simple bowl of rice for each customer seems so important. Preparing food and feeding people is a trade that is held in high esteem. A merchant arranges his fruit in a perfect mosaic, while another carefully spritzes his vegetables with a spray bottle to make them glisten with freshness. Three hours spent watching how others live their lives invigorates my own life.

With the constant clamor of honking cars and the blight of poverty all around me, I'm shaken back into reality. But maybe having seen this sorry scene so often on TV makes me feel less guilty about being relatively well off and in good health. Who knows? Maybe our values and our material comfort would bring these people even more suffering. Anything is possible here; even seeing a legless man, strapped to the lid of a trashcan, still managing to cross the street.

After coming back from a third-world country, bragging about seeing "real" poverty is just a cop-out. It gives us some peace of mind as we return to our safety cocoons, with the certainty that our world is better, that our life is enviable. Here, I've often heard, life has no value. There are so many people that what do a few more deaths here and there really matter? At home, we deny death but gladly kill ourselves working. With all the effort required for modern, material comfort, we hasten our own demise without knowing it, and we live without taking time to live.

Those of us living in rich countries look for a happy life, while those in poor countries are just happy to be alive. Isn't awareness of the gift of life enough reason to find happiness? At our frenetic pace of life, I wonder if we haven't bypassed happiness and raced so far ahead of it that we'll never find it again.

But I talk about happiness without really knowing where it lies. According to my father, I'm not lucky, because he maintains that happiness can be found "in our own backyard." So it's not as if I have to go halfway around the world to to figure that one out.

I feel much better tonight. Is my Christmas present late, or will it be an early New Year's gift? No matter, let the good times roll regardless.

Happy New Year!

* * *

Chapter 9

·····································

The Himalayas: First Meeting with the Earth's Giants

DAY 171
Lahore, Pakistan—January 1, 1995

I cried victory too soon. My diarrhea's back. I pick up some 7-Up, bread, and water-soluble gastrolyte powder (a sodium, potassium, and sugar mix that helps rebalance the body's electrolytes), and I stagger off to my bed. My trip to Islamabad is postponed for now.

I use my last ounce of energy to crawl to the hospital. I'm not sure if the dehydration has caused me to become disoriented, but I wander around in circles for a good forty-five minutes. Eventually, I find the hospital. Now, where can I find a doctor? Under a scorching sun, people of all ages wait patiently on the main steps—the hospital's makeshift waiting room. Before getting discouraged, I discover that being a Westerner apparently gives me an advantage; namely, I soon find myself at the front desk. I gladly pay the two-rupee registration fee, and I'm invited to take a seat.

A doctor, either just-plain curious or keen to practice his English, hurries over to examine me. He makes me lie down on a stretcher and gives me the once-over, even though we're surrounded by curious onlookers. Thank goodness I'm not here for a prostate exam! But I have to say I much prefer to be examined as if I were a Martian rather than have to wait outside for the whole afternoon with the rest of the anonymous mob. My blood pressure is good, and he deems that I should fully recover with some rest. Taking Flagyl® was a good move, because he's just prescribed me some more. I return to my room to lie down, reassuring myself that it's about all I can do for the moment. This hospital visit turned out to be more of a hassle than a whole day spent on the bike. I'm a faithful diarist, but I have to stop because even my pen is too heavy for me right now.

DAY 173
Lahore, Pakistan—January 3, 1995

Well settled in my room this evening, I play the health freak and put my mess-kit gear to work preparing steamed cabbage, eggplants, carrots, and potatoes. Plus, no spices are in sight, just a little cheese and a slice of bread. My digestion is much better thanks to my conscientous efforts.

DAY 174
Lahore, Pakistan—January 4, 1995

Late in the evening, strolling along a deserted alley, I stumble across a large gathering. Excited kids scramble to catch coins that have been tossed into the air. An immaculately dressed man, in a brightly colored get-up and riding a superb, white stallion, leads a cacaphonous fanfare. The procession comes to a halt, and people begin shuffling into a hall. Suddenly, somebody pushes me inside. Even though I'm just wearing shorts and a T-shirt, I've been spontaneously invited to a Muslim wedding. Among lively musicians, a luscious buffet, and a kaleidoscope of celebrating guests, I stick out like the proverbial sore thumb. But nobody seems to mind. People act like it's their last meal, with plates emptying as quickly as they're filled up again.

In Pakistan, a wedding is a joyous occasion. On such a day, everybody gives money as a symbol of celebration and abundance. The way this is done, however, is slightly unconventional. One-rupee bills are stuck to the heads of the guests, whoever they may be, and someone is designated as bill collector. This is how newlyweds are given their wedding presents. As the festivities unfold, everybody dances their feet off, until finally exhausted. I don't join in the dancing, but I do enjoy myself immensely, taking in this spectacular scene, sharing in their happiness.

DAY 175
Lahore, Pakistan—January 5, 1995

Posting letters is quite the feat in this town. The post office randomly opens and closes whenever it suits the staff, and once inside, you invariably find yourself at the wrong counter. A real tower of Babel, where line jumping is rife as each desperate customer tries to steal the other's spot. More often than not, I lose out.

I've come to know this city of 3 million quite well. Walking around, I discover a nice restaurant where they serve peppered steaks. Tonight, I'm treating myself to a belated birthday present—from me to me, with all my love. For sure, my stomach is ready to celebrate.

DAY 182
Islamabad, Pakistan—January 12, 1995

I'm to receive my crucial parcel from Canada, as well as my visa for India, in Islamabad, Pakistan's capital city. Long live bureaucracy. Surprise, surprise . . . my hotel room is as filthy as it gets. Maybe not so surprising, because in Urdu there is no actual word for "hygiene." And when you see how food is prepared, it's little wonder why so many travelers are sick. But hey, it all adds to the charm, right?

I'm back from a week-long stay in the Karakorum Mountains. Here, before the road was completed in 1978, travelers had to journey on foot, on horseback, or even by donkey. Villagers along the route had very little contact with the outside world. It's amazing to think that they managed to adapt and survive in such an isolated and inhospitable region. Fortunately, there's plenty of water, the very source of life. Locals have developed ingenious ways to channel this pure, pristine water.

Since the construction of the Karakorum Highway (KKH), the local way of life has changed dramatically. Newfound prosperity has drastically affected the formerly undisturbed villages. It has also changed the deep-rooted values of the villagers themselves. The old are complaining that people are becoming more materialistic, whereas the younger generation readily welcomes these changes.

Because Pakistanis didn't have the necessary expertise, Chinese engineers built the road. They only had one choice when it came to construction, namely, to find a river going upstream from south to north and to follow its path all the way up to the Tibetan plateau. So they followed the Indus to the Hunza River, which flows northeast toward the Chinese border.

A million years of erosion has worn through the soft-rock face, and the river has carved out its riverbed 500 feet deep into the mountains. Following the course of the river, the road was cut straight into the mountainside at the very edge of its vertical drop. This is what makes it so spectacular, so treacherous, and so thrilling. The road's maintenance is difficult, and it's hard to always keep it in good condition. Sometimes it becomes practically impassable in some areas, particularly after a heavy downpour or with the onset of melting snow. At any given moment, the bus might have to get around a huge boulder or two that have fallen into the middle of the road. Bordering the road like milestones, the many grave markers are a constant reminder that natural selection takes care of bad drivers. To call this a "highway" is a bit of an overstatement . . . it took seventeen hours to travel the 385 miles separating Rawalpindi from Gilgit.

After arriving in Gilgit, the largest village in the area, I take a minibus to Baltit, about three hours or seventy miles away. This lost enclave, a splendid marvel built into the side of a mountain, is utterly magnificent and a favored haunt of tourists during the summer months. Never would I have believed that such impressive mountains would appear to be so small at close range. The surplus of majestic scenery tricks us into forgetting that we're on the doorstep of the world's mightiest mountain range. From my room, I can see Raka poshi (25,550 feet), whose peak looms over my head, *two and a half* miles into the distance. That's thirteen times taller than the Eiffel Tower.

In winter, there is not a single tourist to be found, so I have all the time in the world to chat with the shopkeepers and artisans, who sell delicate embroidered pieces, typical of the valley. One of them receives me at his home as an important visitor, all the way from Canada, "a country that has never known war." He offers me a job as an English teacher in the community. It's a service they really need, because English is becoming increasingly necessary in their daily lives. He wants to keep me here forever. This is a happy man. Living in synch with nature among these resourceful people must be a truly rewarding experience. I don't say no, but if I want to continue my adventure, it will have to wait until another day. And so he invites me to return in the summer to enjoy a spectacular, four-day excursion to admire K2, the second-highest summit in the world, up close.

We head back into a full-blown snowstorm. Nobody dares disturb the concentration of the driver. Our lives rest in his hands, tightly clutching the steering wheel. At one point, fallen-rock debris blocks two-thirds of the road. With rocks on one side and no railing against the precipice on the other, the bus crawls to a standstill at the narrowest point. There's not a spare inch on either side. From my window, I see nothing but a slither of the river, 500 feet below. Looking straight down, I can't even see the outer edge of the road. A shiver tingles my spine when the driver tentatively steps on the gas. Was it just me or did we really slide a couple of inches downward before making it through? An inch either way, and that would have been the last hurrah for me and my journal.

DAY 183
Islamabad, Pakistan—January 13, 1995

Today is the big day. I'm off to the airport to pick up the precious parcel that my parents have sent via British Airways Cargo. They moved heaven and earth to forward the package as fast as they could, a real *tour de force.*

The service at the airport is quintessentially Pakistani. I bounce around from one desk to another, accompanied by a gentleman who has taken me under his wing, because he knows that I would never get anywhere by myself. After an hour of carting myself from one officer to the next, I manage to obtain the seventh (and hopefully final) required signature. My guide then leads me to a huge holding area where parcels end up from every corner of the globe. I lay down my requisition order, which is whisked off once more to god knows where. I'm quite excited. The package will be here any second now. Right next to me, in a semi-windowed office, some clerks quietly take a break, sipping their tea.

An hour and a half later, and I'm still hanging in there. I glance over at my gentleman guide, who informs me without batting an eyelid, that they're still waiting. "Waiting for what, exactly?" The answer flabbergasts me: we're waiting for one of the tea-sipping officials in the adjacent office to affix his John Hancock on the requisition form. Pinch me, somebody, quick!

Now that my form is riddled with equally useless initials and signatures and after a three-and-a-half-hour delay plus $40—"You pay or you wait"—finally, the package. Now I know why Friday the 13th is not my lucky day!

Back in my room and after a much-needed cold (naturally) shower, I'm as fresh as a daisy and ready to rip open the cardboard box. My new wheel is in perfect condition. The latest news from Canada, however, dates back to September 15, already four and a half months ago.

DAY 191
Lahore, Pakistan—January 21, 1995

Tomorrow, I leave Pakistan for India. I've installed my brand-new wheel, and my visa is good for six months. I feel like a kid looking forward to his first day at school.

Chapter 10

....

An Unbridled Country

DAY 192
Amritsar, India—January 22, 1995

What a beautiful day to cross the border into India, under a warm breeze and summerlike weather. Everything seems so different here. Turbaned Sikhs, with their impressive stature, imbue the country with a regal touch. Cows plonk themselves down in the middle of the traffic. Garbage lines the streets. Rickshaws manage to weave their way through this mayhem. Slow-moving cars, stuck in a tidal wave of man and beast, inch along. Smaller and niftier mopeds cut in and out, filling the air with a nonstop din of beeps and honks. Pedestrians (quite used to this chaos) amble along the road as if it were a sidewalk. Indeed, the traffic means good business for merchants and roadstall owners, pitching their wares. Finally, as if this wasn't enough, I spot a dying cow, lying in the middle of the road, guts spilling out. A sorry victim, probably knocked down by an errant vehicle, yet no one will dare put her out of her misery . . . she's a sacred animal.

I'm in Amritsar, capital of the State of Punjab, where stands one of the most beautiful temples I've ever seen: the Golden Temple, on Sikh holy ground (gurdwara). It is filled with such a deep spirit that I remain transfixed by the site. Built in the fifteenth century, it is center of the Sikh religion founded by Guru Nanak Dev in 1469. He is one of the Sikhs' great, spiritual leaders, like the Dalai Lamas for Tibetan Buddhists and the Prophets for Muslims. His objective was to draw from both Islamic and Hindu influences while establishing the unique faith of Sikhism.

From the main street, you can see the outer wall, which encloses the Temple's central square. Before taking the steps leading inside, both body and soul must be purified. This rite is piously observed by worshippers. Footwear is removed, and feet are thoroughly scrubbed with water from a small basin to cleanse the body. For the soul, a small mouthful of the same water is gurgled and partially spat out again. Having seen the hundreds of followers preceding me, it goes without saying that I opted out of this particular ritual. . . .

Nothing indicates that behind these walls sits a majestic monument, completely covered in gold leaf. On the walkway, small shelters mark guru shrines. Inside one of these shrines, an old man reads aloud from the Sri Guru Granth Sahib, the Sikh holy book, which must be all of eighteen inches thick . . . as impressive as my kid's-eye view of Fanfreluche, Radio-Canada's hit TV show.

The Temple, rising from the center of a pond, is connected with the walkway by a narrow footbridge lined with lanterns. Pilgrims solemnly cross it to reach the sacred inner sanctum. Once inside, they make a repetitive motion, bending and placing one hand on the ground then onto the chest, as if by good fortune divine power might enter them. They recite a short prayer, after which they toss some coins on the ground, unsolicited. In return, a garland of flowers is presented to each pilgrim, which they kiss and press against their foreheads before placing the wreath devotedly in the center of the temple.

Music adds to the mysticism of the setting. From outside the walls, it can be heard clearly via loudspeakers, leading me to believe that recorded music was being played. But I'm surprised and touched when I enter and spot a trio of musicians playing and singing this soft and intoxicating melody. The first is on a tabla drum, the second on some type of accordion, while the third plays the harmonium. They are all in their sixties. In rich, soft voices they sing in chorus or take turns performing solo, beautiful, poetic hymns that, sadly for me, I cannot make any sense of. Sitting directly behind them, a changing chorus of about ten or so pilgrims accompanies them. The Temple's acoustics, the ubiquitous glint of gold, the innumerable icons adorning the walls, and billows of flowers all contribute to the splendor and beauty of the ceremony. Up on the second floor, sitting peacefully on a fabulously embroidered carpet, I get an even better view of the scene. Truly a delight for the senses.

DAY 195
Amritsar, India—January 25, 1995

Pilgrims and visitors alike are offered free food and lodging if they so wish it. Everything is arranged so that both the rich and the poor may take part in spiritual practices at the Golden Temple. Even me! Too lazy to leave, hooked on a book I can't put down, India Wins Freedom, and pampered by my hosts' generous welcome, I decide to stay a little longer.

In India, the police are given free rein to get creative and use their imagination when it comes to meting out punishment to those who flout the law. I see a good example of this when one such careless motorcyclist gets nabbed, right before my eyes. Realizing the poor guy certainly has no money to pay the fine, the cop decides on an alternative—he deflates the motorcyclist's tires! Pushing his bike to the next garage is, presumably, punishment enough.

Everywhere in villages and in the countryside, peasant women go about their business sporting incredibly ornate and precious bracelets, necklaces, rings, and earrings. Gold is the only cashable asset that they'll accumulate during their active lifetime and, therefore, their only nest egg and safety net for old age. Since most have no bank account or, even less likely, a safety deposit box, they carry everything they own, wearing all their wealth for all to see.

And so it happens that a thief who attacks a defenseless old lady to snatch away any gold she is wearing will receive rough and merciless treatment if caught.

If ever a cry of "Stop, thief" rings out, the idea is to immediately get down on the ground and stop moving, so that the only person left standing is the guilty person, trying to run away.

I've just come back from the soup kitchen. There were about two hundred of us, sitting on the ground in perfectly straight rows. When everybody is ready, and the noise dies down, the service begins. Everyone gets a metal plate and a small bowl while we wait for the food. I feel like a child who has been given toys to keep myself busy. First up, chapati, the round flatbread commonly found in both India and Pakistan. To get a piece, you need to open your hands, as if to receive an offering, otherwise it's "sit on your hands." Then comes the dahl, a lentil puree dished out by the ladleful. Finally, water is poured straight from an old, rusty jerrycan. All a bit sketchy, if you ask me.

In India there are thirteen official languages and more than 700 dialects. Since practically nobody speaks the same language, when the servers come back to offer the hungriest a second helping, you must raise your plate if you are still hungry, your bowl if you are still thirsty, or put out your hand if you want more bread. Just like when I was a kid, lifting up my plate and pronouncing the magic words: "More, mom!"

When we're done eating, everyone brings back their dishes to be cleaned. Plates are washed in water, whereas cups undergo more unorthodox treatment. They are manually washed with some fine sand by women sitting on each side of a large, open container filled with sand. Cups are scrubbed one at a time, until fully dry and clean. I'm told that it's the only way to do it properly, but I suspect they want to get as many people working as possible. So the cup-cleaning women all pitch in, creating a family atmosphere of fun and self-help.

In a park close to the Temple, some men are repairing a canal. Every able-bodied man willing to volunteer is welcome. The work entails toting a load of dirt from one point to another by means of a big, straw basket, balanced on the head. My participation in this collective effort draws some attention. An Indian takes a snap of me doing my bit. For this brief moment, I'm no longer a visitor, I'm one of them.

DAY 196
Amritsar, India—January 26, 1995

This morning, my fate takes another tack; I meet up with a friendly couple. My general dress, demeanor, and boldness intrigues and impresses them. Both are dentists living in Chalisgaon, a small village in the State of Maharashtra, which is northeast of Mumbai. We chat for quite a while, and they strongly recommend that I visit three important sites that one should not miss during any sojourn in India. These three must-see sites are the cave paintings at Ajanta and Ellora and the Kanha National Park, the wonders of which they passionately describe to me. Plus, they live close by to all three sites. They absolutely insist on having me as their guest, so they can introduce me to their friends and guide me around the area. They leave me their address and phone number and even offer to collect my mail until I arrive. I hardly know them, and we're already bantering away like old pals. My route sets its own course. And my guardian angel is definitely hard at work.

Back on the road (and for the first time, I should add), I am pestered by three larrikin youngsters who grab at my bike and try to open my saddle-bags. Despite my polite resistance, they persist. I have to resort to force to get them to back off.

I followed two men on their bikes this morning. They are selling their vegetables in the nearby village. Loaded with a hundred pounds of cabbages, onions, and carrots, they even transport a basic weighing balance on the top of their cargo. The only cost of this operation: bike, balance, and heart, lots of heart. When they finally manage to sell all of their stock, they'll be the happiest marketers in the whole wide world. Who could make a living back home with a bike and a boxful of onions?

DAY 198
Khana, India—January 28, 1995

I'm hanging out in the small village of Khana along the Great Trunk Road, a route that crosses the entire Indian subcontinent, from east to west. From the restaurant's first-floor balcony, I can contemplate all the bustle below along the main drag: barbers, tailors, vendors of every kind, people selling vegetables off the back of their carts, rickshaw drivers making their deliveries, peanut sellers stacking their displays in perfect cones, even bike repairers tinkering away on pre-World War II models. A blacksmith could do a better job since this "repair" consists of banging away at the bike with a hammer until the problem goes away. On the other hand, some artisans seem more meticulous in getting the job done right. Watching a cobbler restoring a saddle to near perfection is quite a show.

DAY 199
Kurukshetra, India—January 29, 1995

After a few days of foot-dragging, my knee is a little better today. Whatever the thousand and one projects I may have planned, it's my knee that has the final say on whether I follow through on them or not. My journey is being held together by a mere ligament.

I leave Khana under the watchful eye of curious spectators. Two locals that I've met accompany me by bike to the outskirts of the city. We have breakfast together and share our views on India, Canada, politics, journalism, sexuality, and religion, obviously. As India was under British rule for a century and a half, city dwellers are relatively fluent in English, which is not necessarily the case for rural villagers and farmers. It's my treat, but, as usual, I also take out my yogurt, bananas, and walnuts. With my voracious appetite, I don't want to run up the bill any higher than it has to be. They see why, as I vacuum up all the extra food I've brought along. One of them gives me his ring as a keepsake so that I'll never forget him.

DAY 200
Panipat, India—January 30, 1995

I pay extra attention to the traffic, which is getting heavier and heavier as I approach Delhi, India's capital city. I would like to find a cozy corner to sleep for the night before actually entering the sprawl around this enormous town, home to more than 10 million people.

I notice the word "English" on a sign. A worker, busy building a house on the side of the road, directs me to the end of the alleyway. There, another elegantly dressed man is getting ready to leave. I politely introduce myself, telling him about my trip, like I do several times a day. He is a school superintendent and is willing to let me crash for the night inside these newly-completed walls. He also kindly extends an invitation to join him for a breakfast of tea and pancakes tomorrow morning. I appreciate the fact that I'm lucky to be sleeping inside, but I pitch my tent all the same, because I'm wary of mosquitoes. You never know which ones carry malaria.

* * *

Here I am in Delhi, staying with family friends, the Guhas. I listen to some music with weary eyes, doubtless because of lack of sleep. Last night was not great, because an old, Indian night watchman, in charge of I-don't-know-what, slept on a chair next to me, coughing all night long.

I must admit I'm feeling homesick tonight. I feel so far away. It's the first time I've felt like this. Maybe it's because of the comforts of a real home. I've upset my solitary routine. I don't know any more. When you're tired, you shouldn't think about it, you should just sleep. So grab some shut-eye, and see how you feel in the morning.

DAY 202 and after
Delhi, India—February 1 to 5, 1995

I had a relaxing time in the Guha home—warm, friendly, and comfortable. I took full advantage to rest up, listening to music, reading, making inquiries, eating properly, and generally getting used to living in the luxury enjoyed by Delhi's professional class. Here, the dismantling of social classes is unthinkable. Every well-to-do family has a slew of servants. I'm not talking about millionaires, but rather college graduates with good jobs. In the Guha residence, someone takes care of the mail and the wretched paperwork, and others look after domestic chores and meals, 24/7. This "cheap labor," as they call it, is commonplace for those who can afford it.

Because the city is so large and with the important sites spread out almost everywhere, I discover Delhi as part of an organized tour, like a proper tourist. I really enjoy the visit to the home of Indira Gandhi, Nehru's daughter and the first woman to be India's Prime Minister, who was later assassinated by her Sikh bodyguard in 1984. The numerous newspaper articles detailing the events of her political life pique my interest and give me the taste to read her autobiography. Currently, I'm reading about Mahatma Gandhi, India's spiritual father, and reading up on Ali Jinnah's story, statesman and founder of Pakistan.

I'm incorrigible. Although I want to reduce my bike load, I can't resist buying the autobiography of Jawaharlal Nehru, one of the instigators of India's independence; the book is a brick, 500 pages thick. I can't help it. Having great reading material handy comforts and reassures me. With such good companions, how could I feel alone? After I've read up on modern times, I'll go back in history and study the Mughal Empire. I'm fortunate to be able to learn on the spot, and I take advantage of it. Certainly, I would never leave behind my dog-eared copy of Lonely Planet, the bible for travelers in India. If it did disappear, it would be like looking at the stars without a telescope!

Unless I change my mind again, my itinerary is pretty much set: Delhi–Jaipur–Agra–Khajuraho–Varanasi–Jaigaon–Ajanta (to visit the dentist couple)–Mumbai and along the west coast until I reach Goa. Then I'll bike back up. How exactly? I dunno.

Going far away
Far from all my loved ones
Going far to discover I don't know what
Simply some peace, maybe Going far to realize
That in the end
Happiness is not found
At the other end of the world But in the backyard
Of my own little world

* * *

Every state has its own, unique character. I am entering Rajasthan, "the land of kings." It's everything exotic about India to the fourth degree. We're in the territory of the Rajputs, a warrior clan that controlled this part of the country for over a thousand years. This hilly state is one of India's least densely populated.

In the the arid region to the west lies Thar, a vast desert area. Cows and oxen are now replaced by camels to transport goods between villages. They are everywhere. Impressive, proud, standing tall, the camels stride impassively through the heavy traffic. Floppy cheeks falling down on each side of their snouts, droopy eyelids covering huge, bulging eyes, a mouth in a perpetual half-grin, they look at me with haughty disdain. I love photographing them.

I'm riding on a semi-paved country road, full of potholes and rocks. Road maps are so pathetically bad here that I can't help but get lost in the wilderness. A guy on a bike offers to help me, so I ride with him for a bit. Along the way, he greets his friends proudly, happy to be putting this lost sheep back on the right track. For the villagers in these remote places, with my bright-white, streamlined bike, my flaming-red saddlebags, my Captain Cosmos helmet, and my Martian glasses, I might as well be an extraterrestrial.

Women at home would surely admire the way Indian women and girls dress here. They wear stunning fabrics, in colors of fiery red, sunflower yellow, and forest green, all embroidered with gold stitching. Dresses here are as varied as they are sensational. I understand why Rajasthan is called the Colorful State. The women are so beautiful with their long, dark hair falling against their fine-featured, dark-brown faces. They watch me riding by and smile at me, showing off the brilliant whiteness of their teeth. A striking contrast with Islamic countries, where black chadors serve as the predominant color and cover.

I'm snugly lying in my cocoon, my mini-tent. It's really quiet. All I hear is the soft chirping of crickets and a few mutts barking far off in the distance. Two old farmers sleep right by me in a shelter that looks more like a woodshed than a house. No matter, they look content.

India's workers are honest and make do with what they have. I can't help but be charitable to those who are no longer in any condition to provide for their needs: the elderly, the sick, the physically challenged. To them, just one rupee is a big help. Fortunately, local shopkeepers are generous. They give away fruits and vegetables to the needy. As for the rest . . . I hate to think. I wonder who attends to those who die in the middle of the street, at night, alone: the morgue, the garbage collectors, the dogs, or the vultures?

* * *

Chapter 11

. . . .

Nothing But Jungle

DAY 211
Sariska, India—February 10, 1995

Hemmed in by barren mountains, I'm traveling along a stunning route through a freakish forest, with trees so strange that I can't tell whether or not they're still alive. Arriving at noon, I stop for lunch at a small roadside restaurant where there are as many monkeys as diners. They are everywhere! During my meal, a gust of wind blows a stale bread crust off the roof. It lands directly in my bowl of lentils, tipping it straight into my lap. After a perfunctory wipe with a suspicious-looking rag, the waiter serves me up another bowl, and I keep on eating. Suddenly, a monkey jumps headlong off the roof to land, once again, in my plate. This time, he promptly makes off with my two pieces of bread! And as if this wasn't enough, a bird passing overhead leaves its calling card on my head. Look! Up in the sky! It's a bird . . . it's a plane . . . it's a . . . it's . . . it is a bird. No Superman, but an entertaining meal, to say the least.

DAY 211

Sariska, India—February 11, 1995

I get up early to visit the nature reserve. We take a jeep ride on the dirt trails of this large national park, covering 300 square miles. Several temples, built by maharajas long ago, are scattered throughout the site. Regrettably, the three-hour excursion doesn't yield any tiger sightings, but we are lucky enough to observe an incredible number of wild animals in their natural habitat: wild boars, stags, blue bulls, proboscis monkeys, and some brilliantly plumed peacocks.

At the national park's exit, a long, tree-lined road leads to the entrance of the spectacular Sariska Palace, built by the Maharaja of Alwar. This is where India's ruling class met and socialized, hunting tigers from the backs of elephants. Thousands of the big cats were killed in this fashion every year.

The palace is surrounded by an immense garden, perfect for a relaxing walk. On the terrace, musicians play sitars and tablas. If you close your eyes and let yourself be carried away by the enchanting sounds, it's not hard to imagine yourself as a privileged participant in one of the rich and extravagant ceremonies from times past. This evening, however, having sat down to a royal buffet in the palace's large hall, I can now only afford the luxury of sleeping out in the open, under the stars with the monkeys and wild boars.

DAY 213

Jaipur, India—February 12, 1995

I begin the day's bike ride right at sunrise. The mountainside is shrouded in mist. On the side of the road, monkeys sit like cherubs on cotton clouds, casually watching me drift by. Sunlight gradually filters through this milky veil. A new day begins. The comings and goings of the lively countryside begin to break the silence. At this early hour, people are taking a moment to appreciate the calm before the storm. They watch me passing by, smiling at me as if I'm a regular part of their daily life.

Thirty-five miles farther along, I'm out of this hilly region and can now join the main road. Regretfully, I leave behind camels and monkeys for a rush of cars and trucks, in the hundreds. A cow, probably hit earlier this morning, is lying on the side of the road. Fifty or so vultures are busily at work transforming this once sacred beast into an unrecognizable carcass. A debaucherous feast? Or a holy communion? They are so hungry that my presence, just a few yards from their meal, doesn't bother them in the least. A dog sneaks up for a feed, but the enormous birds have no intention of sharing.

I clock up seventy-five miles without feeling tired at all. I've got my old legs back, as well as all the energy of my earlier days. My digestion is excellent. It's as if my bike is rolling along by itself. I feel as free as the air. It looks like I've found my second wind. I enter Jaipur, the capital of Rajasthan, on a road shared by both elephants and semitrailers.

What's the big rush?
Why not take a moment
To savor the present moment
Why fret about what comes next?
What will be, will be It's no use to quicken your step
Because once you're there, you'll see It's only lost time you'll regret

DAY 215
Pushkar, India—February 14, 1995

I get up this morning itching to get going. It's seven months, to the day, since I started my trip. I'm setting out on a two-week tour to the western part of Rajasthan. My mechanical "donkey" stays here for a well-earned rest.

Pushkar is a lovely town of whitewashed buildings located in the hollow of a valley lost in the middle of the desert. At its center, there is a lake that fills and empties with the seasons. Pilgrims come from every corner of India to bathe in its sacred waters. From my room, I have a bird's-eye view of the ghats, steps that lead into the water where religious rites are performed. Near the water's edge, a young child is in tears. Despite his protests, his head has just been shaved in readiness for this first, purifying dip. Further along the edge, people are washing and rinsing their clothes in the lake, which serves all purposes, except for the drawing of safe drinking water.

Contrary to other towns and villages in India, Pushkar is generally quiet and calm. Not a car on the street, just a menagerie of cows, pigs, dogs, oxen, and camels, of course. Pigs root through the garbage and any other scraps lying about. Cows, much more picky, cross the streets in search of banana and orange peels, as well as the melons that vendors have tossed out onto the road especially for them to eat. Amazingly, the cows are even into paper recycling . . . by eating it! Yesterday, I bought some bread wrapped in paper, and rather than throwing the wrap in the trash can, I went looking for a cow. Are they working on a shortcut to supply milk already pre-packed in cartons?

I'm totally in love with these bovine beauties of every color and size. They have beautiful teardrop eyes with big, bold lashes; it looks like they're wearing mascara. Their jet black snouts are covered in a stubble of stiff hairs. They're everywhere.

Locals recommend that I climb the rise to Hilltop Temple toward the end of the day to catch the sunset. This means a one-hour hike up a steep path paved with loose rocks. I make it to the top with several exhausted seniors, in sandals and pressing hard on their canes. The expansive view is a delight. The desert's parched ground turns redder as the sun goes lower. The blue surface of the lake becomes even more intense as the color of the village houses subtly changes to a pearly white. Soon, you can feel the onset of the desert's crisp-night air. The sun squeezes out the last rays of light. Already the crowd is making its way back down, a descent that will be a long and painful one for some.

* * *

DAY 218
Jaisalmer, India—February 17, 1995

What is life?
The most beautiful thing on Earth?

What's the Earth?
This big ball that I might possess
With all of my own might, no less

But might self-possession come first?
A painful journey, digging down
To the depths of my guts, until I burst

Do I have the guts, the spirit?
Yes, it's on fire, I can feel it
Consumed by my love for adventure
And burning for a challenge, but what?
To accomplish the impossible, or so it was thought

What is this impossible dream?
To know myself for who I really am
Not for what I ought to be, or so it would seem

DAY 222
Jaisalmer, India—February 21, 1995

I'm now in Jaisalmer, called "the Golden City" because of the color of its fortress ramparts at sunset. It's one of the major towns in the Thar Desert. All goods going westward pass through here. The fortress is the real thing. Built in 1156, it has stood the test of time. Once inside the city, you get the feeling that the inhabitants have been living the same way for centuries.

To experience caravan life, I leave for a two-day excursion on camelback, right into the heart of the desert. That's a twenty-five-mile romp that will take us to the dunes along the Pakistani border, where we'll spend a night under the stars.

I learn that camels need only one hour of sleep a day, that they eat ten pounds of hay daily, that they can travel hundreds of miles, and that they can go three days without drinking. No wonder they are ideal for crossing vast tracts of arid desert. Along the roads, there are water holes at regular intervals where they can have a drink and feed on leaves and shrubs. Their master makes sure they have food for the long journey across sandy dunes.

The caravan team, sitting sphinxlike and loaded like mules, is ready to go. I climb aboard my ride and sit pretty. The leader's instructions make me a little nervous: "Hold on tight, you're going to feel it!" Then he pronounces the magic words: "Chik, chik, chik." The camel unfolds its back legs, then those in front, so fast that I'm nearly catapulted face-first over his head. Perched up like this, I now feel even taller, which is weird since I'm already six-feet-four in my socks. Despite being a complete novice, I'm given full reign over my camel, as if I've spent my entire life in the desert. But the saddle is too wide, and it tilts forward. My inner thighs are chafing nonstop. Five or six miles along, we make our first stop. I'm already suffering from a "charley horse." (I guess that's a "charley camel.")

We walk around what remains of a maharaja's palace, abandoned and in ruined decline. But it gives me some idea of the importance and the wealth of these Indian princes. A pool, carved out of the rock base, is directly connected to a subterranean aquifer. During the monsoon, as the level of the water table rises, so does that of the pool. Yet the villagers still don't have running water. Women line up with their carriers to draw water from the maharaja's wells. They take great care not to spill a single drop. In the desert, water is life.

Along our route, we arrive at the cemetery reserved for members of the royal family. Here, women and men are buried separately. Each tomb has its own unique, intricately sculpted, dome-shaped monument. It's like coming across an ornate display of miniature temples. Regard for royalty has long since disappeared, because the site is now partially destroyed. Before too long, nobody will be taking care of these works of art, which were once so preciously guarded.

Farther along is another village, where houses are built from earth mixed with cow dung and water. This place was an ancient caravan watering hole. Its inhabitants have never left the area, despite the barren soil. Their ancestors were once prosperous, thanks to a water tax on every caravan that stopped. Today, the sale of Thumb's Up—India's version of Coke—and some arts and crafts is their only source of income. This hamlet exudes peace and quiet. Maybe too much so. I can hear the silence roar.

Arriving at the renowned Sam Sand Dunes, we set up for the night. But first, it is de rigueur to take the customary, posed snap, perched on our mounts as real-live caravan nomads. A chilly breeze reminds us that nights here are particularly cold. We spend the evening huddled around a campfire. Our guide hums some traditional-folkloric songs passed on by these desert peoples. In this total darkness, it's as if you can reach up and touch the stars dotting the night sky. The silence is interrupted only by the rustle of the camels, licking their chops and jingling their bells.

For someone who thought he was completely cured of giardia, I sure picked the wrong time for a relapse. I am sick all night long. Vomiting, diarrhea, and cramps have doubled me up since I finished the peas from last night's supper. Now I have to grimace and bear it until it goes away.

DAY 223
Thar Desert, India—February 22, 1995

A second busy day awaits me. Very early in the morning, I climb back on my camel, without having a bite to eat. I'm told that the way back will be longer. We have to pick up the pace and move along at a trot. That's the kicker . . . I'm in for a whole-new world of pain. The guide doesn't want to slow down. My delicate derriere is being pulverized, my back feels like I'm water-skiing across the desert sand, my arms ache as if I've been lugging logs all day long, and the palms of my hands make me a candidate for the stigmata. Amen. Plus, I had the bad luck to get stuck with the youngest camel; he has just had his nose ringed, so he's pretty cranky about being ridden at all.

DAY 224
Jodhpur, India—February 23, 1995

After a six-hour bus ride, I'm really feeling it. I spent the rest of the day visiting Mehrangarh Fort, which dates back to 1459, built much more recently than that of Jaisalmer. At more than 400-feet high, it looms over the city center. All along its six miles of walls, you can view the whole city, including the distinct blue of the old town. Only the highest-caste Brahmins had the right to paint their homes this color. Why blue? For health and as a sign of well-being. Sitting on the rampart, feet dangling into the void, I listen to the sounds of the city, carried up here by the wind. High in the sky, eagles glide over the fortress.

Inside the fortress is the former, palatial residence of the Maharaja of Jodhpur. The master bedroom is immense. With only a single bed in its center, the room's walls are covered with tiny mirrors. A single flicker of a candle reflects a thousand, dancing glimmers of light. Here, the master received his nine wives and thirty-one concubines. In a nutshell, not just a bedroom but also a workout gym.

DAY 226

Jaipur, India—February 25, 1995

Around the world, Jaipur is widely recognized for its precious and semi-precious gemstones. "Come to my shop. Just have a look!" These are the friendly and persistent phrases that I've heard repeatedly since my arrival. Every conceivable technique is used to coax me to buy. In the end, I must admit, I'm curious.

I meet a character who is just as slick as any vendor. We start to chat about politics and religion. He's interesting and knows a thing or two, so we decide to have a coffee together to continue the conversation. Although I thought he was merely trying to lure me to one of the cursed gemstone shops, it's not the case. Much to my surprise, he invites me to a wedding, to take place that very evening. I graciously accept, and we fix a time to meet tonight. At the planned hour, we head for the ceremony. He wants to buy me a beer, but because he's a bit short, I lend him four dollars, which he promises to repay tomorrow. I wouldn't bet on it. Bottom line, that's a small price to pay for a wedding invitation. And he's a nice guy, how could I say no? During the celebration, he hits me up for another couple of bucks, this time to convert to rupee notes to be placed on the head of the bridegroom.

Then I learn that he has his own workshop where he cuts gemstones. I intend to buy a ring sooner or later . . . why not get one off him? He offers to give me a tour of his shop tomorrow. I agree, and I call it a night, glad to have attended yet another Muslim wedding with such interesting people.

The next day, as agreed, we head for the workshop on his motorcycle. As his studio is situated on the outskirts of the city, I figure it can't be a tourist trap, like the rest. The visit is fascinating. We drop by an office, where I learn that he's not actually the owner but rather a mere employee. Just as he starts showing me some stones, the boss steps in. Now it's the real owner who takes all the time in the world to tell me about the unique characteristics of different stones. And this is despite the fact that he didn't sleep a wink the night before because of a sick son. Plus, he tells me he's also observing Ramadan and so cannot eat or drink from sunrise to sunset. He does indeed look tired but nevertheless puts in a full effort to show how the gems are extracted from the raw rock and further cut and refined to produce these magnificent jewels. I feel uncomfortable not buying anything and unnecessarily wasting his time. Cautiously, I ask about prices before I commit to anything. He begins by showing me the least expensive. I pick out a few. Then stone by stone, one gem at a time, he reveals his impressive stock with the greatest of care. He proudly tells me that he exports them all around the world.

He recommends that I select a lapis lazuli (for love and loyalty), then a malachite (for health and well-being), and finally a star ruby (for success in life). The prices are climbing steeply: diamonds, rubies, emeralds, and sapphires. He becomes more and more insistent, and this is the moment when I know I've been caught . . . hook, line, and sinker. I become less nice while thinking fast how to extract myself from this bushwhacking. I tell him bluntly that his jewels are well beyond my budget. He has all the right arguments: "You don't pay interest with your Visa card. Your parents can send you money if you don't have enough for your trip. You can always sell these stones if you need money. In Canada, the same worth ten times more!" I'm not going to budge.

I also realize that the less I buy, the smaller the commission for my new buddy who brought me to this sucker's den. Finally, I buy the "loyalty" and "health" stones, although I doubt they are genuine. This lesson costs me a quick twenty bucks and a lot of sweat. By the time I get out of there, I've lost total interest in knowing any more about Jaipur's famed gemstones.

My motorcycle pal drops me off at a nearby street corner, reneging on his promise to bring me back to the city center. He wants to meet up with me again tonight. No thanks, I'm good. . . .

To take my mind off things, I check out the Jaipur observatory, tagging along with a Japanese tour group. Built in 1729, the observatory's sundial still indicates the exact time to the nearest two seconds. Other instruments calculate astrological signs and their ascendants, whereas another device identifies all the constellations.

After this visit, I go to the bazaar and pity anyone who tries to hassle me. Nobody insists. By the end of the evening, I'm wearing a new ring on every finger. And every one I thoroughly enjoyed choosing myself, so who cares what they're worth. I like 'em, and they didn't break the bank.

Tomorrow, I'll do nothing. I'll read, maybe do a bit of washing, but mainly get my mind set, ready to hop back on the saddle.

DAY 228
Mahuwa, India—February 27, 1995

Getting back on the road again is difficult. I'm sick and tired of being asked fifty times a day, "What country, what name?" I have to find a way to ignore these never-ending shouts, coming from all directions, and rediscover the joy of carefree riding. I understand their curiosity, but my own exasperation outweighs this. It's hard to talk with villagers, and it's hard to shake off all these youngsters, running after me, trying to get me to stop. Suddenly, two of them grab hold of my spare tires attached behind my bike. I have to come to a complete standstill to avoid losing everything. At the same moment, other young boys run over from the fields, including a little brat who throws a stone that dings my bike frame, chipping the paint job. What a nice souvenir. And a good thing I didn't get it in the face, I suppose.

En route, I see some twenty eagles lunching on a roadkilled dog. After ten minutes of gorging, all that's left is skin and bones. Without warning, a truck runs over one of the satiated eagles as it tries to take off. It managed to spread its wings but failed to make it down the runway. Now it's just one more serving of roadkill and the next course on the menu.

In India, the road is shared with oxen, camels, motorcycles, rickshaws, farm tractors, taxis, buses, trucks, and semitrailers. Riding on a badly paved, pothole-ridden road or a road without a shoulder can be downright suicidal.

Vehicles speed by in sets, as if they're racing in a videogame. If there's no slot readily available, drivers honk like hell until the smallest, lightest, most vulnerable is forced into the ditch. Every day, I witness accidents.

Low over my handlebars, an eye riveted to my rearview mirror, I'm a hair's width away from being pancaked into oblivion by a truck hurtling down the wrong side of the road. I'm just another annoying fly who could be swatted mercilessly at any tick of the odometer.

While I'm wondering why I didn't go around the world in a Bradley tank instead, I come upon a roadside gathering. A clearly agitated and boisterous crowd of about twenty people is milling around. Two men lying in the middle of the mob are being pummeled. Police burst onto the scene. Both victims are now semi-conscious, unable to get to their feet.

Just as punishment is meted out for thieves, the same applies to reckless drivers. When I get to the next village, I discover the answer. It turns out that a bus struck a motorcycle, instantly killing the motorcyclist's two passengers. Knowing what was in store for them, the bus driver and his assistant took to their heels and tried to flee the accident scene. But both were quickly caught, sentenced, and punished . . . on the spot.

* * *

Chapter 12

....

My "Mule" Gets a Break

DAY 230
Bharatpur, India—March 1, 1995

Today, I visit the bird sanctuary in Keoladeo Ghana National Park in Bharatpur, home to 328 bird species, including some from as far flung as China and Siberia. In this semi-arid region, the Maharaja diverted an irrigation channel to create an artificial pond to attract birds. His intention wasn't to improve the environment but rather to attract birds as target practice for his guests, some of whom killed up to 4,000 birds a day. This type of shootfest was abolished in 1964 when the sanctuary area was declared a protected zone. The sanctuary is scattered with trees, and except for the odd dirt road, most of the surface is covered with water. Birds flock to this man-made swamp to live and breed. Here they also find tranquility, safety, and plenty of food. Indeed, studies have shown that 3,000 storks, living within a 250-acre habitat, can consume up to three tons of fish a day.

DAY 231
Bharatpur, India—March 2, 1995

I've just realized that someone stole my camera while I was in the shower. I'm really upset. All I ask is that I get it back at all costs. Otherwise, the thief will have deprived me of the joy of sharing key moments of my trip with friends and family.

I offer a $20 reward to anyone who finds it, but I don't hold out much hope. The hotel manager is reluctant to get the police involved. I wasn't the brightest bulb in the building to leave my stuff unattended, but what was I supposed to do? Take the bike into the shower with me?

After two hours at the local cop shop, I return to my room with three officers and three hotel employees, including the manager. They're all chatting away, but I can't understand a thing. The police are questioning the hotel staff and taking notes, as if to convince me that a serious investigation is underway. A couple of these Keystone Cops painstakingly recreate the facts: they draw a plan of the room, prod the bed where I slept, and ask me where my bike was at the time of the theft (or time of the "crime," as they call it). In a word, comical. Finally, I'm assured that I will receive the only thing that matters to me: the police report I need for my insurance claim.

DAY 234
Agra, India—March 5, 1995

I'm biking through one of the most polluted regions in India, a dirty strip of territory along the Yamuna River, which flows between Delhi and Agra. It's in the State of Uttar Pradesh, home to 150 ironwork foundries and a glut of oil refineries.

I've just met a Dane, who caught malaria in Jabalpur. All the medication he's been taking is making him as sick as a dog. He can't stop throwing up, and he's so weak he can barely walk. Not very reassuring because I'll be in this city myself within a week. Just looking at him is enough to turn me into a hypochondriac.

One thing makes me forget all of my worries. It's the spectacular sight of the legendary Taj Mahal, a stunning edifice and justifiably considered one of the seven wonders of the world. This white-marbled masterpiece changes shades with the ever-changing light of day, finally taking on a pinkish tinge at twilight. It is to India what the Eiffel Tower is to France. Commissioned by the third Mughal emperor, Shah Jahan, and built between 1632 and 1652, this elaborate mausoleum stands as a memorial to his dearly beloved third wife, who died giving birth to their fourteenth child. This monument of love was designed and constructed by the most talented architects and most highly skilled craftsmen of Iran, Turkey, and Europe.

DAY 242
Khajuraho, India—March 13, 1995

Eight days without jotting down a word. I've been completely floored by a virus, as though a regular cold just wouldn't have cut it. Nothing but fever and chills, which I wrongly mistook for malaria. After three days of fasting, I slowly begin to eat again. I gradually regain my health, but something is bothering me: should I take my bike southward (or not)? It would take me at least five months to bike this part of the journey. If I go by public transport, I'll have more time to fulfill my greatest dream, that is, crossing the Himalayas by bike.

I made friends with a German traveler a couple of days ago, and I'll leave with him tomorrow for Jabalpur, in the south. My "mule" plus all the gear it usually hauls will rest up in a hotel in Khajuraho. The only stuff I'll bring with me is my Lonely Planet guide, a paperback novel, pen and paper, soap, a razor, a T-shirt, a pair of shorts, a long-sleeved shirt, my tough little tent and groundsheet, and nothing more. Given that the weather is sure to be nice and warm, I'll travel light, very light. Plus, this will be a great chance to practice my German, which has inexplicably improved, even though I haven't spoken a word of "Deutsch" in two years.

DAY 244
Panna, India—March 15, 1995

And off we go again. Well, sort of—barely on our way and the bus breaks down. Those headed for Satna, the next village, have to get out and walk. But since our final destination is Jabalpur, 170 miles down the road, we have to hang in there while the bus gets fixed. We're towed to the Panna depot, which looks more like a junkyard than a garage! This eleven-hour bus ride is shaping up to be more like sixteen, if we're lucky.

I go looking for a toilet—not such a simple task. On my bike along the road, it was easy to find somewhere to go, but in an unfamiliar town? I wander around in a blur before a savvy employee points toward the back, indicating it should be OK outside, behind the building. As I get down to the job at hand, dogs run free, people pass by on a nearby path, cows graze the well-manured (if not manicured) lawn, all while a surly pig impatiently waits for me to serve up his breakfast.

Before the bus broke down, I thought the driver was deliberately driving slowly to avoid any mechanical problems, but after the bus is fixed, I soon realize that this was always meant to be our cruising speed. Driving on this road is a bad joke. In some places, we splutter along at less than 10 mph. The two of us are sitting up front, practically on top of the engine. It's hotter than Hades, and the bus keeps filling up the closer we get to our final destination. I find myself with a couple of kids on my lap and my bag at my feet. I could've done the same trip by bike with a little more effort. But not that much more.

To be honest, you have to be truly stoic to spend sixteen hours traveling by bus, which is only called a "bus" because it's got four wheels and carries an overflow of humanity. The whole contraption is rattling around, regardless. I've never seen such deplorable public transportation in such a pitiful state. Sixteen hours and a couple of hundred miles later, we hobble, safe and sound, into Jabalpur.

It's very late, and according to our information, the cheap hotels are right by the train station. So we head off in the right direction, according to the map. After a few minutes of walking, we learn that the bus has stopped at a new terminus and that those cheap hotels are now three miles away—in the opposite direction. One hour later, we find a place to sleep . . . that's one way out of this nightmare and a hard-earned ticket to sweet dreamland.

DAY 245
Jabalpur, India—March 16, 1995

This morning, we take a rickshaw ride on a road going nowhere. After an hour, us pair of sardines are told to hop out: we've arrived at our destination. This has "tourist trap" written all over it. Our curiosity leads us along a path ending in a cloud of mist and spray from a thundering waterfall. It's still early, but already the sun has some sting to it, so the refreshing mist is a welcome relief. Years of erosion have carved a deep canal through the pink-and-white marble rock. By following the riverbed, workers with picks in hand are able to extract this precious rock, which is used for sculptures that are sold everywhere in the village below. Here everything is done by hand, and quickly at that.

This is such a peaceful setting, a strange contrast to the feverish city life. For a rare moment, I forget that 890 million people call India home.

DAY 246
Khanna, India—March 17, 1995

We leave Jabalpur in pouring rain, as two of the seventy-two ticketholders in a forty-eight-seat bus with a leaky roof and no windshield wipers—for six, long hours on a mountainous road. Fortunately, the air is a little fresher up here.

Today is both a holiday and a day of celebration for all those living in northern India, because it marks the end of winter and the beginning of summer. It's called "Holi" or sacred day and is also known as the Festival of Colors.

I'm in Kanha National Park, a place isolated from neighboring towns, although the sheer noise of the festivities gives one the impression of being in the middle of a big city. Everybody dances to the pulsating rhythm of drums. Everywhere you look, men, women, and children walk around with bags filled with powder of various colors. The idea is to draw a line of color across the forehead of the person whom we wish to wish "Happy Holi!" In the excitement, that simple gesture degenerates into hilarious fun and games. Now the scene quickly transforms into clouds of color, with a fistful thrown directly into the face of your immediate neighbor. The activity is wholly mutual, and as the chain reaction unfolds, it's not hard to imagine how easily this frenzied event becomes a chaotic shamble of riotous color. I was also a target and a "victim" of the rite but only after my agreement was sought and given.

The party's over, and the forest grows calm again. We request a special "to order" meal. Not only do we get to choose the spices but also the main ingredient . . . a fat chicken, right over there, sitting on death row in its cage. Schwak! That's the end of the line for my now dearly departed, fine-feathered friend.

DAY 249
Aurangabad, India—March 20, 1995

After twenty-one hours by train and bus, I finally set foot in Aurangabad, in the State of Maharashtra. And it was well worth the effort. I visit twenty-nine Ajanta caves, and many shrines (chaityas) and monasteries (viharas) all built between 200 and 600 AD. In every cave sits a statue of Buddha, around which worshippers gather to pray. The walls are covered with paintings of exquisite beauty, but upon which time has taken its toll, requiring much-needed restoration.

If the caves of Ajanta are recognized for their wealth of treasured paintings, those of Ellora are renowned for the abundance, quality, and beauty of their sculptures, still in very good condition. All the works were carved directly into the rock. Any slip of the chisel could have been disastrous, because once a piece was mistakenly chipped away, that was it. The detail on each sculpture testifies to the incredible talent of the artists of the period. The most beautiful temple, in the Kaisala cave, is as large as a three-storied building. Its walls are replete with amazing sculptures of Hindu divinities. From the temple's center rise sixteen columns, intricately carved with scenes from everyday life. It took 150 years to complete this masterpiece.

I'm now ready to set off for Chalisgaon, home of the dentists, a great couple I met in Amritsar, in the North of India. I can't wait to open the mail that I've arranged to have sent there.

DAY 259
Chalisgaon, India—March 30, 1995

I've been in Chalisgaon for nine days now, and my hosts really have gone to a lot of trouble so that I can make the most out of my stay with them. I don't have an idle moment: one day I'm invited to a village farm where the local denizens include snakes, parrots, and peacocks. The next day, I'm off to an English school where I'm asked to talk about my journey, my homeland, and my studies in front of seventy or so wide-eyed kids. Their ages range from ten to thirteen, and they hang on my every word. A few days later, a judge invites me to attend a courtroom trial. He then insists I come back to his place to celebrate his daughter's twelfth birthday, with several of her friends in attendance. The girls chat with me incessantly and want to know everything about how women and girls live in Canada, especially customs related to marriage.

That same day, I hardly have time to take a shower and eat a quick meal before I have to leave for a meeting where I'm the guest of honor. This time, I'm sharing my adventure (so far) with sixteen members of the International Rotary Club. They offer me a welcome flower, then I'm invited to speak, something I manage to do with effortless aplomb, much to my surprise. The next day, at 6 AM on the dot, a family friend drops by to pick me up for the daily yoga session. Tomorrow, it's another day on the farm. My stay was not supposed to be so long, but with everyone being so welcoming, I could hardly do otherwise. The village jeweler even popped in to give me a silver chain as a goodbye present. I promise him that I'll always wear it.

DAY 261
Mumbai, India—April 1, 1995

Yesterday morning, I entered India's industrial and economic heartland. What was once a bevy of seven, small islands has now morphed into a megalopolis. At 14-million strong, Mumbai is one of the world's largest cities. I prefer village India to big-city India. Mumbai does not truly reflect the beauty and charm of this wonderful country. Gone are my beloved cows. No more vendors with their wagons brimming with fruits, vegetables, goods, and supplies. Walking along Marine Drive, I might as well be in Florida.

Today I visit Gharapuri, an island fortress, six miles out of Mumbai. It was renamed "Elephanta Island" by the Portuguese. Here, you'll find temples dating back to 450 to 750 AD, whose inner walls are covered in sculptured gods, enormous in size and in near-perfect condition. They're the major attraction on the island.

The entry into the port is spectacular. The "Gateway to India" is an immense arch that commemorates the visit of King George V and Queen Mary in 1911. With a little imagination, it's easy to take myself for an Englishman who has come to deal in spices. But I come crashing back to earth when I discover not sumptuous spices but, rather, shocking prices . . . a bottle of Coke costing six times the usual sum, for example.

Sightseeing tourists, their pockets filled with foreign coin, are fresh meat and easy prey for the lions lurking in the jungle that is Mumbai. Beggars are content with a few rupees of loose change. Softer hearts tend to dig deeper into bottomless pockets, but for others, as far as poverty is concerned, the obscene might as well be unseen. Merely acknowledging this poverty has little impact on India. In any case, who wants to change India? Behind all this misery hides a world rooted in its own traditions, a world that reveals itself only to the more curious and persistent traveler.

DAY 263
Mumbai, India—April 3, 1995

While waiting for my friend in the post office for more than an hour, I run into an Iranian whom I met in Lahore, Pakistan, three and a half months ago. During our chat, he mentions "bedbugs" or, better yet, "bedbites," the intimately intimidating tiny critters found almost everywhere in Asia. These miniature bloodsuckers seek refuge and proliferate in the wooden bed bases in unhygienic settings. They carry all sorts of germs and cause unbearable itchiness. That's what happened to me in Aurangabad, where I spent several diabolical nights scratching myself more furiously than a dog with fleas. My dentist friends surmise it's a simply an allergic reaction. My biggest problem? My portable tent and my clothes are riddled with them. Plus, they're unkillable. My Iranian friend, finishing up his Ph.D. in chemistry in Mumbai, has chosen to study these charming little creatures, just for the joy of it. So far, he has concluded that they can survive in water and that no known chemical has any effect on them. "But, just like Count Dracula, they can't handle the sun!" He's quite proud of his discovery. Me too. My gear is now lying around, soaking up the sun, all day long.

* * *

Big disappointment. I just phoned the dentist in Chalisgaon, and still nothing received for me. I have had no written news for three months. I'll have to wait for Delhi to get my next package. This is the second time that my mail has been lost. I have to find another means of delivery, because the post office can't be trusted.

Tomorrow I leave for Goa, a magnificent, seaside-resort town. So not everything is a lost cause.

* * *

Chapter 13

....

Never Without My Guardian Angel

DAY 265
Colva Beach, India—April 5, 1995

After a twenty-six-hour, 340-mile jaunt, I've finally arrived at Colva Beach, in Goa. As weary as I am, I'm nonetheless thrilled to have made it to this gorgeous beach, right on the Indian Ocean. If Mumbai reminded me of Florida, this certainly feels more like India to me. In small boats, industrious fishermen sort and clean their catch. Here, just like everywhere else in India, all work is performed by hand, with handcrafted tools. Close by, some workers busy themselves either building or attending to small boats, typically used for fishing in this area. These remarkable vessels are built out of horizontal wooden slats, roped together with old fishing nets. Coconut scraps are woven into the netting to help make the boat waterproof. The sea can be stormy; therefore, to increase stability, wooden skis are attached to the craft by means of two poles. This simple construction makes the boats well adapted to the fishermen's needs. It is amazing to see how much they can do with so little. Their ingenuity fascinates me; I never grow tired of watching them at work, always busily improvising.

DAY 271
Colva Beach, India—April 11, 1995

The sea is beautiful. I laze around for six days, taking advantage of the downtime to study the roads through the Himalayas . . . connecting Srinagar in the Kashmir region, Leh in Ladakh, and Manali in Himachal Pradesh. That's a 900-mile route that crosses eleven passes, all more than 13,000 feet, including the renowned Taglang La Pass, at 17,480 feet, the second-highest roadway pass in the world. Taglang La is even higher than Europe's tallest peak, Mont Blanc, which rises to 15,770 feet. No wonder this region, recently opened to tourism, is one of the most spectacular in the world. This upcoming expedition will require meticulous planning and rigorous mental preparation. I plan on stopping in a couple of the hamlets, hanging precariously on the side of the mountain, to rest up and to see how the locals live. I'll follow the Indus River for a good fifty-five miles, similar to what I did in Pakistan, biking the Karakorum ranges. It should be an epic journey in wonderland. I was bowled over by the sheer splendor of the Himalayas in Pakistan. Just thinking about crossing these mountains on my bike gives me goose bumps. What a dream come true. Even though I know it'll be physically demanding, I also know I'll make it. More than ever, I have faith that the body can be pushed as far as the soul will venture.

DAY 277
Hampi, India—April 17, 1995

I'm in Hampi, the ancient capital of India's southern empire. To get there, you have to really want to go, and I really wanted to go. First up, six-and-a-half hours to Hubli, in a bus bursting at the seams, hot enough to melt the soles off your sandals. From there, I transfer to another bus, but since I'm the last one to hop on and since there's no more available space inside anyways, I get to sit on the roof. Easier said than done. I haven't even had time to settle down before we suddenly take off. Because I'm so tall, I come within a hair's breadth of being guillotined or electrocuted by the overhead wires criss-crossing the street. Like a big bumblebee mashed up against the windscreen, I stick low and lie as flat as I can.

* * *

Since yesterday I've been traveling with a couple of Brits, checking out some ruins. From the roof of a temple, we look down on a fairytale landscape: a desert panorama, flecked with bright flourishes of banana trees, a shimmeringly clear thread of river, boulders the size of houses, sitting bare and brash, and mountains as far as the eye can see. It looks like Bedrock, from The Flintstones. The stark contrast of the lush greenery of the banana groves set against these grey, arid mountains intensifies the beauty of the scene.

I'm like a leaf in the wind, with plans that are constantly taking unexpected turns. I decide to take the route south with my two new travel companions. Afterward, I'll return to the North to tackle the Kashmiri mountain passes, as originally planned.

DAY 279
Hampi, India—April 19, 1995

Up at sunrise, we take advantage of the crisp morning air to go for a walk along the Tungabhadra River, which runs through Hampi, eventually taking a break in a nice, little cafe aptly named the "Tea Shop Under the Mango Tree." Mango season is in full swing, so we quench our thirst and get our fill of this delicious fruit, very much appreciated all over India, where more than one hundred varieties are grown.

I head down toward the hottest part of the country, the extreme South. Because of chronic itching on my scalp, caused by the dust and the excessive heat, I decide to give my "nut" a full-razor shave, ending up with a noggin as smooth as a billiard ball. That, plus a dollop of moisturizing cream, applied several times a day, solves my problem. With my John Lennon glasses, my lithe look, my frugal clothes, and my cleanshaven head, some smart-ass train passengers are calling me "Gandhi!" as I walk by. I'm as proud as a peacock.

DAY 280
Bangalore, India—April 20, 1995

After a whole night on the train, we get to Bangalore, India's answer to California. As soon as we get off at Bangalore Station, we rush to buy a ticket for Kochi, in Kerala. There's a train leaving at 9 PM, so there's still time to nab the last seats. Later, ticket counters will be swamped, and the entire station, overrun with travelers, will begin to look like a supersized ant colony.

Walking through town, we decide to escape the stifling afternoon heat by going to see a movie. Hum Aapke Hain Koun, one of the greatest Indian films ever made, is currently playing. It's a story of an "unarranged" marriage for love, a musical comedy that features the greatest hits of the wildly popular Lata, a seventy-year-old woman whose singing is said to seduce all men, both young and old. She has a shrill, very stylized voice, and her song melodies are quite unique.

DAY 281
Kochi, India—April 21, 1995

After a thirteen-hour train ride, we arrive in Kochi. You might think you were in a fishermen's village in Portugal, and that's no coincidence, because Kochi was once a Portuguese enclave. The Portuguese explorer, Vasco da

Gama, was the first European to discover India, and on this small peninsula he established India's first church in 1503. Of Kerala's 29 million inhabitants, 20 percent are Catholic, and most live here in Kochi.

Among other things, Kochi is famous for its "Chinese" fishing nets. They are immense, 100-plus-square-foot contraptions, whose four corners are attached to a rope connected to a long, wooden pole and positioned in an estuary. When drawn in, such a net is filled with fish of all sorts.

The night was so hot and stuffy I thought I would suffocate. So that makes me appreciate this boat trip through the cooler backwaters even more. We're gliding through a series of canals lined with palm trees on narrow strips of land. Here, people live in houses made of stone or hand made brick. A different family resides in a dwelling every couple of hundred yards or so. On both sides of the canal, women wash clothes, men fish with small nets, while other people fill their boats with dried coconut and palm-tree fronds to be used as fuel by locals. One woman empties her basketful of grass into a boat, which will be sold as feed for dairy cows. Going further into these canals, which get tighter and tighter as we advance, I see two laborers collect the mud that stagnates on the shallow bottom of the canal, which will be used to fertilize rice paddies. Here the waterway is the focus of human activity, and nothing is left to waste.

For lunch, we eat thali, a typical Indian dish. It's served on a metal plate divided into three compartments to separate the rice, the fried vegetables, and the meat. All three are generously doused with a kind of homemade, spicy broth. Since everything is eaten by hand, chapatis conveniently fill in as utensils. Here, as it is everywhere in the Middle East, the right hand is used exclusively for eating—no prizes for guessing what you do with your left. My most recent adaptation to Indian customs? Getting up to speed on the "left hand rule.". . .

DAY 285 and following
Kovalam, India—April 25, 1995

Kovalam is about fifty miles from the southern tip of India. Streets are packed with small shops, including excellent restaurants where the local speciality is freshly caught fish grilled over hot coals.

With enormous waves rolling in, the turquoise sea is the backdrop to today's more temperate weather. Yesterday, we were struck by a hurricane. Lashing rain and frenzied winds swept everything away in its path. In its fury, the sea battered the cliffside with angry waves. Lightning flashes unrelentingly lit up the night sky, which helped us find our huts in the darkness. The bathroom was flooded and all my gear soaking wet.

Today, with some difficulty, I managed to book my train passage north. After a nightmarish lineup and no choice but overbooked trains, I could only get a ticket for Madras, eighteen hours and 625 miles farther away. From there, I hope to transfer to the Madras-Varanasi Express. All in all, fifty-seven hours in steam-train purgatory, not counting the usual delays and cancellations.

I meet a girl who's been traveling by herself for eleven years. She is following a therapeutic cure that involves fasting and drinking her own urine. Wow-wee-wee! She's wowed by the fact that I'm traveling around the world on my bike. Me, too! I'm wowed at her "piss is bliss" regime! To each his or her own, I guess. When it comes to our good-byes, I give her a hug but forego the customary farewell kiss.

Up early, I wander over to the nearby village beach to see what the fishermen are up to. At this hour of the day, the beach is plastered in gobs of blobs . . . big, small, hard, soft, brownish, greenish, dark amber, and bright yellow. Yessiree, excrement is what I'm talking about, and the beach is full of it.

When I say plastered, I'm not kidding. In the towns, it's the railroad tracks that serve as a public toilet, but here, it's the beach. It may seem gross, but at least the pigs are delighted with this arrangement. I notice a big, fat pregnant sow feasting on the leavings. Pity the poor, little piglets-to-be. . . .

The fishermen, who left a lot earlier, are now returning with their bountiful catch. As soon as they arrive, they throw hundreds of fish on the sand to be cleaned by wave and tide. The women crowd around, making sure not to miss a bargain. They buy fish for their family or to resell to fishmongers. The bidding starts high then comes down until a buyer is hooked. Even then, the buyer inevitably haggles for an even lower price. Selling, like the fishing, is all part of the sport.

DAY 293
En route to Varanasi, India—May 3, 1995

As if the lengthy train ride wasn't enough, my shoes (and my orthopedic insoles) are stolen while I was asleep. Maybe my guardian angel was taking a shower. . . .

Joking aside, here's a theory I came up with when I was alone in the Iranian desert.

On a long trip, just as it is in our daily routine, both fortunate and unfortunate events are bound to happen. Among family and friends, you stick together when times are tough, and you make merry when the good times roll, praising each other's triumphs and celebrating joyful occasions in unison.

From the moment Jean-Pierre left me, I found myself alone. Solidarity gave way to solitude. As part of the pack, like wolves, we bare our fangs as if nothing could stop us. With energy to spare, full of vim and vigor, we feel invincible. Being alone is another matter. On your own, you become aware of just how small you really are. You soon realize that your actions can have a direct bearing on what happens next, sometimes they may even affect your very survival. You learn to be wary and fearful of the unknown, while trying to tame it at the same time. You become acutely aware of your strengths, your weaknesses, and your limits. And finally, you realize that if you were really alone, you could never really make it out there. When I'm under extreme duress, the force I call my angel, so full of wisdom, shows me the way and lays out the road ahead.

My guardian angel is my truest friend, my teacher, my guide, and my protector. In short, he's my partner, and he's with me every single day. Regrettably, when all is well with the world, when life unfolds without a hitch, I forget to talk to him, and I'm especially remiss in not asking for advice.

Mine is very versatile, as far as guardian angels go. He can be a teacher who places pitfalls in my path, so that I might learn how to react and to deal with them. Or a guide who sends clear signals on the best choices when I'm feeling unsure. Lastly, he can be a protector who leads me away from the precipice, sometimes throwing me for a loop, only for me to later find out that this is what saved me.

Do we deserve all the help we receive? And what should we give in return? Do we make our own luck? I have no exact answer. I can only say that everything happens for a reason, and if you're ready to forgive your guardian angel some minor missteps, he will repay you a hundredfold.

Am I talking about a good guardian angel or simply a good theory? It doesn't matter, life smiles down on me. Anyway, I'm especially privileged, because I have two other guardian angels, my mother, Lili, and my father, Victor. I can't see any of the three right now, but I know they're there.

DAY 294
Varanasi, India—May 4, 1995

While still getting over someone swiping my shoes, a young punk dashes past me, hotly pursued by a woman screaming behind him. At first I thought it was a fire, but quickly realized her gold necklace has been snatched by the fleeing youngster. It all happened so fast that I couldn't help her. Indeed, the thief had already jumped off the train.

We're now crossing a bridge that spans the legendary Ganges River, the lifeline of an entire people since time immemorial. On its banks, devotees in the hundreds are bathing in its sacred waters, whereas from the train, passengers are tossing out offerings. I stick my arm out the window, to feel how hot it is. It's like I've waved my hand over a barbecue grill.

Appearing shoeless and with a shaved head apparently elicits sympathy from a fellow passenger: a Nepalese monk who has been studying Buddhism in Sri Lanka for the past nine years. On the way to Katmandu, he is making a three-day stopover in Varanasi and invites me to stay in the temple with the monks. I feel privileged to be able to share their lives for a few days.

When it's 106°F in the shade, you can sizzle steak on the asphalt. So before my toes become ten charred cocktail hotdogs, the monk finds me a shoe store. There's not much choice, and it's too expensive, so I opt for a pair of $1 flip-flops while waiting to step up to more serious footwear later on.

As soon as we arrive at the monastery, we leave for Sarnath to visit another Nepalese Buddhist temple and meet the monk's friend, who teaches the Tibetan culture to children. He's writing his doctoral thesis in Sanskrit, the Indo-European language that is to Hindi what Latin is to English. These monks personify kindness, serenity, and a joy of living. I am impressed by their young ages. They easily communicate their peace of mind, and the prevalence of their orange robes imbues the monastery with warmth and radiant goodwill. A tree, which bore witness to the Buddha's first teaching in 1525 BC, stands testament to his ongoing spirit.

This short day hike was long enough to make an impression on my feet: three big blisters, two of which are oozing and bloody. Anything to save a buck. . . .

Today, I rented a boat, and I've been cruising the Ganges since 5:30 AM to observe the activities taking place on the numerous ghats lining the river's edge. A ghat is a succession of steps leading down into the river, where certain religious rites are practiced. It is also the place where cremation takes place. People from all over India come here on pilgrimage, mourning the death of a close relative or making offerings. The woman who had her necklace stolen on the train has come here to mark the fifth anniversary of the death of her husband.

According to the Hindu custom, to be cremated and have the ashes cast into this sacred river leads directly to Nirvana, which is the extinction of all pain, thereby liberating the soul from the cycle of reincarnation. That's why so many Indians dream of ultimate fulfillment in these sacred waters.

Drifting with the wind and current, I find myself on the opposite bank. The Ganges is very low at this time of the year, because the monsoon has not yet begun. You only have to look at the high-water marks left in 1944 and 1972 to appreciate the difference. This bank looks more like a beach. I get out and take a stroll, but not too far for fear that my boat might get nicked. I wouldn't like to swim in this gigantic, public sewer. This is also the bank where they dump rabid dogs.

I make a discovery: an intact and very dry human bone. A tibia, I believe. This find in Varanasi is a real kicker.

I continue my boat ride toward Dasaswamedh, the main ghat, where they seem to be waiting just for me. Full preparations are underway for the cremation of six bodies. It's a simple ritual: the body lies on a bamboo stretcher, swaddled in a funeral shroud. It is left for thirty minutes, resting in the water of the sacred river. It is then briefly wrapped in a silver cloth, which is removed before incineration. This cloth will also be used for the same purpose for other corpses. Meanwhile, the funeral pyre is built in such a way that enough heat can be produced to completely reduce the entire body to ashes. That doesn't always happen, so it's believed that the dolphins who swim in the Ganges sometimes dine on the rest of the remains. Yes, as surprising as that might be, there are dolphins in the Ganges.

The family participates fully in this rite, but once the incineration begins, attendees take refuge in the temple to pray and possibly to find a little shade, given that the heat in Varanasi is intolerable this time of year, particularly when you're standing next to a raging fire.

I know nothing about this man going up in flames. He was surely poor, because the pyre is a modest one: the body is lying at the center of the blaze, but the head and the feet hang just outside the fire's reach. Worse still, his genitals are covered with only a few sticks of wood. I am hypnotized by this scene, and I watch the burning from beginning to end. As the skin shrinks, the toes swell up, and the arms lift toward the heavens, as if to implore the spirits above. Soon the ankles melt like wax, and the feet drop off. The skin of the stomach becomes a whitish mass from which the intestines pop out. Yet the inert face has a peaceful countenance. What is painful for us is a relief to him; his ashes will soon be cast into the Ganges. . . .

DAY 296
Khajuraho, India—May 6, 1995

I'm back in Khajuraho. And after twelve hours of travel by train and bus, it's great to get back to my bike and familiar ground. Sitting on a terrace overlooking the lake, I watch the sun's last rays filter away. Mercifully, with the sun's disappearance, the temperature becomes gradually bearable once again. However, tonight I'll have to sleep in a hotel room that is little more than a concrete box, now transformed into a furnace after accumulating the day's heat. I dream about the air-conditioned home of the Guhas, where I'll finally be able to read letters from home in pure comfort.

DAY 197
Jhansi, India—May 7, 1995

Holy heavens (and it has to be spelled out), it is goddamned H-O-T. After a sleepless night, I visit the last of the Jain temples, where I have breakfast. I gather up my gear and get to the bus stop early, so I'll have plenty of time to tie my bike securely to the roof. After five hours and 100 miles down the road, I have to bike another three miles to get to the train station. During this short ride, the mercury tops 108°F, and combined with the exhaust-fume stench of the passing trucks, it gives me the distinct impression that I'm being burned alive at the stake.

But I'm not at the end of my martyrdom. The worst is yet to come. I want to book a passage on the sleeper car. We're in India, alright . . . all the signs are in Hindi only. Everybody is pushing and shoving—every man for himself. I'm in line for more than two hours, sweating and jostling to hold my own, only to finally hear, when I reach the front, "Delhi not here, next line across!"

Tired, defeated, done in, I plop down on my small camping stool as I slowly work my way toward the counter. The clerk looks at me, surprised. All sleeper cars are fully booked. The next available passage departs six hours from now. I've got no other choice than to get a third-class ticket: in other words, spend the night with ten fellow third-classers all over me. I'll try and sneak into a second-class carriage where at least I can sleep on the floor, stretched out in front of the door. Hey, I can even double as a guard dog for the carriage. I've already used this trick before.

* * *

Chapter 14

···

The Kashmir Valley: A War-Torn Paradise

DAY 303
New Delhi—May 13, 1995

Back at the Guhas' for four days now, and I've just received my mail: orthopedic insoles, my new camera, and, best of all, letters from home.

I put in a phone call home, and I get the good news that my thesis will be presented at the ACFAS Congress (Association canadienne-française pour l'avancement des sciences/French-Canadian Association for the Advancement of Science). Even better, my university diploma came through, too. That should put an end to the recurring nightmares I've been having about not receiving it at all. I give my parents a heads up: they won't be hearing anything from me during the next seven weeks, that is, until I return from the Himalayas.

Everything is set. I leave at ten past four, tomorrow afternoon, on the Shalimar Express night train, bound for Jammu. Then I catch a bus right to the foot of the Himalayas, in the Kashmir Valley. And that's where I climb back on my bike.

How long I stay in Srinagar, the capital, will depend on the political situation and whether the 11,800-feet-high Zoji Pass will be opened or not. This pass, which always gets a lot of snow, marks the end of the Kashmir Valley and the beginning of the Buddhist enclave of Ladakh, a subregion within the Kashmir. This very dry part of the country is completely sheltered from the Indian monsoon and gets about as much precipitation as the Sahara Desert.

I'm lukewarm about embarking on this new adventure. I'm still not too worried, but then again I don't want to move mountains either. I'm familiar with this state of mind, and I know that I can handle it. Put it down to a temporary lack of confidence due to a long spell without pushing a pedal, without burning up the bitumen. . . .

There's another problem: my right knee, which I stupidly hurt playing soccer in France. It's not too bad, but I feel an occasional, worrying twinge. The ligament hasn't got back its tensile strength of the good old days. It doesn't affect my cycling capacity—at least not yet. In fact, I'm hoping that more pedaling will strengthen the muscle structure and stabilize the knee joint.

The clock has just sounded the twelfth stroke of midnight. It's time to draw on my strengths. Tomorrow, a new stage begins, and I must face it head on. Meanwhile, my sore toe, courtesy of the infamous $1 flip-flops, is still oozing pus. We're talking twelve days later, here. . . .

DAY 304
Shalimar Express, India—May 14, 1995

I've taken my seat on the Shalimar Express. It's 4:01 PM, and the heat is so intense that it makes a grown man weep. I took a shower (fully dressed!) on the platform, hoping for some relief. It seems like my clothes will never actually be dry again, because I'm sweating so much. The forecast was for 111°F, and I believe we've already reached that. There are twelve of us in a six-seat compartment. We are scheduled to pull out of the station in five minutes, thank Buddha, because I'm melting away here. If all goes well, my bike should be following me. I tipped the porter generously, counting on him to take good care of my precious ride. My wish is granted: it is 4:11 PM, and we're choo-chooing out of here.

Ten months ago, I was flying to Paris. Now I'm in Jammu, sans bicyclette. "Don't worry," I'm assured, "it's on the next train."

Army trucks line the entrance of the station, and as I get off the train, I'm directed to register at the army control. No doubt it's for my own safety, because the Kashmir and Jammu region is a war zone. When the Indian subcontinent, which then encompassed modern-day Pakistan, India, and Bangladesh, was granted independence from the British, borders were drawn up to separate these nations according to region. Not everybody was happy with the location of these borders, hence the conflicts.

The latest train from Old Delhi has arrived and still no bike. The next train will be here within an hour. With few tourists this time of the year, the guy responsible for registering new arrivals is not very busy, so he volunteers to help me find my bike. As usual, we make the tour of numerous offices, as we're shunted from one place to the next. The stationmaster, a no-nonsense Sikh, tells me to calm down. In 105°F heat and after a fourteen-hour train ride, a sleepless night, and five hours of hanging around here waiting for my bike, he obviously thinks I am Gandhi. He assures me that my bike will arrive by tomorrow, at the very latest. I'm going nuts. Is my guardian angel watching over me, or would he rather see me suffer?

It would seem that not a single tourist has been sighted in Srinagar since a curfew was set four days ago, after a terrorist group set fire to a 500-year-old religious monument in Charari Sharief. Locals may only leave their home for three hours a day. A soldier tells me not to worry, the army is everywhere, and, besides, tourists are not targeted by the terrorists. If anything happens, he advises me to go to a military outpost. He also informs me that Zoji Pass will be open to bus travel toward the end of May, when it will be completely cleared of snow. Since I'm on a bike, I might be able to cross it earlier. Apparently, this pass is no pushover, especially when the two-mile plateau, right along the top of the summit, is covered with snow.

The registration clerk who took care of me at the station invites me back to his place for supper. I hope I'm not heading into another trap.

DAY 306

Still in Jammu, India, waiting for my bike—May 16, 1995

As soon as a train comes in, I check both the front and back luggage compartments. Still no bike. As I head for the stationmaster, my new pal from yesterday comes running toward me, yelling out he's found my bike. I follow him, blindly asking a thousand questions. Too good to be true? But no, there it is over there, on top of a pile of burlap sacks.

Barely back in the saddle, I get a flat tire riding over the Tawi River bridge. . . .

Last night, after (count 'em!) one, two, three showers, I finally managed to fall asleep by wrapping myself in a wet sheet. The fan's cool air gave me some relief, but I would wake up as soon as the sheet was dry. This will be the last night I'll sweat like a pig. Closed doors help to keep the blazing heat out, but I'll wait for sunset before repairing my tire.

And to think that, in Iran, all I dreamed about was being warm.

* * *

My bike well secured on top of the bus, my saddlebags safe in the luggage compartment, I'm sitting pretty, ready to go. I would have preferred to be in better shape. I'm having trouble digesting yesterday's meal, and I'm not as gung ho as usual. Is it the heat? The stress? Or maybe just plain fatigue, bad digestion, or another giardia outburst?

The bus leaves right on time. Only ten minutes into the trip, and we're already beginning our ascent up into the mountains. In spite of the beauty of my surroundings, my upset stomach manages to steal the show. I soon face the urgent fact that I need to get off and answer the call of nature, but where and how? I relive the nightmare trip between Nok Kundi and Quetta in Pakistan. At the exact moment I'm about to beg the driver to stop, he pulls over for gas (thank you, guardian angel!); it's time for the bus to fill up and me to empty out. At breakneck speed, I duck behind a low wall. In supreme peace and tranquility, I let loose and exorcise the devil from my system. Now I'm back on track.

Cut straight from the side of the mountain, this sinuously winding wayfare is a thing of beauty. The army also uses this route to reach the occupied territories. Convoys made up of several hundred soldiers cross here daily to ensure supply lines and security. Oddly enough, there are very few roadblocks.

I've still got the runs. Another five minutes, and that'll be it. I'm sizing up the distance between me and the nearest exit, I check if the aisle is free. In short, I'm on emergency high alert. Amazingly, the bus pulls over once again. Another lucky break—it's time for breakfast.

The scenery changes from one minute to the next. We reach Patnitop, at 6,758 feet, according to my altimeter. The air is cool and fresh . . . finally. The bus goes through a two-mile tunnel, connecting the rest of India with the famous Kashmir Valley, an immense plain surrounded by the world's most imposing mountains. As we near Srinagar, the valley narrows, and mountain peaks get closer and become more and more impressive. We stop at a lone roadblock. It's completely bogus. One by one, we file past a guard using some sort of low-tech scanning device, which detects god-knows-what, badly at that. After a half-hearted and random ID check, we're on our way. Next stop? Srinagar.

DAY 308
Srinagar, India—May 18, 1995

For those living on the plains, Srinagar is heaven on earth. For those who live there, it's a place torn apart by political and religious conflict, where prosperity is but a distant memory. For me, it's a pristine village in the heart of the Himalayas. It's also a restful place in a valley where the air is so pure that it makes you quickly forget India's mind-boggling heat.

Built on the shores of Dal Lake, the Kashmiri capital was once a magnet for tourists. Here, we find the famous floating houseboats, dwellings built on wooden hulls. The houseboat phenomenon was created by the British colonials at the beginning of the twentieth century. Varying in length from sixty to eighty feet, their width rarely exceeds twenty feet. The interior furnishings range from the simple to the more opulent, according to the relative wealth of the owner. In general, their decor is somewhat sober, with Kashmiri carpets and varnished wood walls often a common feature. If the owner lives full-time on the houseboat, he will add a kitchen; otherwise, there will be just two or three bedrooms, a lounge room, and a washroom. Since owners usually prefer to rent to foreigners, they typically live next door with their family, in a small house built on stilts. In this way, the houseboat becomes a business, ensuring a seasonal income.

Moored one alongside the other, the houseboats create a "floating village," with the channels between them acting as streets. To get from one house to the next or to get to dry land, locals travel by shikara: small boats hollowed out of tree trunks. Vendors also use these vessels to hawk a whole slew of farm produce, handicrafts, and other goods and knickknacks.

Aside from the houseboat district, there is also the village around the lakeside, which is inaccessible at the moment because of the ongoing conflict. From the houseboats, you can clearly hear gunshots. The army is at war against the rebels, and raids occur at any hour of the day or night. I hear a woman screaming about her son having been arrested. Soon enough, it all quiets down again . . . until the next crisis, that is.

In spite of all the hostility that runs rife throughout the town, the lake remains mirror still. I write on the deck of my boat until sunset. If it wasn't for this war dividing India and Pakistan, a conflict that has resulted in thousands of deaths over the past ten years, Kashmir would be the undisputed jewel of India.

DAY 309
Srinagar, India—May 19, 1995

Today is Friday, a day of rest for Muslims. The curfew continues. Since people have nothing better to do than look for trouble, they're kept indoors for the day. Tomorrow, when the curfew will be lifted, it'll be a different story. I think it's a great idea to go for a stroll through the town's center. I'll try and pick up some tourist brochures on Ladakh and some info about the route ahead. I'll study the situation and do my best to memorize the roads and mountain passes to be crossed. All my energy is focused on my mental preparation. I still have a lot to learn, but I'm heading in the right direction. With the help of a few flyers, I'm hoping for the best. "If you can dream it, you can do it"; a simple maxim, but it does the trick.

Clouds roll back a little to reveal a breathtaking sight: a towering summit in full view. I am overwhelmed with joy. This spectacle rekindles my longing for adventure. I feel uninhibitedly courageous, looking up at these stunning mountains.

DAY 310
Srinagar, India—May 20, 1995

I am in some emotional turmoil, and I can't quite put my finger on what's bothering me. Something is sticking in my craw. Here's what's probably upsetting me: my houseboat host doesn't stop whining about how poor he is and how he hasn't got any money. This houseboat was passed down to him by his father, but he lives in a house just behind it, with his wife and three kids. In the Kashmir Valley, you're either an artisan, a landowner, or a houseboat entrepreneur. For the past six years, since the political conflict intensified, people have been complaining that the economy has gone bad. To drum up some business and make ends meet, just about anything is offered to fewer and fewer tourists. My host wants to sell me a guided boat excursion across the lake. Putzing around in a dinghy for four days with somebody who can barely string together three words of garbled English is not my idea of a fun time.

He gave me a break on my first day, but today he's back on my case . . . this time with photos, itineraries, and, most importantly, how much this one-of-a-kind sortie will cost. He promises that I'll be back by May 30, when the Himalayan road is set to open. All this seems to make him happy, but what makes him think I'm going to dive right into his ever-growing, steaming pile of bullshit, I haven't a clue. Mind-game giardia strikes again. "You know, people come to India just to do that. And the price I told you is a student price plus a little bit profit for my family" and on and on, the dung heap grows even higher.

If I accept, no doubt he'll hire a local peasant for the length of my boat trip and pay him a ridiculously low sum, keeping the lion's share of the cash I hand over without lifting a finger . . . I don't actually help out anyone by accepting this type of deal.

Furthermore, he keeps pestering me to buy "at least one Kashmiri carpet and one wood carving for your parents. If they are happy, God will be happy, and you will be happy, too." Although I've explained that I don't have money to splurge on pricey souvenirs, not to mention the trouble of carting them around with me, he retorts, "It doesn't matter, if you don't have the money, you can buy it and your parents can send the money after." And on and on it goes. For a rich fat cat, this could be fun, but for a back-alley stray like yours truly, it's a real nightmare.

He might be poor by our standards, but in Srinagar, he is among the privileged. Compared to rural workers who live along the Ganges and other parts of India, he's a millionaire. Plus, he enjoys a smoke. His cancer sticks cost him at least thirty rupees a day, that's roughly a dollar a day or $365 per year, a significant amount here. He confides in me that he took his son out of school a week ago, because he can no longer afford the tuition fees and that the lad is now distraught at seeing his schoolmates leaving without him every morning. If he can manage to scrape up the money to pay his son's school fees in the next few days, the boy can pursue his studies. On the surface, this sob story is a real heartbreaker, but I did some digging and learned that it has been two years since our young scholar has actually attended the school. I also found out that the annual tuition fee was about $100 or approximately three months' worth of cigarettes.

I should have been firmer, right from the start, but I let my guard slip earlier on. He won me over by taking care of me and my bike at the station and by inviting me to supper at his place on the night of my arrival. This puts me in an awkward situation. Because he's so nice, I feel guilty refusing his entreaties. I want to switch houseboats immediately, but his two sons are so kind, his nine-year-old daughter so cute, and his wife such a good soul and devoted mother. Even the small income I bring in affects the whole family. I don't know what to do or where to go. If I stay, I'll have to put up with his begging and unseemly whining, and if I leave it will probably be more of the same the next place I go. Kashmiris have this bad reputation of taking tourists for a ride.

All of this may seem fairly humdrum, but I feel quite isolated with nobody to talk to. Every so often, I have to stop and ask myself if I'm making the right decisions and whether my principles are the right ones. Fortunately, I can vent my frustrations in my diary. But this trusted companion is not very talkative and, so far, has kept mum.

DAY 312
Srinagar, India—May 22, 1995

The curfew has finally been lifted, and shops open their doors once again. My health isn't improving, so I check into a medical lab to have my stool tested. You really have to want to do it: the sample flask is just two inches high and hardly wider than a pencil. Hey, if you have to get your hands dirty, so be it.

I'm sure I've welcomed aboard some new parasites, a near certainty since I saw where the tap water comes from. The houseboat owner swore to me that it came from the filtration plant, but I have just discovered that it's pumped directly from the lake, the one used by local inhabitants as a public sewer. Smile! That's the same water I've been brushing my teeth with. To think that I've been filling my mouth with this shitty concoction has the steam blowing out of my ears. And what about the gentle bathing of my infected big toe that I've been doing dutifully for the past nineteen days? What hope have I of clearing this up by dipping it daily into my very own eau de toilette? The important thing is that at least I've tracked down the cause of my problem. My food intake will now be limited to that which doesn't come into contact with the tap water. I wanted exotic; I got it.

DAY 313
Srinagar, India—May 23, 1995

My lab results come back negative. All I've got is a minor-intestinal infection, probably caused by drinking the water. Once again, I'm prescribed Nidazol to "de-bug" the parasites. Prescription or not, I would have taken it anyway. I am also told to take isabgul, a natural product that is used in Ayurvedic medicine. Originating in India, it's the world's most ancient medicine. It must be the real deal, because, as far as I can tell, India is still going strong.

Fate has sent an honest man my way, as if our paths were meant to cross. Today, I meet Shahan, a dwarf, who takes me under his wing. He knows everybody, forever waving at people like a political candidate on the hustings. He's friendly, smiling, and cheerful. Having discussed everything and nothing, he invites me to meet his family. I'm surprised at seeing how old his father is and how young his brother is. He corrects my false assumptions by pointing out that the young boy is actually his nephew and this old man, his grandfather. They all live together as a family, four generations under the same roof. The house is tiny, and he tells me that the key to living in harmony together is respect. You got that right, Sherlock.

I speak to him candidly about my recent health problems, and he tells all sorts of crazy stories about the houseboats on this subject. Because of Kashmir's political instability, the tourist industry has all but ground to a halt over the past five years. The owners, whose income depends only on tourism, are the big losers in this downturn, and it seems that they sometimes use drastic measures to keep visitors as long as possible on their boat. Shahan tells me it's not uncommon to see houseboat guests mysteriously falling ill, especially after they've said they were about to leave. I suddenly remember telling my own host that I plan on leaving as soon as my health improves. My new friend points out that it would be inadvisable to make false accusations, but that I should be doubly cautious or, even better, change houseboats completely. I hope I'm not one of these victims. Only time will tell. . . .

DAY 317
Srinagar, India—May 27, 1995

The end of the month quickly approaches, and I'm still in Srinagar. I left my pain-in-the-neck owner and his parasitical houseboat to install myself on dry land at the Island Hotel, to join a throng of other dissatisfied tourists. Here, nobody disturbs us, and the hotel manager seems more honest. Wonder of wonders, my health recovers. After a six-day fast of almost total abstinence, I must now fully rebuild my strength.

The curfew is officially lifted, but a general strike has just been called by the Kashmir Liberation Front. There is tremendous apprehension surrounding the upcoming elections, to be held in mid-July. The various governmental authorities haven't ruled out the possibility of cancelling the elections to avoid an escalation of violence. One can sense the palpable unease and dissatisfaction of the population. Frustration is brewing, and it's going to get ugly, but I should be out of here before it all boils over. In the meantime, it appears that the road connecting Leh with Manali has been been made impassable by numerous landslides and that it might be closed for the next three years. I can't get any concrete information, and nobody dares elaborate further. Confidentially, Shahan tells me that this type of road closing has happened before, but this time, he suspects his fellow countrymen sparked this rumor to keep the tourists in the valley. Right now, whether it's opened or not, nothing changes my plans. Once I reach Leh, I'll simply retrace my steps if the road is really closed. There is far too much uncertainty in the air for me to know exactly what's going on. The most urgent thing for me is to fully recover my health, and then I'll leave everything to fate.

DAY 318
Srinagar, India—May 28, 1995

A quiet Sunday, all peace and serenity. After eleven days in this town, I'm practically part of the furniture. I'm starting to know a lot of people. I'm glad of that, but the call to adventure is becoming more and more insistent.

The fear persists, as well. Most of all, I am afraid that I won't have the courage to give up, if that's what it comes down to.

As if I needed any more worries, I meet an Australian medical student, who scares me with tales of hypoxia (altitude sickness). At 13,800 feet, he suffered it himself, and I'm going even higher. Unable to continue, he had to come down again and rest for three days before resuming his ascent. He also tells me that two Japanese adventurers died recently in Nepal because of the same sickness. "When you hack up a pale-pink thingamabob, it's already too late, you've only got twenty minutes to live." He's not really reassuring me. I feel like I'm suffering from it already. The prescribed medicine, acetazolamide, is sold under the brand name of Diamox. It helps prevent altitude sickness but also relieves symptoms. It's possible that I'll need Diamox for the ride along the Taglang La Pass, at 17,500 feet. Nobody can predict one's reaction to extraordinarily high altitudes, but imagining the worst surely doesn't help any. Nevertheless, I listen to his advice and take careful note of the warning symptoms.

* * *

Chapter 15

....

Tackling the World's Highest Roads

DAY 318
Srinagar, India—May 28, 1995

After this leg of the journey, I'll be off to Thailand, where I'll rejoin Caroline. The thought of seeing her again is a great motivator. I've got such a lot to share and catch up on. She does, too. Six months after my departure, when she finished her studies in occupational therapy, she flew to the United Kingdom to learn English. She quickly got a job in a vegetarian restaurant and found a flat with five American girls the same age, whom she met by chance in a youth hostel.

In Sariska, India, I met two Brits who had just returned from a ten-month stay in Australia. They were so taken with their time Down Under that I'm thinking maybe I could meet Caroline there, in June, later this year. I want her to join me for part of the trip, so that she might live, experience, and understand what it has been like. The snag is that other globetrotters have already told me how difficult it is to get back to "normal" life after you've been traveling for more than a year or so. I have often asked myself if I should prolong my stay on a whim. This might be a stupid, or maybe even a dangerous, decision. Since my "mind spin" in Iran, I feel at peace, and I want to go on . . . but first I need the point of view of my parents and the wisdom of their counsel.

With their sound opinions and their moral support, it didn't take much to convince me. My father tells me about the recession and about how some of my engineering colleagues had yet to find work. He encourages me to pursue my education in the School of Life, to earn a diploma that no university can give me. My mother, who loves traveling, always dreamed of going round the world. She reckons I'm a lucky lad and encourages me to keep on keeping on. She says that now's the time to fulfill my dreams before really settling down—if I ever do settle down. My parents are living this adventure vicariously through my journal and letters, which they devotedly transcribe, word for word. They just want to see me happy, and I'm gladder for it. I even suggested to my mother that she should join me for three weeks in India, but she was bedridden with the flu, so our plans never materialized.

After speaking to Caroline, we decided to change our plans somewhat. First, we'll meet up in Thailand, after which we'll travel through Malaysia and Indonesia before reaching Australia. We haven't decided how we'll get there, but her enthusiasm reassures me, and I'm definitely hot to trot. She's loving her time in England, and, like me, she's not ready to go home just yet.

DAY 320
Kangan, India—May 30, 1995

Time to break the ice, one more time. Back on my bike, I'm as free as a bird again, wistfully leaving Srinagar and my new friends behind. Cycling for forty miles or so, I roll into Kangan, at an altitude of more than 6,500 feet. The road getting there is a difficult one. My knees hold up OK, but I feel like I asked them for too great an effort. Tomorrow's 9,000-foot ascent leads me to the village of Sonamarg. Far off in the distance, I see an immense rock massif at the end of the ever-narrowing valley. Speckled with snow, the setting sun brings out both the color and the sharp relief of the stone. It sits there like the almighty local head honcho. Tomorrow, as I pass alongside it, I'll get yet another perspective on its spectacular presence.

The muezzin has just started chanting again: "Allahu Akbar, God is Great. There are no gods but only God. I witness that Mohammed is God's Messenger. Come to prayer, come to prayer. Come to prosperity, come to prosperity. Allahu Akbar, Allahu Akbar. I witness that there are no gods but only one God, Allah." And when it's proclaimed five times a day, ten minutes at a time, how could they forget it?

The sun slips shyly behind a jagged peak, and the hubbub of the village dies down with it. Night starts as soon as the last, faint rays of sunlight disappear. Traffic is quiet except for some military vehicles streaking across the valley. Dogs are lying low; cows are busy at work. They saunter around, eco-grazing on anything edible on the ground. From my balcony, I watch the quiet, empty streets below. I feel the cool air rising. High up in these beautiful mountains, I feel so free. I've waited for this moment for months. Tomorrow, another beautiful day unfolds. I now have to unplug my buzzing thoughts to give my soul a little freedom, as well.

DAY 321
Sonamarg, India—May 31, 1995

Every mile of road is a hard-earned victory. I arrive in Sonamarg, nestled at the bottom of a tiny valley. It's a small locale but still home to fifty or so villagers. Guided by the looming rock massifs on both sides of the valley, a rumbling river of melted snow tears through the stillness. I pick a quieter spot along its banks to take a wash. It's growing dark, so it's time to set up camp for the night.

I'm writing by candlelight. The whole village is pitch black, because there's no electricity whatsoever in these remote Kashmiri mountains. It all adds to the mystique of the place. I'm at 9,000 feet. Except for the desperate whir-ring of a moth, which has just flown into the candle wax, everything is dead silent. It's early to bed for me. Tomorrow is a big day: I'm tackling my first Himalayan pass and entering Ladakh, the Buddhist enclave within Kashmir.

DAY 322
Dras, India—June 1, 1995

The sun shines brightly this morning in a clear and cloudless blue sky. I kick start my departure by filling up with calcium, complex B, multi vitamins, vitamins E and C, plus one-and-a-half ounces of protein concentrate, three eggs, and a side of red beans, all washed down with a quart of water. I'm ready to cross Zoji La (Zoji Pass), at 11,750 feet. My legs are metal rods, my heart is steel, and I've got just one idea in mind: make it to the top, no matter what.

I follow the course of the river for the first ten miles or so. Everything is hunky-dory until the road forks to abruptly face a sharply rising incline. This wall of rock is so high that I don't even dare to look at it, for fear that the sight itself would crush my morale. The road becomes a series of switch-backs, cut straight into the rockface. Beneath me, at every bend, I see the rungs that I've climbed. Above, I look up to see those I have yet to conquer to reach the summit.

My efforts are rewarded, and, much to my relief, the lofty altitude doesn't affect me. At least, not yet. I've never climbed so high or scaled such a long slope: eighty-five miles of continuous ascent over two days of riding. At the summit, I'm totally alone. A small lunch—a tomato sandwich, a walnut, fruit salad, and a chocolate bar—should give me enough energy to make it back down again.

Gazing westward, I take one last look at the lush Kashmir valley. To the east, I check out a forbidding and barren mountain range: Ladakh, also known as "Little Tibet" because of its large population of Tibetan refugees.

As I was previously told, Zoji La Pass is a flat two-mile stretch, right at 11,750 feet. Six-foot-high snowbanks on each side are slowly melting, thereby transforming the road into a shallow stream of water. Now I see why it's closed to cars. . . .

And here I am, thinking that going down would be the easy part! Perhaps it's less tiring, but it's decidedly more dangerous. The first six miles are fairly treacherous. In fact, half the road has been washed away. I'm thrashing through a constant stream of pebbles and rocks swept in by the current. Farther down, a surging torrent completely cuts off the road. Attempting to cross here would be suicidal. Finding a spot where the gushing stream peters out into a trickle, I decide to clamber up the cliff with my equipment, one piece at a time. This, of course, takes forever and a day. I'm looking forward to the end of this bike-water rafting, even more so now that there's a vicious headwind. I actually have to pedal to go down; otherwise, I would remain at a standstill. Without quite knowing how I manage it, I ride into Dras just as the sun goes down. At an altitude of 10,500-plus feet, this village is renowned for its deathly cold winters. Indeed, it's among the coldest settlements on earth.

It wasn't easy, but mission accomplished. My reward? An ice-cold shower. It's so dark out now, I can't see anything, anyway. I'm going to bed.

DAY 323
Kargil, India—June 2, 1995

The cool breeze makes you forget how strong the sun can be at these heights. I probably got a touch of sunstroke when I took off my helmet to have lunch. I learned my lesson. I'll be more careful in the future.

My bike chain has been creaking ever since my spin through the water, pebbles, rocks, and sand. I don't have any oil to grease it, but I come across a road crew unloading 265-gallon barrels of oil for roadwork. They can spare some, and in no time at all, my bike chain is squeaklessly clean. These friendly guys are happy to see me. The feeling is mutual.

As I approach Kargil, the valley becomes more and more narrow. Rocky crags are huge shards, tearing up the sky. The wind is howling. The village is covered in a cloud of dust so dense that I can only make out the peaks surrounding it.

After strolling through the village streets, I sit down in the middle of the bustle to people watch. A cobbler repairs shoes with the single-minded dedication of a Benedictine monk. He doesn't even realize that I'm watching him. I never grow tired of the show. With hammer and nails (lots of nails) he resoles a shoe using a rubber material that I immediately recognize. As he turns it over, I can see that it's clearly marked "Goodyear." He nails a pre-cut sole into place but realizes that it doesn't quite hold at the heel. His solution is to hammer home a longer nail. This poses another problem: the nail goes right through to the inside of the shoe. A few discrete hammer blows to bend it flat, and the job is done. Close by, someone is selling eyeglasses. An old mountain dweller tries to find a pair that suits him. I'm not talking Giorgio Armani high fashion, here. He tries them, one pair at a time, squinting to see if he can read the sign on the other side of the street. And in a nearby booth, a beaming Sikh offers a full display of pre-owned dentures. I approach and ask him if they're really for sale, plain and simple. "But, of course," he says, flashing his own fangs at me, as if I had asked the dumbest question in the world.

My Ayurvedic intestinal cure is giving me the kind of results that would amaze any traveler in India. This morning, instead of mixing it in water and drinking it down immediately, as instructed, I waited. After ten minutes, I see that not a single drop remains in the glass—just the powder, now as hard as dough. Not surprising that a clod like that can romp through your guts, cleaning out the bowel like a Zamboni in heat. A traveler's health in India is fixated on the scatalogical and brings a whole new meaning to the Freudian "anal stage." We don't so much talk about the weather but, rather, chat about our latest (and greatest) bowel movements.

My legs feel like they're set in concrete. I'm tired and tense. Although I need to relax, I can't settle down. I'm getting up as early as I can tomorrow, because I'm on a roll. A wholesome diet helps me stay in shape. It's not exactly epicurian, but I'm getting everything I need. It's 7:40 PM, and I am about to drop off to sleep. My body is begging me to give it a chance.

DAY 324
Mulbek, India—June 3, 1995

Less than a mile from Kargil, there's a T junction. One way leads to the Zanskar Valley and the other to Leh, where I'm heading. I follow the sign to Leh, which leads me up a steep road, going up and up and up . . . and then up some more. At one point, I meet a local who is quick to tell me I'm on a dead-end street—a Kashmiri cul-de-sac. I've just put myself through a grueling nine-mile trek for no apparent reason. Back at the T junction, I realize that the signpost has been loosely planted in the ground. It's surely been moved around a couple of times.

It's now 7:30 in the evening. I finally found some water to have a wash. I sleep under the stars, on the roof of a rest-stop building. This close to the heavens, you can't help but feel good.

DAY 324
Mulbek, India—June 3, 1995

Another pass, this time Namika La, 12,800 feet above sea level. Since yesterday, the landscape has changed dramatically. Mountains of hardened sand have replaced the solid-rock peaks. From a distance, it resembles marbled chocolate cake.

In this part of the Himalayas, a region as dry as the Sahara Desert, both crop fields and homes are supplied with water by a complex system of canals, built out of mud and stone. In certain irrigated zones, to grow rice, for example, some conduits are opened and others closed. Blocking a canal is done with anything at hand. It's interesting to see how much this engineering work respects the laws of gravitational flow, while reducing erosion to a minimum, and all to provide the best irrigation possible. This innovative construction is a cornerstone of survival for these farmers.

Fortunately, I always carry extra provisions! It takes me no time at all to prepare an excellent supper made with a packet of dried noodles, pan-fried onions, and tomatoes, as well as two eggs added to the noodle broth. It's delicious. But suddenly, I feel another giardiasis attack coming on. Generally, I've had peace since Jammu, but I know the symptoms like the back of my hand. Extreme cases require extreme measures! I pop two grams of tinidazole . . . just like that. It's similar to Flagyl, except it acts instantly. At 12,000 feet, in the clouds, in a godforsaken village where you can't buy anything to eat, and a mountain wall topping out at 13,500 feet to cross the next day, a night of diarrhea and puking is not an option. I'm sure I made the right decision. I'll know by tomorrow. Anyway, that's not going to stop me. When you've emptied your guts, alone, half naked and half frozen in the middle of the Iranian desert, you're ready for anything. That was my true test of courage, an experience that has given me all the moral fiber and fortitude I'll ever need.

I made the right call. The Leh-Manali road is not closed, after all. It was a scam dreamed up by unscrupulous Kashmiris. A truck driver, who regularly drives the route, confirmed that the road was, indeed, open. Others told me that tourists even had access to the Nubra Valley, where the highest pass in the world is located. At the summit, a sign boldly proclaims, "Khardung La, 18,392 feet above sea level, the highest pass in the world. Here you can chat with God!"

DAY 326
Khalsi, India—June 5, 1995

The dose I took yesterday worked wonders. I slept like the king of diamonds. On the other hand, my breakfast was more suited to the two of clubs. I managed to rustle up four eggs to make an omelet. One contained a speck of blood, and, of course, it had to be the last one that I cracked into the pan! Since Ladakh is isolated from the plains for more than six months of the year, the produce you get at this time of year is often past its prime and/or quite limited. After my "deviled egg" disaster in Italy, there's no way I'm risking it, especially just before climbing a 13,400-foot pass. I still have some protein powder given to me by the Aussie, as well as heaps of vitamins. That should do. It will have to do.

Pedaling across the pass was no problem at all. The view on top is superb, but I immediately start down again, to Lamayuru. After a failed attempt at breakfast, I'm starving. A short, half-hour break is enough for me to recoup my strength. I don't know it yet, but I am about to encounter one of the most beautiful vistas I'll ever see, anywhere. It's just around the last bend, as Lamayuru village finally comes into view. This breathtaking sight gives me goose bumps, and I shout out loud with sheer exhilaration. I'm simply awestruck. Never would I have imagined that such natural splendor could possibly exist on Earth. I marvel at a rocky mountain mass from whose base flows the source of the Indus, and whose summit, covered with a skullcap of snow, points directly at the sky. On my right, a series of ridges and ridge folds, like giant serpents etched into the rock, clearly reveal the imprints of the past. Behind this prehistoric tableau lies a succession of peaks, soaring higher and higher as I glance toward the infinite. On my left, rain and wind have sculpted the terrain into a lunar look-alike landscape, a "moonland" as they call it here. The color, shape, and layout of the mountains form a kind of dreamlike reality, proving emphatically that not every fantastical set comes out of Hollywood.

Suddenly, I want to make myself very small, to shrink into oblivion. It's like brushing shoulders with death itself. I always imagined that such beauty would only be revealed to us in the afterlife. A rush of ideas, one as crazy as the next, swirl around my head until a mountain dweller, hauling his load on the back of a donkey, snaps me out of it. He stops by my side and, without a word, looks at my bike and then at his donkey. I smile at him, but he's already on his way. Maybe he briefly thought about making me an offer: his mule for mine?

On the way down, I arrive at a road with numerous hairpin bends. And I believed that the sharpest turns were in the Alps! By comparison, these hairpins are certainly fit to coif a giantess. This road is unnerving. On the left, where I usually ride, the road is carpeted in with rocks and pebbles that have fallen down from the cliffs above. So I have to stick to the other side, where, less than three feet from the edge of the road, opens the yawning maw of an unforgiving precipice. Twelve miles down, including half a mile of flat, is a gravity-defying, roguishly rough road of seductive beauty. Sure, it charms and transports you, but with one little distraction, it can also "rock" you into the timeless beyond!

After a couple of breaks to cool down the wheel rims (and to avoid melting my inner tubes), I finally join the Indus, the very same river that I followed along the Karakorums in northern Pakistan, five months ago. Here in the Ladakh ranges in India, we meet up once again, as old friends. And this same old friend will lead me to Leh, sixty miles down the road. In a month, it's Thailand and my sweetheart, Caro.

At high altitudes, the sun is less filtered and beats down hard. When I stop for a few minutes to catch my breath, the hot road surface underfoot and beneath my wheels is sticky, like glue. Whatever. It didn't stop me—I make it to Leh. I figured on resting up for a week, but as fate would have it, I meet a German guy, Patrick. He invites me to share his room, one with a spectacular view of the mountains. He's here for a month, also on his bike. Somehow he's already heard about me. He fills me in fast on what he's been up to. And he also wants me to accompany him to Lake Tsomoriri, wildly singing its praises. This lake is perched at 15,000 feet, just ten miles from the Tibetan border. It's been open to tourists for only one year and only with a permit! "If you don't come with me," he admits, "I'm not going there by myself . . . it's too dangerous."

It involves a six-day trek, off the beaten track, where the possibility of getting help if you need it is very thin. Just a few nomadic tribes live in this remote region. The road doesn't even exist on official maps. My new friend has met one of Ladakh's best guides, who said he'd give us a hand-drawn map of the area. Patrick has already crossed South America and Canada, he is experienced and confident, but I'm not ready to give an immediate answer. I'm still knackered from my day of biking. Plus, I want to take time to think about it and, most of all, to personally meet the guide and ask him my own questions.

As if the challenge of heading straight back to Manali wasn't enough, I accept Patrick's offer. We leave this morning, loaded like mules: eggs, dehydrated meals, walnuts, dried fruits, and protein nuggets that look more like dog food. The guide hands us a map on which he scrawled some information regarding the various heights of the passes, distances between certain landmarks, water sources, rivers to be crossed, and finally a few directions so we won't get lost.

This evening, we sleep in a cramped room at the Hemis Monastery. On the edge of a tributary of the Indus River, it's the only one in Ladakh to have never been plundered by invaders, probably because it's not visible from the road. We had to climb a 400-yard path before arriving there. Built in the seventeenth century, the interior is decorated with images of Buddha, sculptures, and silk paintings (thangka), typical for this part of Ladakh. On the outer walls, there are a series of prayer wheels, a common feature of Tibetan Buddhist structures. These ornate, wooden spindles are fixed alongside the wall and turn on a vertical axis. By following the walls of the monastery, devotees turn one after the other by using the palm and fingers of a single hand. It is their way of engaging with God.

There are eighty monks in this monastery. Two of them prepare butter tea ("po cha"). As the name implies, it's made by blending yak butter and tea. First, they brew four cups of tea and pour them into a metal cylinder, at the bottom of which sits a half a pound of butter. Then, they vigorously churn the contents until it's completely mixed. Finally, they pour in another eight cups of tea and stir once again.

The monks explain that this beverage is an excellent source of fat, much needed to get through the harsh winters. Still, I have to wonder how they can resist the brutal Himalayan cold in dwellings made of stone and wood and devoid of insulation.

Tomorrow, we shall follow the Indus until Mahe, where we'll turn off onto a dirt road. The day after that, we'll follow the 16,750-foot pass to Lake Tsomoriri, where we'll definitely spend a few days more in the place they call "the lost paradise."

DAY 331
Chumathang, India—June 10, 1995

We biked fifty-seven miles before stopping near a small cluster of homes. We just have to say "julley"—"hello" in the local dialect—to bring a smile to the faces of the locals. We've barely poked around, and already the welcome mats are out. A man, joined by his son, offers us a friendly roof for the night and tells us that we'll be served a proper "Kashmiri meal." This is a dish of mutton and vegetables in a rich-bone broth.

As is my habit after a hard day of biking, I look for a small brook so I can wash myself. The wind is biting, and the air is chilly. Some kids gawk at me splashing around in this icy water and can't understand why I would torture myself in this way. Patrick doesn't get it, either.

Before the end of the day, the mother comes to meet us, dressed in traditional getup. After a series of shy gestures, she makes us understand that she would like it if we take some photos of her family and then send them back to her. In next to no time, we're having a photoshoot in their small inner courtyard. Mom, Dad, the kids, and a few close friends take their shot at posterity. For them, as it is for us, it's a joy to share this moment fixed in time.

It's very unlikely we'll reach Lake Tsomoriri tomorrow, because the distance is greater than anticipated. The guide's information is already a bit iffy—not that reassuring for what comes next. We still have another twenty-five miles along the Indus before we really get into unknown territory. According to our map, the nomadic village of Korzok, south of Lake Tsomoriri, is thirty-five miles from the place where we branch off from the Indus. I'm very apprehensive about this route. Patrick, with his mountain bike, is much more confident. I may even turn back if conditions prove to be too difficult. But at the moment, I'm vaguely hopeful, especially since I feel no hint of altitude sickness. It's a good sign, because I won't be coming back down again to anything less than 13,000 feet for at least fourteen days.

* * *

Chapter 16

....

Unforgettable Smiles

DAY 332
Sumdo, India—June 11, 1995

We have just left the Indus River road and branched off toward our destination: Lake Tsomoriri. A harsh reality strikes home. I soon understand why the road doesn't appear on any map: it's no road at all, just tracks left by four-wheel-drive vehicles snaking along a nameless riverbed. The first three miles are atrocious. I can't even pedal, nor can Patrick, even with his fancy mountain bike. Our only choice is to walk our bikes. Luckily, the "road" becomes less rocky as we trudge ahead. Frustration and anguish subside once we're able to ride again. Eyes riveted to the ground, I concentrate on avoiding the bigger rocks. Now the challenge is not doing the miles but rather the yards and the feet. I'm scared to look up and see how little progress we've made, despite our best efforts. Around each bend of the river, it's more of the same. Four miles along, still transfixed by the track scrolling under my front wheel, I suddenly find myself on a lush plain, the first greenery I've seen since I left Leh. Farther, I think I see a kind of grey-stone building. As I approach, the moving shapes I took for animals are, in fact, kids playing around.

It's a school—even out here in the farthest reaches of the Himalayas! A teacher comes out to greet us in impeccable English. At 14,500 feet, Sumdo is, in fact, a school for Tibetan refugees. The surroundings are breathtaking: lush green grass unfurling below snow-capped peaks against an incredible expanse of blue sky. We're so high up, yet it feels like we're on a flat field surrounded by modest hills. The sun is strong, but the chilly air reminds us that we're sitting on top of the world.

Day from Hell
Korzok, India—June 12, 1995

We traveled twenty-seven miles over sandy tracks and riverbeds covered in rocks and pebbles; nine unrelenting hours of pushing our bikes. In other words, a day to forget. The guide's info is still off the mark. I'd like to throw a tantrum, but just like a kid, I won't, because no one's paying attention. It's important to stay positive. On the bright side, I can boast about having absolutely and totally regretted at least one day of my trip.

I'm in Korzok, a small, nomadic village at the edge of the renowned Lake Tsomoriri. It's hard for me to appreciate the beauty of this spot since I can't stop thinking about our inevitable return back to Sumdo on that soul-destroying ride through hell. No view on earth is worth all the agony and effort getting here. Patrick agrees, even more so now that he's feeling some altitude sickness. We're at 14,900 feet, and between us and Sumdo is a 15,750-foot pass. If that turns ugly, there'll be nobody to help us. I do my best to reassure him. Ideally, we would rest here for at least another day, but that's out of the question now. We must leave first thing tomorrow morning. I get furious just thinking about that cursed road. I throw a worried look Patrick's way. At least I'm healthy, I tell myself. . . .

Our Lucky Day, a Day for Diplomacy
Sumdo, India—June 13, 1995

It's our lucky day: an Indian minister and a researcher, accompanied by their three servants, are heading to Korzok. Also a day for diplomacy:

I manage to convince them to give us a lift to Sumdo. Better yet, would it be possible to get our bikes and gear aboard their already jam-packed Jeep? Their generous response is music to our ears: "If you can squeeze it in, we'll take it." The very thought of not having to ride on this road again is incentive enough to try and cram an elephant into a glove box! In the end, we fasten our bikes on the roof, we stuff one hundred pounds of gear inside the Jeep, and we take a deep breath so that the driver can close the door shut. No worries. How did we manage to pull this one off? Patrick gives me a wry smile that speaks volumes. Every minute in this can of sardines takes us sixty seconds closer to Sumdo. I'd rather be a sardine in a Jeep than a fish on a bicycle, any day.

After a tightly squashed four-hour drive, we finally make it back to our cherished school. We can't thank our deliverers enough. A funny thing: Patrick feels much better. So do I, and my friends, my very dear friends, whose Jeep now sits out in the direction of Leh. I'm wondering if we shouldn't have stayed onboard. . . .

The schoolteacher offers us a spacious, empty classroom to stay in. I feel like I'm back home. We're invited to have supper with all four teachers. As we start talking, we learn about their particular plight. In 1949, the Chinese Red Army invaded Tibet. Then, after the Tibetan Uprising in 1959, the Chinese exiled the Dalai Lama. A massive exodus of Tibetans soon followed, with refugees fleeing mainly to Nepal and India. The region of Ladakh, sparsely populated at the time, quickly became their adopted homeland. It's now known as "Little Tibet." The kids attending this school come from nomadic families searching for newer, greener pastures to graze their cattle. Too young to follow their parents as they roam the area, here, they are housed, fed, and taught the Tibetan language and the culture that they will someday champion. The teachers, themselves refugees, have been educated in India and are now back to share their knowledge, because, they say, a good education is the best weapon against the Chinese. They insist they need help from democratic countries, and so they must be both credible and informed—in a nutshell, educated. The school principal interrupts our conversation and mentions that the kids are taking their lunch break. It's the best time for us to meet them.

Sitting directly on the ground, they form a rectangle, each one tight up against the other, and wait patiently to be served their lunch. While the principal says a few words to them in Tibetan, they all start sniffling and using their sleeves as handkerchiefs. They all have colds, their clothes are ripped and torn, and their shoes no longer have soles. Yet somehow they still shine as radiantly as the sun. They all stand up en masse and say "Welcome to Sumdo" in chorus and sit back down again. Now with the niceties taken care of, the cook brings in lunch. Each looks around, without knowing exactly what to do next. They must be hungry, but rather than just diving in, they look to each other, trying to figure out what to do. For them, a banana is a play sword. The bowl of boiled cabbage, for washing fingers, and the bread a napkin to wipe them on. Meanwhile, their runny noses drip and drip! They live like a litter of puppies and have just as much fun. After the meal (I've got no idea why), they jump up and prepare to change clothes. Digging through four big, metal boxes, filled to the brim, they randomly choose raggedy uniforms that they'll wear for afternoon classes. Their dirty linen is thrown into the boxes and will be reused the next day. If you think these rags will be washed tonight, you'll also believe that I'll be continuing my trip on a flying carpet!

Now that I've regained my spirits, I'm better able to describe the setting at Lake Tsomoriri. Not only a large lake (fifteen-and-a-half miles long by four-and-a-half miles wide), it's also at very high altitude, surrounded by mountains all greater than twenty thousand feet: a gigantic swimming pool with walls more than a mile high.

Except for that horrific road, whose existence I'm trying to forget, there are also a few nomadic-tent settlements. Wearing several layers of ragged clothes, they go on a walkabout around the entire lake circumference, so that their animals can always graze on fresh grass. They have herds of sheep (for wool), cows (for milk), and yaks (as beasts of burden).

We head for the Manali Junction tomorrow. We'll have to ride over a 16,500-foot pass. We don't know exactly where these nomadic tribes will be, so it will be hard to rely on them for provisions. We'll figure it out when we get there.

DAY 335
Nowheresville, India—June 14, 1995

It is with a heavy heart that we say goodbye to the Sumdo kids. Patrick had set out on this trip with the intention of helping out the Tibetan refugees in Ladakh, so he gives the school 900 German Marks. We are both tremendously moved by the genuine joy we see in the teachers' eyes. Their work, the children, and the land itself have touched us so deeply.

Five miles further on, where the nomadic village of Puga was supposed to be, we find only abandoned, ramshackle huts and a primitive fence. No luck with a water source either (as promised by our guide), but we should have enough water before we reach the next nomadic camp situated at Tsokar, a dried-out salt lake.

I'm in amazing shape. I'm zipping up slopes without a problem, as if I was a well-oiled, mountain-climbing machine. Indeed, the height doesn't bother me in the least. Feeling so fit is a wonderful sensation. I arrive at the summit a good two hours before Patrick, so far ahead that I wonder if he hadn't given up on me. It's a good time to eat. When he gets to the summit, he's happy to quickly scarf down some walnuts and dried fruit. And we're off again.

The descent offers us a unique view. The salt lake, also surrounded by an array of impressive peaks, seems quite close and easily accessible from where we sit. But, as we've noticed before, amid these colossal mountains, it's impossible to estimate distances correctly. That's why we pedal another twenty-two miles before reaching the lake, first pushing our bike across a flat of sand, which finally turns into salt. My front wheel is too narrow and bears too much weight, so it sinks into the ground. There is no sign of life for miles around, and the village of Nuruchang, as indicated on our map, appears to be a mere fiction. Patrick insists on continuing. He believes there have to be people farther along waiting to welcome us. I'm hoping he's right, but I also know I can't waste another ounce of energy going nowhere.

Once the sun goes down, Patrick fully realizes that it's time to stop. I feel guilty about riding for such a long stretch. These past thirty miles in such difficult conditions have totally exhausted us. We're at 15,000 feet, in the middle of nowhere, on a salt lake, between a rock mountain and a hard sandy place, as far as the eye can see. We saved on water all day long, and, even so, a couple of pints are all we have left. We knuckle down to cooking our supper. We're lucky enough to find ourselves in an unlikely spot: there's enough firewood here from the dead shrubs lying about. So we start a fire behind a big rock, shielded from the wind, and cook up some dehydrated protein. Plus, I sacrifice a chocolate bar, hoping that it gives me the energy to get a good night's sleep. Fear is no match for weariness as I drop into the arms of Morpheus.

DAY 336
Taglang La, India—June 15, 1995

Wow! What a sunrise to wake up to. It's time to get going; we've got a big day ahead. We still don't know how far we are from the main road. Worse yet, we're not even sure we'll find it. The guide had recommended we take the northern side of the salt lake, but apparently we're on the southern side. Yesterday, we followed tracks left by some off-road vehicles. They must lead to somewhere.

The first few miles fly by at a good pace. Then we hit another tract of sand. This time, it's damn near impossible to pedal. To be honest, I barely manage to drag my bike through it.

Big problem. Now our route splits into a two-way fork, with neither direction marked on our map. We don't know where we are anymore, and it's decision time. The tracks on the left point straight ahead, whereas the other path, forking off to the north, faces a huge mountain in front. My gut feeling tells me to go left. I look at Patrick. "If we don't get back on the main road within the next three hours, it's because we're really lost, and we'll have to backtrack." That puts us at least two days from Sumdo and the Tibetan kids' school. We'd better be quick, because I don't intend to die of thirst, stranded in these mountains!

We dribble along at a snail's pace, despite tremendous effort. I resign myself to simply dragging my bike, trying not to think about whether or not we went the right way. I stop frequently. It's been two hours since we left the fork, and I sense that the noose is tightening. The sun beats down harder and harder, the air becomes more and more dry, and I'm getting thirstier by the minute. My lips are parched and burned. I feel like a live lobster dropped in a pot of boiling water. If only we could get some shade. But nothing rises above ground level. Here, only mountains reign supreme.

Suddenly, far off, we spot a nomad tending his herd of yaks. We pick up the pace as much as we can. It seems we'll never reach him. After twenty minutes of this cat and mouse chase, I decide to leave my bike and run toward him, water bottle in hand. Patrick stays behind patiently. As I approach, I realize that the herder has nothing but his staff. Getting desperate, I repeatedly spout out the words "Manali" and "Leh." Unfussed, he raises his arm and points a knowing finger southward. At that very moment, I hear Patrick shouting with excitement. In the distance, he sees a strip of asphalt. Is it a mirage? I run back to my bike, while Patrick heads toward the road to make sure he's not dreaming.

Finally the road! I empty the sand out of my shoes while Patrick figures out how far it is to Manali. He must be there by June 20, at the latest. For my part, I won't be going there until I make my round trip to Taglang La. Nothing will dissuade me. It's my ultimate dream, and I'm not backing off now that I'm so close. Patrick respects this decision, even though he'd like us to continue riding together. It's 1:00 PM, lunchtime. I haven't eaten yet, and a solo, sixteen-mile upward slope is my next challenge. We exchange addresses hastily. Patrick apologizes for talking me into such an "interesting" trip. I reassure him by telling him that he never forced me to tag along and that he's got nothing to feel guilty about. It could have been a lot worse, tragic even. We kept our cool all the way through. Being in top shape didn't hurt either. We shake hands, and we go our separate ways, hoping to meet up again in Manali or (to quote Willie Nelson) "on the road again." Both of us head off in opposite directions, Patrick southward and I northward. I've only got one idea in mind: to get to the world's second-highest pass before the end of the day.

Climbing toward the summit means I soon have to cross a series of small streams of melting snow: pure, crystal-clear water trickling over a stony bed.

Unabashedly, I drink straight from the source and take full advantage to fill my water bottles and wash up a little. And I have to say, this ice-cold wash is a real treasure, even though it does shrink the "family jewels" somewhat!

I take my pulse regularly as I progress. It varies between 140 and 165 during the final three hours of the climb. Two-and-a-half miles from the summit, I want to cry. Every push of the pedal is excruciating. My body cannot take it any more. But my merciless mind tells me that I can't stop now, so close to my goal. The lack of oxygen makes my feet feel like they're made of lead. My legs are gone, I'm totally out of breath, my energy completely depleted. All that's left is my heart, my will, my courage, and a bike full of pride.

My headache instantly goes away once I see the summit. After a five-hour climb, just as the sun is setting, my dream comes true: I'm on the second-highest pass on the planet Earth, Taglang La, 17,582 feet above sea level.

Now I'm inside a tiny, albeit brand-new, stone temple, where I'll kip down for the night. It's not warm, but at least I'll have some shelter.

I still have 240 miles plus three passes (all exceeding 16,400 feet) to be crossed before reaching Manali. Having endured these last few days, nothing can stop me now. Tomorrow, I'll watch the sun rise out of the infinite sky. This night on Taglang La will be my last flirtation with madness. Biking in the Himalayas has been a mysterious and magical experience. I thank God for giving me the strength to meet such a challenge . . . as for the rest, I have only myself to thank. It is 8:15 PM, and I'm lying on top of the world, all 17,582 feet of it, to be precise. So close to the stars, I can't help but have sweet dreams.

DAY 337
Pang, India—June 16, 1995

I was right to sleep inside the shelter. Overnight was very cold, and it's hard to get out of my sleeping bag. The sun hasn't risen yet, but already I can see its first beams piercing through the horizon. I take a photo of my bike, propped up against the sign: "Taglang La, altitude 17,582 feet, you are passing through the second highest pass of the world, unbelievable, is it not?"

My lower lip is seriously burned by the sun and dehydration. It cracks and bleeds continuously, weighed down by a thick crust of blood. I start my descent wearing all the clothes I've got.

After a sixteen-mile ride, I'm back at the place where I left Patrick yesterday. For the next eighteen miles, I ride across a bleak, barren plateau at 15,100 feet, ending abruptly on top of a cliff. Then I go down a zigzagging road, cut directly into the mountainside, to join the river again. Here, there is a permanent camp set up by the Himank company. It's the base settlement for workers who built the road and who now maintain it and clear the snow. During the summer season, some local entrepreneurs set up their tents and provide meals for those traveling between Leh and Manali. Finally, some food. I had none left.

The locals inform me that the road to Manali is still covered in snow and that the next village, Sarchu, will only be a ghost town until the road is opened. I reckon I can get there by bike. I take a day off to rest up for the next leg. Manali is less than four days away. Now's not the time to give up.

I borrow some blankets from the locals and sleep in a tent made from a World War II parachute. The propane stove breaks the silence, but I can't do without it.

DAY 339
Sarchu, India—June 18, 1995

As I expected, I find absolutely nothing in Sarchu. I'm in an abandoned Himank hut, and there isn't a soul within a forty-mile radius. I crossed Lachlung La—16,620 feet—without any trouble. However, I wasn't aware that another pass followed shortly thereafter. I couldn't catch a break, riding three hours through a relentless headwind. I'm done in but glad to be under cover.

* * *

A Day of Surprises
Darcha, India—June 19, 1995

According to my Lonely Planet guide, "a short climb will lead you to the Baralacha Pass." As a surprise, it's quite a big one. Yes, this description is true enough . . . if the road is open.

I set out feeling cocky, confident that everything will be fine. The more I ride, the more I'm convinced that snow won't just appear out of nowhere. Once again, I must have heard wrong.

As the road becomes ever steeper, the real climb begins. I can now see that there's snow ahead, and the road is getting more difficult to climb. In a few places, big boulders block the passage. Certainly, a vehicle could never get past these obstacles. I get a kick out of the fact that the road is closed, yet I can zip along, no trouble at all. Long live the mighty bike!

After 650 feet of a very steep climb, I come to a plateau, surrounded by mountains. The pass must be somewhere near here, but I'm not sure which way the road goes . . . it's white, everywhere you look. I go another mile, and the snow is denser and denser. And I've still got five-and-a-half miles before I reach the top of the pass.

The aftermath of a small avalanche spills across the road. No big deal, I still manage to carry my bike through the snow pile. A little further, a river is the next obstacle to overcome. The bridge that normally crosses it has not been put back in place yet, ready for the road opening. During winter, bridges are dragged to dry land, so they won't be swept away by the strong floods caused by melting snow. Not a new situation for me. As usual, I take off my shoes and socks and wade across the river barefoot. You can guess how warm and cozy the water is. My cockiness has gone down a few notches, and it's not so funny anymore. Five miles to go. Around the next bend, I'm not laughing at all: a twelve-foot-high snowbank and a rush of water have taken out the whole road. The cliff is too steep for me to go around it from below.

I study all my options. The most realistic is to tackle the wall head-on. A dangerous operation. If I slip, I'll slide down and land in the rocks below. First, I check the surface. It is frozen solid, and I can hardly get a grip. There'll be no traction at all if I'm to climb such a slope with a bike on my back. That would be a suicidal maneuver. And that's why carving out steps in this hardened snow strikes me as a brilliant idea. Using my knife and carefully selecting particular rocks, I cut out a staircase. The end result proves satisfactory. I hurl my saddlebags one by one over the wall. Now for the bike: I lift it above my head and anchor a pedal solidly in the snow. I climb past it, up to the top, reach down to grab the handlebars, and give it a final hoist to the top of the wall. I then enjoy a forty-five feet snowslide, toss my gear down to the other side, and Bob's your uncle.

I can't go back. I've got one meal left and not enough food to make it through the night. The stress of all this mountain climbing, and the walls still to come, is getting the better of me. I take a moment to wolf down the last of my food. Then, there's just one thing to be done: get on with it.

If my guardian angel is close by, he certainly heard my triumphant yell. I shout out in relief when I see a few snowplows. Although they're abandoned on the side of the road, I can be sure that there won't be more snow patches ahead. I'm relieved, but there's more punishment to come. This is a "short" climb, according to Lonely Planet, but it turns out to be a thousand times more difficult than I had imagined. The road is clear of snowslides, but it's still covered in snow and ice, under which a steady stream of water trickles. The weight of my bike is enough to constantly break this thin, frozen layer. I sink all the time. My feet are blocks of ice, and I'm forced to wheel my bike. I'm exhausted and close to tears. My sole comfort is knowing that civilization welcomes me on the other side of this trial.

I finally reach the summit. It took me three-and-a-half hours to splish-splash through the last five miles. I'm far too exhausted to smile and too frozen to jump for joy. The surroundings are bleak. Everything is white. The whole area is blanketed in snow, with the exception of a few peaks timidly poking through. The contrast with this morning's weather is striking. How to explain such a change? I don't even want to know.

As a reward, I eat my last chocolate bar. I slip on my GORE-TEX® socks, the best thing I can do to warm up my ice-cold feet, swishing around in my soaking-wet shoes. As the sky clouds up, the wind screeches ominously, as if it wanted to warn me to run away as quickly as possible. I don't have a lot of time to waste, because Darcha is still thirty miles away. At least I know this village really exists. The way down starts similar to the Zoji La descent: rocks and water everywhere. The road improves as I get lower. I see another cyclist, resting in the distance, his equipment spread out on the rocks. He tells me he met Patrick yesterday. Apparently, my friend wasn't able to cross the pass two days earlier—he had to abandon his bike and continue on by foot. The next day, when he returned, someone had stolen all his gear. But fortunately, the thief left behind his bike. I feel sorry for Patrick. As I know Patrick, he would say it was all just stuff . . . and he'd be right.

The cyclist points to the stream just down the road. "Be careful, it seems shallow, but I had some water up to my chest, and I lost everything when I waded across." No sweat; with me at six-feet-four inches, the water should only come up to my well-worn bum.

If the other cyclist hadn't been there to warn me, I would have lost everything as well. I untie my saddlebags once again, and I cross. The current is so strong that my bike floats sideways. I use the bike as a buoy, because the bottom is rocky, and I risk being swept away in the torrent where, about 100 feet downstream, around thirty workers are more concerned about staring up at the sky, divining the weather, than putting a bridge back in position. I wave back at my fellow cyclist and wish him good luck on the road ahead, the road I've so painfully managed to cross. God knows what waits for him, and for me, too. I'm hardly on my way when I meet two other rivers hindering the road. They're quite shallow, but I have to take off my shoes all the same. For sure, my toes are popsicles.

I get into Darcha just as it starts to rain. Upon my arrival, the locals imagine that the road is finally open. With a heavy heart and in a halting voice, I explain that this isn't the case. I was really quite worried.

* * *

Chapter 17

· ·

A Precarious Success

A Triumphant Day
Manali, India—June 21, 1995

I caught up with Patrick again in Kosar, and we're heading off to Manali together.

An unwelcome wake-up call . . . it's precisely 4:24 AM, and giardiasis is on the attack. It's raining cats and dogs outside. There's no toilet in here, and I absolutely, positively, must go, urgently. We're shacked up in a cattle shed, so if the veranda is good enough for the cows, it's good enough for our bikes, too. I have to go on the spot, and since the end result looks nothing like cow dung, I carry my mess outside where the rain makes short work of it. I don't want anyone to think my mother didn't raise me properly.

Starting at dawn, this already looks like it's going to be a rough day, so I don't take any chances; I swallow my magic pill. After forcing myself to eat breakfast and still suffering from piercing cramps, I leave anyway. I know that once I'm on my bike, the pain will shift to other areas. It's miserable weather. The rain and wind require us to take special measures. My good old plastic garbage bag does the trick. And for Patrick, I've found him a plastic fiber number lying around the cowshed. I tear off a small piece and slip it in under my helmet to stop the rain from trickling down my neck.

The rain is pouring down harder, but my getup holds out. I don't feel tired anymore. Patrick is overdressed, and his perspiration freezes every time he stops. This means he closely follows my lead without taking his usual breaks. We climb ever higher, all while approaching what looks like more snow. It's 113°F in Delhi . . . and snowing on the Rohtang Pass. Go figure.

Less than a mile from the top, and here we are right in the middle of a blizzard. A violent wind lashes us; there's nowhere to hide. We can't see the sky above . . . or the ground below. The cold bites right through me. The last quarter mile seems endless, but I'm almost there. Another bend and there it is—the Rohtang summit, the final Himalayan pass. I shout out in hysterics, unable and unwilling to contain my excitement. Patrick wonders if the heady heights haven't finally driven me completely bonkers.

We shuffle into the temple marking the summit. My hands are so frozen that I'm having trouble opening a saddlebag to dig out a change of clothes. I quickly get undressed and put on all the dry clothing left: a singlet, a cotton sweater, a windbreaker, a plastic trash bag, a scarf, a pair of Chlorophylle shorts, and GORE-TEX® socks. I have to keep wearing my completely soaked shoes, because I don't have another pair.

After a three-hour climb, all we have to do now is go down again. Manali is located thirty miles away and one mile down. In my head, it's already a done deal, but reality proves otherwise. "Hellish" is a mild way of describing this descent. There are rivulets, puddles, potholes, pebbles, and rocks everywhere. The wind is wickedly cold and visibility nonexistent. We ride through a devil's brew of cloud, fog, and rain. About a mile down from the summit, there's a winter sightseeing outpost for Manali vacationers. And of course, there's India-style traffic mayhem. These knuckleheads think they're on a racetrack, where charging ahead, honking, and tooting take the place of studious braking and cautious slowing down. On a flat stretch, this can be vaguely tolerated, but on a road whose entire route is hairpin bends, with one side a solid rock wall and the other a dizzying precipice, it's another story. Coming down, my brakes wear thin as my frustration rises. It's getting dangerous. Still raining, I'm bobbing along like an onion in a bowl of soup.

My glasses are fogged up, my windbreaker is no longer waterproof, and my arms and hands are like blocks of ice. Patrick is still following me and is worried about my bike not holding out. All of a sudden, we both burst into tears and laughter. We're bewildered. Are we expressing our joy or our pain? Just when I think I can't keep going, I remind myself of the times when I was able to pull off the impossible. My spirit will rise to the occasion and get everything back on track.

It takes us just over four hours to put away the thirty miles from the top of the pass down to Manali. The passes are now a thing of the past. Such an experience adds fuel to an already-burning fire. If you approach this blazing fire tentatively, you'll get burned. But if you engulf yourself in it wholeheartedly, it will consume you. Fired up with adventure, this flame has fueled my rides to the highest summits in the world.

DAY 343
Vashisht, India—June 22, 1995

Patrick left this morning for Delhi, where he will take a Lufthansa flight back to Germany. Rather than staying in Manali, which is invaded by Indian tourists, I prefer Vashisht, a much smaller and quieter village. Here, Indian hemp is widely cultivated to produce marijuana and hashish. Surprise, surprise, it's also the preferred joint for hippies or the "flower power," as they're known to the locals. Yesterday, when we rode in on our bikes, decked out in our plastic bag, wet-weather gear, we looked like two extraterrestrials infiltrating a band of wandering wonderers. Each to their own trip, right? The hippies are high in the clouds, while we're lost in the mountains.

Tonight, I air out my gear and do some repair work on my wheels. Tomorrow, I leave for Shimla.

DAY 344
Manali, India—June 23, 1995

Having just spent thirty-eight days up in the mountain air, I'm now back at a lower height—and a higher temperature. Not for long, though: I have another thirty-six mile climb toward Shimla before finally biking back down to Delhi. After three consecutive, rainy days, the sun is out. If my calculations are right, I should enter Delhi at the same time as the monsoon begins. And then I'll have known all of India's seasons.

Day of hurt
Bilaspur, India—June 24, 1995

Earlier in the day, while I was going down a hill and getting ready to cross a bridge, a pedestrian popped up out of nowhere. He steps in front of my left saddlebag, and I go flying over the handlebars. Skidding along the asphalt on my left side, I end up with a grazed knee and shoulder, plus a skinned hip and elbow. My head struck the ground, too, but my helmet protected me well. I go berserk. I look straight into the eyes of this contrite halfwit and bawl at him in the plainest English I can muster: "When cross street, you look. If me truck, you dead!"

I get back on my bike, but I don't feel so good. I take a spell in a nice, quiet spot. Using my first-aid kit, I clean up my injuries the best I can. Later, at the hospital, my scrapes and gashes are disinfected once again, and as an extra precaution, I get a prescription for antibiotics, too. Here in India, we pop 'em like candies, but, hey, I'm not complaining. Maybe they'll even help cure the open wound I've been sporting on my toe for the last fifty-three days . . . and counting.

I get out of this dodgy town fast. I'm so shaken up that I'm startled by any little thing. My head is somewhere else. Although I'm short on energy, my heart is pumping full of rage. I wish I had set that reckless fool straight with a proper tongue-lashing, or worse. I was way too kind. But I'm as peaceful as any hippie. My only consolation is reminding myself that it could have been a lot more serious.

Goodbye freezer. Hello furnace. I'm not used to cycling in such heat, and I have to make sure I drink plenty of water. At this road stop, I drink ten pints of lemony water while catching up with my journal writing, and I didn't even need to take a leak.

My Unlucky Day, Number Two
Shimla, India—June 25, 1995

After a painfully still night, my fresh scabs want to crack into a million pieces.

Last evening, as I was pitching my tent, five young brats came snooping around. I didn't worry about it. I should have, because they pinched my bike pump. It took me two hours to find them. They swore they didn't take anything. To let them know I meant business, I grabbed the biggest by the scruff of the neck, glued him against the wall and started squeezing his throat until he stopped squirming—the Ghandi-like pacifist at his best. I know I'll never get my pump back, but at least I'll leave a lasting impression.

Negative thoughts spawn negative events. Six miles later, I puncture a tire. No pump, so I have to walk a mile or so before being able to inflate it. It's already noon, and I'm quite worried about this relentless sun.

I cap off the day with a steady climb of 4,750 feet. It's a big detour, but I don't regret this side trip. Located at an altitude of 7,400 feet, Shimla is an awesome city. Everything is green, with the farming terraces carved into the mountainside, looking like the staircase to the Jolly Green Giant's house. I spend the rest of the day watching the townsfolk stroll by in the "pedestrians only" area of the old part of Shimla. It's a great feeling to wander about without being honked at, or worse, getting knocked into next week by unruly traffic. I still have a four-day bike ride and 245 miles of road before reaching Delhi. Once there, I'll take the opportunity to put in a phone call home. It's been impossible to give my family any sign of life for these past forty-five days.

DAY 348
Saharan, India—June 27, 1995

Murphy's Law strikes again: I've had two flats in the last two days since my pump went missing. This time, I had to walk five miles before finding the right pump.

I'll soon be leaving these mountains . . . a long and beautiful stage drawing to a close.

DAY 349

Badshahi Bagh, India—June 28, 1995

I slept behind an abandoned house, shielded from the wind. It's 5 AM, and I'm already back in the saddle, tearing down the hill toward the plain. For a fabulous, final farewell, the sun rises over the Himalayas to say goodbye. It's dressed to the nines. A bright and lively red, only the morning's early risers get to see this sun at its most beautiful. As I zigzag down my last mountainside, I see the vast, open plain on my right, stretching out in front of me as far as the eye can see.

Much to my surprise, I happen to be on a road that crosses a national park teeming with antelopes and birds of every kind, living in this tranquil wilderness. No doubt about it—I've definitely reached the plain—there are flies everywhere. Just breathing makes me sweat. Worse, I have to deal with at least three million cursed flies that cheerfully nibble away at both my patience and my grazed knee, which they think is an all-dressed slice of pizza.

DAY 350

Saharanpur, India—June 29, 1995

There's no hotel in this neck of the woods and no way was I going to sleep in my tent in this unbearable heat. So lucky for me, I met two brothers, both doctors, who invited me to sleep at their place. Or, in other words, in a driveway ten yards from the main drag and within earshot of an overnight police outpost monitoring the road. I spent the entire night listening to the radio, not the one by the rocking chair, but rather the one that's used for police-dispatch calls. Similar to a taxi radio . . . only louder. And let's not forget the voracious, insomniac flies and the sweltering heat. Before becoming completely unhinged, I should pack up and leave. Make my getaway, but where to? It's too dark, and I'm dead tired. At four o'clock, I get up, as sticky as if I'd been dipped in a honeypot. The sun finally knocks at the door, and the horizon opens up. Pedaling along on my bike, at least I get some relief thanks to the moving air.

After a thirty-mile spurt, I stop at a small hotel. There's nothing else around within reasonable distance. I can't bear to spend a second sleepless night under my tent.

DAY 351
Panipat, India—June 30, 1995

No matter where I stop, I always attract a flock of curious people eager to see me up close. For greeting purposes, social hierarchy and pecking order is key. The most distinguished person, as established by the group, leads this sea of humanity to meet me. This is also the only person I need to address, a bit like paying full attention to the lion king who emerges from the pack to sniff at the newcomer. Of course, they want to know all my reasons for existing at this time, in this place. The head honcho wants to know everything: my name, my nationality, the full story of my adventure so far, where I've been, and where I'm going. He translates my words into the local dialect, which reverberate through to the back of the crowd by "bush telegraph." He's also the person responsible for taking care of my bicycle. He makes sure that nobody gets near it, much to the disappointment of the youngsters who have been ogling those great big, red saddlebags. Better yet, he organizes a place somewhere private so I can eat in peace. If this didn't happen, I would be sure to be dining with someone on my lap. Every crowd I encounter always wants to close in on me and swallow me up.

Today, the company is so pleasant that not even the flies manage to spoil my meal. Regrettably, I can't stop for very long, because without my bike-riding breeze, the heat is downright unbearable.

So far, we're into a two-day heat wave. It's 130°F . . . in the shade! My T-shirt is covered in white patches of perspiration salt. I should drink up to five gallons of water a day to avoid dehydration, but I can't do it. I'm neither thirsty nor hungry. Tomorrow, I'll give myself a day off to recoup. I'm less than sixty-five miles from Delhi, so there's no point in overdoing it. I'll have another two whole days to get ready for my departure to Thailand. Tonight, I pamper myself with a rare luxury: a $16 hotel room.

DAY 352
Panipat, India—July 1, 1995

This time, I've topped every record. I wake up at midnight with nausea. A short time later, unable to sleep, I throw up. Hopefully a good thing because having expelled the culprit, I'll feel better. But later in the night, the cramps, vomiting, and diarrhea get worse, twice as bad as before. My trips from bed to toilet, although only a few steps away, are quite the achievement. It feels like I'm attempting to wretch up my heart as well. I'm writhing in pain. I want to go to the reception desk, but I can't even walk. I'm about to faint. In one last desperate effort, I crawl out to the reception office and collapse on the floor. I knock weakly on the reception door until someone opens it. I make a sign to the clerk that I want to drink some water. He returns—in leisurely India time—with a quart of water, which I guzzle down in one long gulp. He explains that I should force myself to throw up to clean out my stomach. He promises to bring me some more water, with lemon and salt. I hesitate, but I follow his advice, in spite of all the pain inflicted by this gut-wrenching process. Then he helps me get back to bed.

The lemon water fails to materialize. I beg him to bring me two quarts of mineral water and two Cokes. Twenty minutes go by before he returns with the latter only—sorry, fresh out of mineral water. The town center is just a ten-minute walk away. I plead with him to find somebody who could go fetch some for me. I'm ready to give a healthy tip. He replies that he can go there himself, but only at 4 PM when his shift ends. I tell him, "Too late, I'll be dead by then . . . fallen off the twig, for sure."

I never did get the lemon water. I ask to see the manager, hoping that he'll better understand my distress. He arrives two hours later, and I immediately see that he's just as heartless as the other guy. In such a precarious situation, I realize I have to get to the hospital as quickly as possible—under my own steam. But before leaving, this moronic manager obliges me to check in again, because I originally reserved for one night only. I explain to him, as I would to a two-year-old child, to just cross out the "1" and mark in a "2." Then he asks me to pay for the room in advance. Obviously, he thinks I'm about to die (the ultimate "check-out") before I settle my bill. How very touching.

At the hospital, I'm rushed onto a stretcher and hooked up to an IV of saline solution. I spend all day on the hospital bed. They tell me to come back tomorrow to receive two more quarts of this magic potion. It will replace the significant quantity of mineral salts that I lost through perspiration. Everyone needs a good amount of mineral salts to keep healthy, as these mineral salts conduct electricity through the body. If left untreated for a few days, a major imbalance of electrolytes can cause cardiac arrhythmia and, eventually, death. I was riding along the precipice, that's for sure. If I had a biking partner, this would never have happened.

The doctor strongly recommends that I take the bus to Delhi.

The only thing on my mind right now is Thailand and my sweet love waiting for me there.

* * *

Chapter 18

....

Thailand and My Sweetheart: Second Wind

DAY 356
Bangkok Airport, Thailand—July 5, 1995

Caroline got her man back, still tall and lean, but now twenty-five pounds lighter. We've been apart for a whole year. I hug her without saying a word. Our gestures are hesitant and shy. Even so, a Thai couple would never dare to display such emotion and affection in public.

I can't wait to savor our beautiful adventure together, but at the same time, there's an emotional barrier between us. I have lived in the moment for nearly a year now, and my outlook on life has changed. India has completely transformed me, whereas I find Caroline exactly as I left her. Both of us have lived different experiences, and we'll need to spend some time to get to know our "new" partners.

From pillow to lamp post, we catch up on a thousand and one topics. She's already been here for two weeks, and I'm curious to know about her first impressions of Asia. How did she like Europe? What's the latest news on friends and family? Has Jean-Pierre fully recovered from his trip since we parted ways in Tehran? How did his final university internship go? I want to know anything and everything. The sound of her voice soothes and comforts me. When she takes a breather, I repeat the same questions, hoping she'll add a new tidbit. Even the most banal details pique my interest. And the gossip! When I let her get a word in, she shyly asks some questions about my own trip, as if she's afraid to hear the answers.

I only tell her about the good times, worried that all my pain and anguish will come flooding back. But I'm much more chatty about how free I've felt since I left Iran. "I have the world at my feet," I tell her, "and I feel as light as the air, with no stress and no social pressure." Suddenly, Caro seems distant and sad. She confesses she's not following me anymore. She can't relate to this sense of freedom that has brought me such intense joy. "Don't worry," she says, "I've been dropping out now for six months already. Accept whatever Asian culture throws at you, and give yourself the time to enjoy it." She confesses that she stopped reading my journal ever since I described the cremation ritual in Varanasi. She was even apprehensive about our seeing each other again.

On the train to Bangkok, she tells me about her stay in England, a decision that she has never regretted. Before leaving Canada, she had stopped being Caroline and had become "Pierre-Yves' girlfriend," left behind while he was on his jaunt around the world. The first six months, sans Pierre-Yves, were atrocious. She was quite miserable and bored to death, constantly being asked what her adventurer boyfriend was up to.

England freed her. There, she no longer felt as though she was just waiting around for me. More like herself, she began to live her own life again. She dived into an unknown world where nobody knew who she was. And she was the happier for it. She no longer wanted to live in a situation where she felt robbed of her own identity.

These five days in Kanchanaburi give us an insight into the horrors wrought by war. On the brighter side, we visit beautiful national parks and take advantage of the sumptuous charm of our floating hotel. This alone would have made the trip worthwhile. Built on empty oil drums, the floating building has a fixed mooring on the edge of the River Kwai. The gentle lapping of the water is like a lullaby. At dusk, the last sun rays flicker off the water, coloring the aged-wood facade of the hotel a lively red. I'm with Caro, and all is well with the world.

DAY 383
Surat Thani, Thailand—August 1, 1995

We've ridden more than 300 miles so far. Caroline has no problem adapting. She's a good traveler, just like her brother Jean-Pierre. Tough and tenacious, she's ready to get her feet wet, no matter what. We camp out on deserted beaches or on uninhabited terrain away from the road. Sometimes, we stay with the local farmers.

Off the tourist track, English is virtually useless. That means we have to redouble our efforts and patience to make ourselves understood. It's easy enough when asking for a drink, but another matter entirely when we're looking for, say, eggs. That usually involves five minutes of role-playing a hen laying her eggs in front of fifteen or so Thai, who look askance at us, as if we're completely bonkers. At night, it's always a question of which one of us will inquire about the possibility of a shower. Vigorously scrubbing under the arms or scratching at our hair like a monkey with fleas . . . all meant to convey we need a wash. More often than not, our gestures for showering and washing plus the word "water" are off the mark, because our Thai friend ends up dutifully bringing us a glass of water!

This time, we finally find a washing area around the back of the house, amid the chickens, pigs, and garbage: a small, muddy corner with an immense terra-cotta jar (the "shower") from which water is scooped using a cup. The men keep their shorts on, whereas the women stay wrapped in a sarong: a large, lovely piece of batik cloth, dyed by local artisans. All this takes place with amused glances from the matriarch who prepares supper under a thatched hut.

Once shiny clean and freshened up (and finally free of grunge, road dust, and sweat), all we have to do now is ask for permission to set up our tent somewhere. We make a triangle with our hands over our heads and mime someone sleeping on a pillow. If that doesn't do the trick, we add copious snores. The answer is automatic: nodding "Yes! Yes!" at us with a smile. With our camp set up, we then prepare a meal of vegetables, rice, or fish. All fresh, straight from the small, local market.

At night, sleeping in the stifling heat, we fall into a deep sleep. Once, I shared this tent with Jean-Pierre on a certain rainy evening in a tobacco field in Italy. Now, I share the same tent, not once but every evening, with his sister. Sorry, Jean-Pierre . . . you don't even come close.

DAY 393
August 11, 1995

How can you talk about this country without mentioning the Golden Triangle? Located on the borders of Thailand, Myanmar, and Laos, this place is said to be the world's largest opium-trafficking zone.

Opium, a sap extracted from poppy pods, has been used as a narcotic since the time of the ancient Greeks, but it's during the reign of the Mongolian emperor, Kublai Khan, in the thirteenth century, that Arab traders turned the Chinese onto the drug. The opium poppy plant grows easily in mountainous regions with nutrient-poor soil. Southern China proved ideal for this type of cultivation, so much so that poppy farmers not only paid off their debts to the local government, but they also grew rich. The Asian market had become so prolific that rebels from the Burmese Communist Party and Chinese Army nationalist refugees wanted their slice of the pie. But not until the late 60s, as the war raged in nearby Vietnam, did opium see its biggest economic boom.

As the story goes, US planes stopped by to pick up opium loads before heading back to Vietnam, where the drug was blatantly exported under the very nose of the authorities to every corner of the globe. Because of this, the CIA could supposedly finance some of its operations in Indochina. Later, the government's laissez-faire attitude contributed to the drug-fuelled prosperity of the area. The main players were businessmen with links to the Burmese and/or Chinese Army, whose soldiers took care of transport. As this vicious cycle gained momentum, even small-time nomadic farmers became full-time suppliers to the drug trade.

After several raids, Thailand managed to expel Khun Sa, the Golden Triangle's most powerful warlord, from its territory. Then, financially backed by the Americans, it ordered the massive destruction of opium fields and established crop-replacement programs: tea and coffee plantations, corn, and Chinese herbs. While Thailand has changed horses midstream, Myanmar and Laos remain the top two opium producers in the world.

In Thailand, the big players took off with the big money. The former nomads, now sedentary, find themselves saddled with herb gardens that pay much less than before and not enough to live on. A responsible government would have provided an alternative solution that took into account economic, social, and cultural factors. Thailand failed to do so. Burma, which is also trying to abolish this massive trafficking, is no doubt hoping to learn from its neighbor's mistakes.

DAY 395
Pattani, Thailand—August 13, 1995

We're never going to bike on a Sunday again—it's simply too dangerous. Besides the usual traffic, we share the road with a gaggle of young, reckless (but not wreckless) motorcyclists whose inexperience is all too plain to see. Barefoot or wearing flip-flops, no helmet, three on the same bike, they use the main road for their crazy, clueless racing. These rubbernecking young punks swivel as they zip past, just out of curiosity or to make idiotic gestures. And so today, in front of our very eyes, two kids on the same motorcycle land in the ditch. Naturally, the driver at fault gets out of it without a scratch, whereas his friend bangs his head up against a rock. He's bleeding and semi-conscious. He vaguely answers the questions of his obviously worried friend. Since we couldn't do much for them, we left, but only after the driver had promised us that he would take his injured buddy to the hospital.

We get back on the road, doing our best to forget about the accident, when, suddenly, two other motorcycles smash into each other. More scared than hurt, four more punks emerge with a few little scratches and a mighty big fright.

OK, before it's our turn, let's just stop!

It begins to rain. Comfortably settled in our tent, well away from the road, we suddenly hear a long, drawn-out screeching of tires, followed by a sickening crash of metal. We're among the first to arrive at the scene of the accident, but seeing the extent of the damage and knowing how Caroline feels about death, I tell her to stay back. The scene is terrible. A truck loaded with a cargo of fish on ice is upturned, and now its contents are completely sprawled across the road. It looks as though the driver had swerved the truck right before hitting an oncoming car. Several people are lying on the ground. An injured woman holds a baby in her arms. All seem alive, except for the driver of the truck. Stretched out on the ground, her feet still stuck in the door, she is not breathing anymore. Her face is covered in blood.

I later learn that the injured woman I saw was riding a moped with her baby in her arms when she was sideswiped by the truck, which spun out of control after the impact. A visibly upset man tells us, "When it's raining, the road is as slick as glass, but people still won't slow down."

DAY 398
Ton Sai, Thailand—August 16, 1995

We're now hearing the Mosques call to prayer again, here in the province of Narathiwat, a buffer zone between the Theravada Buddhism of Thailand and the Islam of Malaysia. Even if we are gradually approaching a more Muslim area, we will only find a truly radical cultural change when we reach Malaysia, seventy miles away.

The monsoon seems to have spared us but not the heat. At night, we try to stay out of the rain as much as possible without suffocating under our waterproof and airtight double cover. We're able to sleep a little more comfortably once the cool night air comes in. Last night, we slept right under the stars. It had to rain, of course, so I installed our double roof. Finding it impossible to sleep, we could hear some kids rustling around our tent, surely looking to steal some of our equipment. I trailed them into the woods for a good half hour without ever catching them. They didn't take anything, but, as we went back and forth from the tent, it quickly turned into a mosquito den. They feasted on us the rest of the night. When we woke up this morning, Caro counted at least thirty buzzing around like kamikazes, engorged with our blood. Maybe this will qualify us as experienced donors for the next Red Cross blood drive.

Unlike India, where there are plenty of little, cheap lodging houses for local and foreign travelers, Thailand has very few accommodations outside of the big city centers. And so, we're obliged to camp out almost every night. Tonight, we're getting a bit of luxury. We've set up camp at one of our coveted gas stations. Here, we can enjoy some shelter against the rain, some peace and security, and as much drinking water as we want. Tonight's menu: freshly caught fish and rice. That's two-and-a-quarter pounds of mouth-watering fish for the ridiculous sum of 60¢. My adored lady friend (or, as I call her, "La petite Doré du Lac-Saint-Jean") cuts off the fish heads, while I, the great chef, fry them up. Like my mother would say, "Ça se mange sans faim!" (Which roughly translates to, "You eat without being hungry!")

The sky is about to burst as the chickens scurry around our feet. They should count themselves lucky that we've already planned out our menu for tonight.

* * *

Chapter 19

....

My Love for Adventure Takes a Hit

DAY 406

Kota Bharu, Malaysia—August 24, 1995

Selamat datang ke Malaysia! Welcome to Malaysia! We fell in love with this country the moment we arrived. Here, Malay, Chinese, Indian, Thai, and Indonesian cuisines live side-by-side, with choices to please every palate. Indeed, the Kota Bharu night market, as big as a football field, has one of the most diverse arrays of food offerings in all of Asia. Squeezed tight together, stalls and temporary stands spring up as soon as the sun goes down. Exquisitely delicious dishes are whipped up right on the spot for just a few dollars apiece. Laid out on tables propped up on the back of tricycles, you'll find blue rice, quail eggs, grilled stingray, chicken on bamboo skewers marinated in a peanut sauce, coconut rice, fried fish in tamarind curry, lentil soup, hot dumplings filled with meat or vegetables, and egg noodles sautéed with pork, tofu, and ground meat.

We've been here for five days now, and our main focus is waiting for the nightly food market to open. A food lover's paradise: no wonder "Malaysian" rhymes with "epicurian."

DAY 413
Cherating, Malaysia—August 31, 1995

Despite the lighter traffic, better roads, and more courteous drivers, fate soon flexes its muscles once again. After leaving Rantau Abang, a beach where the giant leatherback turtles come to lay their eggs at night, we are now heading for Cherating. We're riding along peacefully without a car in sight. Today marks the fiftieth anniversary of the country's independence. It's hot and humid as usual (after all, we are on the equator). We're really looking forward to a day off tomorrow.

A car approaches us, and, as is my habit, I check my rearview mirror to make sure that we're not blocking the road. A moped is behind us; it seems to me to be quite far away. However, I start to worry, because as it approaches, it appears as though the moped rider hasn't seen us yet. I keep an eye on him, but he quickly moves into my blind spot. Tightly gripping my handlebars, I expect to see him go flashing past. Without warning (and certainly with no time to alert Caroline), I'm thrown off my bike, smashing into Caro before finally finding myself scraping along the gravel on the road shoulder. The moped hit us from behind. Fortunately, there was no car coming the other way. Caro doesn't realize what's going on. She didn't see or hear it coming— everything happened so fast. Now she lays spread-eagled in the middle of the road. I shout out at the top of my lungs for her to get off the road.

When I took my spill, I managed to crush my precious "family jewels" on the stem of my handlebars. I have road burn along my entire right-hand side, and I'm bleeding profusely from the hip to the elbow. I have a stone embedded in my ankle. Caro has some scrapes on her knee and elbow but swears she's OK. The motorcyclist has a bit of blood on one arm but nothing more. Our bikes are in no condition to ride. A car stops immediately to offer some help.

DAY 416
Cherating, Malaysia—September 3, 1995

Thinking I could take care of myself, I applied some talcum powder to my injuries. It should help dry up the wounds and form nice, crusty scabs. This doctoring served me well in India, but this time round, an infection develops under the hardened crust. After three days, pus seeps out everywhere. I've got no other choice but to go to the hospital in Kuantan, which is an hour and a half away by bus.

At the hospital, I pay the $1 medical fee, and a doctor immediately takes me into his charge. Laying stark naked on a table, I get ready to undergo a torture I hope I never have to endure again. Two male nurses hold me down on each side while the doctor, armed with a metal-wire brush, scrubs away mercilessly at my wounds. Bits of talc melded with fresh skin fly off in chunky scraps. The pain is so intense that the tears flow, despite my every effort to stay stoic. Every part gets the scourge treatment: my shoulder, my elbow, my hip, my knee, and, finally, my ankle. The brush leaves behind just raw patches of mutilated flesh. But nothing stops the hand wielding the brush, not while a single hair remains. As the doc explains, "It's the only way to prevent the infection from returning, so that the skin doesn't heal over the impurities."

An hour and a half later, I'm up and about again. The doctor carefully dressed my wounds and handed me a prescription, saying, "If you feel any pain, take a couple!" Well, gee thanks, doc, but I could've really used these before you started your scrub routine. . . .

DAY 417
Cherating, Malaysia—September 4, 1995

Caro has just told me that we've been robbed during the night. One of our four saddlebags was cleaned out of its more precious and expensive items: a Chlorophylle vest, a pair of GORE-TEX® socks, my spare glasses, my razor, a dictionary, and our ground mat.

Here's what happened: during our recent crash, a jar of jam had broken and spread inside one of the bags. Despite cleaning it, some sugary residue remained, and a colony of huge ants was attracted to our hut and feasted on their good fortune. So we wouldn't get completely gobbled up, we decided to put the bag outside. We're in a pretty idyllic spot, so the thought of theft didn't even cross our minds. During the daytime, we left our bikes and bags unattended . . . a thieves' paradise indeed!

DAY 420
Seremban, Malaysia—September 7, 1995

What is my life worth to me? Much too valuable to play Russian roulette with, that's for sure. Should I go on? I'm reluctant to admit that my objectives may have shifted. Am I really ready to weather all these perils simply to realize my dream? Perhaps, but not at the cost of my life.

After a final night in the guesthouse, it's time to get back on our bikes and start pedaling again. We ride through thirty-five torturous miles, always imagining the worst. Totally stuffed and with our morale at a low point, we accept a lift with a truck driver who offers to take us across the entire peninsula, from east to west, to Kuala Lumpur, the capital. From there, we bike forty-five miles to Seremban to pay a visit to Pui-Leng, a girl I briefly met on a boat in Greece. Although we only talked for a few minutes, she left me her address on the off chance that I would wind up in Malaysia. She's surprised to find me on her doorstep, but she greets us as if we were all long-lost friends.

She, along with her family and her extended family, welcome us warmly into their home for a few days. The Malaysian Chinese are like that. We'll use this precious time to refocus and figure out which course our journey should take next.

DAY 422
Seremban, Malaysia—September 9, 1995

You've got to lose some to win some, but if you lose it all, you'll have nothing left to lose. Having endured countless blows to get this far in the fight, I don't intend to throw in the towel now—I'm ready to battle on. But I do have to make some adjustments. Instead of going through Borneo, Sulawesi, Java, and Sumatra by bike (a pipe dream, anyway), we'll travel by bus and boat. After that, we'll get back on our bikes to continue our route to Singapore as planned before taking the boat again, this time for the island of Bali, in Indonesia.

The accident in Cherating not only took a pound of my flesh, but also weakened my desire to succeed at all costs. It sapped a ton of my energy and ushered in a new round of discouragement and fatigue. Although I've been so vigilant, this was my second accident. Will the third be my last?

We'll soon take a car to the Cameron Highlands, a mountain range in the middle of the country, where temperatures are much cooler. The fresh air should clear our heads for the trip ahead.

DAY 427
Tanah Rata, Malaysia—September 14, 1995

Quite the wander through the jungle! This morning we climbed to the top of 6,000-foot-high Gunung Beremban. The way up is a bit sketchy, but the sunlight filtering through the foliage reassures us. The air is thinner. The ominous buzz of insects and assorted jungle noises are a constant reminder to keep our ears and eyes open. Since we've been walking through this rain-forest, we haven't seen a single person. Caro is starting to slow down, and the closer we get to the summit, the more trouble she's having breathing. She's having a kind of panic attack, probably due to the isolation, the altitude, and these confined spaces.

Since I don't want to backtrack down this muddy path, I do my best to reassure and calm her. I'm worried, because her breathing is more labored as time goes by. She's now wheezing like an asthmatic. I sit down by her side and gently massage her neck and back, trying to distract her, reassuring her that she's not all alone in the jungle. After a couple of minutes, the crisis passes.

We stay on track without any more hiccups—that is, until we reach the top. To go down, we opt for the path that will supposedly lead us straight out of the jungle and right past a Chinese Buddhist temple, as indicated on our map. It took us two hours to get to the summit, but I'm sure the way down will be a lot faster.

There's still no sign of life. The trail goes up and down like a roller coaster. Caroline is exhausted. To complicate things, we arrive at a three-way fork with no signs. And since none of the three paths is shown on my map, we take the way that seems the most traveled. It gets worse the further we go. We've been walking for more than six hours and have yet to see a single living soul. The more the minutes and hours slip by, the less sense I have that we're actually going anywhere. Fear creeps in. Caro keeps telling me that we're lost in the jungle. We can always retrace our steps, but we're running out of time with dusk already underway. The path continues to roll up and down, so much so that I wonder if we're simply on the wrong track. We move heaven and earth to jump across streams without getting wet. Caro is in tears when she sees the climb ahead of us. I try to keep my cool to comfort her, but I'm very worried myself. I find it hard to believe that this path will lead to anywhere. The idea of spending a night in the jungle without food and water, but with plenty of venomous snakes, is wearing me thin. But I'm careful not to share my thoughts. I keep on encouraging her, and I stride ahead hoping to tell her soon that I've spotted a road.

Another half hour passes before I give that much anticipated cry of elation: "We're saved! A farm. The road must be nearby." Caro is way too crushed to welcome the good news with any semblance of enthusiasm. This distant vision of a little slice of civilization is not enough . . . she'll shout, "We're saved!" when she's finally back in the guesthouse.

Finally out of the jungle, I wryly mention to her that I hear her mother castigating me: "Good Lord! What are you doing to my daughter, you loopy, lanky beanpole!"

Tropical rain begins to fall just as we make our way out of this claustrophobic labyrinth. Caro laps up the rainwater running down her nose and keeps telling me that from now on nothing will ever faze her again. Nothing.

When you travel, you learn to test your limits. You can do this by adding a link to the chain, but watch out—you might break the chain entirely. Sometimes, it's like playing with fire.

DAY 437
Kuching, Borneo—September 24, 1995

After a ninety-minute flight from Kuala Lumpur, we land in Borneo, the world's third-largest island. Our first stop is Kuching, a city on the Sarawak River and the capital of its namesake state. Kuching is home to a multitude of different tribes. It's in rapid development to accommodate the influx of tourists. Attractions on this large island will soon make it an outstanding destination. National parks, caves, jungle trekking, an orangutan sanctuary, pristine beaches, scuba diving, riverboat tours to the interior, "longhouse" visits . . . Borneo has something for everyone.

DAY 438
Bako, Borneo—September 25, 1995

We leave Kuching early this morning to check out the Bako National Park. It's quite humid and hot. A forty-five–minute bus ride brings us to the quay where we catch the boat: a long, wooden vessel with an engine in the equally long, narrow neck. Totally disoriented, we feel like we're in a James Bond movie. We go back upstream on the Sarawak River at a brisk pace to end up in Bako Park, right on the doorstep of the South China Sea. To my right, there is wide-open ocean as far as the eye can see. To my left lays the river's delta. In front of me, a mountain capped with a ring of clouds. The sunset lights up the sky in such a glitter of fiery red that we could swear we're witnessing a volcanic eruption.

Upon our arrival, the first sight we see is a wild boar sporting a grandfatherly beard. The whole family trails behind the Papa Boar. Everywhere the eye can see, there are different types of monkeys: proboscis monkeys, recognizable by their big, bulbous noses, long-tailed silver monkeys, and finally, cheeky little macaques, who look like stocky little boxers. We're besieged wherever we go. There are also a myriad of snakes slithering along the riverbanks. Meanwhile, a big monitor lizard comes over to sniff out the newcomers.

Maybe Bako Park should be called Monkeys Gone Wild. It's their own amusement park, as they swing from one tree to another using the liana vines, zipping to the top of the tree canopy and back down again. However, they have the most fun fleecing food supplies from the visitors. Their tactic is simple: they eye the prize, approach it, and jump on the table as fast as lightning. This works every time. The best way to avoid becoming their victim is to keep everything you've got sealed up in a bag. But most importantly, never underestimate them! It can get ugly. Walking along these monkey-filled trails, plastic bag in hand, is like stepping into a lion's den with a sirloin steak in your pocket! They've done the math: plastic bag + human = food. They sometimes gather as four or five bushwhackers to block your passage, look you straight in the eye, and then attack. They have a jawful of razor sharp teeth, and their way of hunting and gathering is very intimidating.

In spite of all our precautions, we still get ambushed. They form up across the path, while a big male prevents us from turning back. Realizing too late that they have already smelled the opened can of condensed milk, we sacrifice it, hoping to save the rest of our food. We jam the can under a big, wooden log, thinking there's no way they can get to it. As soon as we put it down, all the monkeys scamper toward the log, freeing up our path. In a flash, they dislodge the can, and World War III breaks out. Gripping the can firmly in his hands, the alpha male climbs to the top of the closest tree. The other monkeys jump around in a frenzied dance. The smaller, less quick give up on the chase, licking the sweet nectar that has fallen on the ground. Meanwhile, the biggest monkeys are the biggest losers, left with a completely empty (and inedible) metal can. The moral of the tale? Better small and cagey than big and stupid!

DAY 440
Bako, Borneo—September 27, 1995

Today, we're taking a stroll along the seaside at the foot of a massive cliff. At low tide, the beach exposes its coral shoals, teeming with millions of crabs. After four hours spent dreamily admiring this natural splendor, we realize that the tide is rising fast. The only way back to shore is by swimming. We keep going until we discover an enchanted bay and a path that goes back to our campsite. We're very lucky, because as soon as we get back, we're hit by a cascade of rain so dense that it instantly eclipses the mountain right in front of us.

Tomorrow, we'll return to Kuching and then go up the Kapit River to visit the "longhouses."

DAY 442
En route toward Kapit, Borneo—September 29, 1995

To save money, we decide to leave by cargo boat rather than by bus. We book with a shipping company whose boat, the "Raja-Mas," will depart at the end of the day, as soon as it has been loaded. We kill two birds with one stone, because besides paying half the cost of transport, a night trip means we don't have to pay for a hotel room.

Worried about "missing the boat," we head to the docks a few hours in advance. A number of freighters are moored there. I say "freighters" only because they float; otherwise, I would call them recycled junkers straight from the scrap yard. Which one is ours? Checking out the loading docks, we spot our home for the next fourteen hours. It's a hideous old tub with a rusty Raja-Mas nameplate affixed to its hull, confirming that this is indeed our river ride. Not being the type to shy away from discomfort and hoping that this rust bucket has a few more hours of floatability left in it, we decide to embark.

Like two clueless tourists, we cast a worried eye over the goods the workers are loading: chicks and hens in cages, countless crates of eggs and bananas, and even massive, concrete pipes. A far-too-young crane operator hoists the goods willy-nilly, as though he was working a video game joystick rather than controlling dangerous hydraulic machinery.

A siren heralds our departure, right on time. Some crew members, exhausted by the loading, take a rest in the bow. While we glide peacefully down the Sarawak River, a tropical thunderstorm is brewing. Just below the horizon, the sun settles down in a cradle of dying light. This grand spectacle makes us forget the grotty filth that surrounds us.

By some small miracle, the crew's noisy TV set goes on the blink. We'll have a calm and restful night after all. Fresh air breezes through our porthole.

We let ourselves be carried away by the rolling waves. Our primal mother, the sea, rocks and cradles us like her little children. Obviously, we don't need to be on the "Love Boat" to be as happy as clams. . . .

DAY 449
Kapit, Borneo—October 6, 1995

A tour of Sarawak is not complete without visiting a tribe living in a "longhouse." From Sibu, where we arrived safe and sound, another boat takes us seventy-five miles upstream on the Kapit River to a tiny village, far from civilization. Since there are no roads in this rugged, mountainous area, you can only travel it by boat. Here, we really do brush up against the end of the world.

There are more than 200 tribes in the north of Borneo alone. Among the most well-known are the Ibans, who, until the late 1950s, still proudly decorated their houses with the decapitated heads of their victims as symbols of their might.

Luck is on our side. Poking about in a nice, quiet spot of the village, a young tribeswoman, Norhayati, approaches us, arms loaded with fresh vegetables. She makes us understand that she wants to invite us to dinner and even stay the night. Without further ado, she brings us to her small boat. Together, we go up the dark, muddy Rejang River (a tributary of the Kapit) for a few miles, in mountainous terrain covered in first-growth forests.

When we arrive at the longhouse, she introduces us to her husband, Frino, her two girls, Kharrumie and Shahira, as well as her sister-in-law, Rohana, who speaks a few words of English. We learn that the young mother is a member of the Orang Ulu tribe and that she was born elsewhere, quite far upstream. As is the case for most tribespeople, her beliefs are animistic, a faith that confers a soul on natural phenomena and makes them act favorably by the intermediary of magic practices. However, her marriage to a Muslim Proto-Malay meant she, too, had to adopt the Islamic religion.

They live in a longhouse—community accommodation consisting of numerous small dwellings sharing adjoining walls and a single roof.

Constructed on stilts, just above the flood zone, some can reach 1,000 feet in length and shelter up to sixty families.

The room we enter serves both as a family room and as the kids' bedroom. And just for tonight, it will be our guestroom. In the center is the main room and, behind it, the kitchen, which also doubles as the dining room. Makeshift doors and windows are cut right into the walls. There is no furniture. Not only do we sleep but we also eat directly on the ground (our own derrieres make great chairs). For the bathroom, that's a simple hole in the floor covered by a sheet of metal. Close by, a large metal tub collects rainwater from the roof, which is used for drinking, doing the dishes, and washing. For a shower, not only do we have to wear shorts or sarong, but also be careful not to step into the drain hole or lose our soap down it.

We can attest to their reputation as a hospitable people; just one hour into our visit, we're already part of the family. The children frolic around us. One by one, they want us to take them in our arms, and they giggle with delight when we badly pronounce the words they teach us. Who knew "Uncle" and "Auntie" could be so hilarious.

They make us taste all their local specialties, which are absolutely delicious, and offer us eats all day long, little treats they rarely enjoy themselves. They're forever apologizing for the supposed lack of comfort.

Rohana tells us how things have changed since she was a child. With the arrival of commerce and trade, the traditional lifestyle is slowly being eroded as people go for better-paid jobs. Frino, the father, gave up hunting, an integral part of his culture, to work for a logging company. But at the rate things are going, the first-growth forests will be cleared within ten years. Hundreds of families will then have no income and no future prospects. The big companies defend their position by saying that it's the local slash-and-burn farming methods, practiced by the tribes since time immemorial, that bear responsibility for the deforestation. This consists of sectioning off a part of the forest, then setting fire to it to sterilize, fertilize, and activate the soil, which is then planted with rice. Year after year, the process is repeated, each time choosing another patch of virgin ground. After about ten years, the new growth on the land they began with will be razed, and cultivation begins anew. Since the same ground is reused, its capacity to regenerate and provide a good harvest decreases. Then, having exhausted all the surrounding resources, tribes are forced to leave the area and move the longhouse somewhere else.

The big companies accuse the local tribes of turning rich, virgin forest (first-growth) into third, even fourth-growth forests by the way they cultivate. Each accuses the other one of being responsible for the degradation.

DAY 450

Niah, Borneo—October 7, 1995

This morning we're at a national park where the Niah caves are located. Among the biggest in the world, these caves contain bones and paintings that prove that man lived in them 40,000 years ago.

From our campsite, we take a trail that delves deep into the jungle, leading us to the Storekeeper's Cave, which owes its name to its resemblance to a typical Asian market stall. We enter the gaping mouth of the cave, which must be around 100 feet high and 165 feet wide. Walking deeper into the vault, the cave's rock walls gradually narrow until dividing into a series of subterranean passageways and canals. A string of stairs and small ladders leads us toward the depths of the Earth. In total darkness, the cave walls glisten under the faint beam of our flashlights. Subterranean waters slowly trickling down the walls give them a varnished look. The cool, dark caves are a drastic change from the jungle's stifling heat and humidity. Meanwhile, the only sound we hear is that of drops dripping metronomically from the ceiling. It's all so spooky! Now that we've grown accustomed to the dark, we veer off to explore even more unusual trails, which will eventually take us to a cave that contains some scattered bones. Sporadically, we catch a flicker of candlelight from the candle held by one of the guides. If you let your imagination run wild, you can easily picture a clan of cave dwellers roasting freshly killed game.

After this long walk through the dim remnants of prehistory, we resurface, completely dazzled by the sun's glaring brightness.

At twilight, as around four million swiftlets return to their nests in the main cave, the bats leave for their nocturnal hunt. Although the bats are far fewer in number, they zip through the oncoming mass of birds like little kamikaze pilots. I've never seen so many birds share such a small strip of the sky.

Swiftlets build their nests in cracks and crevices in the ceiling. These nests are very much sought after by the Japanese. A culinary delicacy, it's like caviar to them. This very lucrative market has existed for centuries. To boost the local economy, the government nationalized the "nest industry" so that only the local Penan tribes have the right to collect them. The nests are harvested each year around mid-October, which means it's too early for us to catch the action, although we've got a pretty good idea of how dangerous it is just by looking at the long bamboo sticks dangling from the ceiling of the caves. To harvest the nests, men must climb over 100 feet without any safety equipment and dislodge the nests using a long pole. Once they're loosened and knocked out, they slowly fall to the ground like snowflakes.

Throughout the year, guano (bird excrement) is also collected inside the caves to be used as fertilizer. The local peasants work tirelessly scraping it off the rocks or heaving large loads, buckling under the weight. To prevent poaching and protect local interests, a military presence is permanently posted at the cave entrance.

We cap off our day with an after-dark walk in the jungle. Since many of the insects and birds are nocturnal creatures, the jungle is particularly lively at this time, and the sounds of the wild abound. The diffuse light of the full moon transforms the dull green of the trees into a metallic grey, and everywhere along the path, the ground is peppered with small, fluorescent mushrooms lighting the way like Chinese lanterns. It's magic.

After visiting Borneo's longhouses, national parks, jungle paths, and cave interiors, we're up for a climb to the summit of the famous Mount Kinabalu, the highest mountain in Southeast Asia. Then we'll pay a visit to the orangutan sanctuary.

DAY 455
Mount Kinabalu, Borneo—October 12, 1995

Accompanied by a guide and two English travelers we met three days ago, we leave the monolith's base camp very early in the morning. It's five-and-a-quarter miles and a 7,200-foot climb to the summit, 13,454 feet high. Since it's impossible to climb up and then back down the mountain all in the same day, we're planning on spending the night at the Sayat Sayat hut, a one-mile trek from the peak.

We spend the first leg of the trip hiking through the dense and humid rainforest, host to a mind-boggling array of plants, including the rafflesgia, which produces the biggest flower in the world (up to three-and-a-quarter feet wide!) and the famed nepenthes, a carnivorous plant that traps any insect that dares to pollinate it. As we climb higher, the vegetation becomes more and more sparse, and the landscape begins to resemble tundra. At 11,800 feet, we've hit bare rock. Although the incline has been gradual up until now, our climb is increasingly more strenuous. Our last mile before camp is so abrupt that two sturdy ropes are fixed as a railing along the trail. It's impossible to climb up without pulling ourselves along the ropes. With our heavy packs and worn-out shoes, we have to be very careful. After eight hours of hiking, we make it to the hut where we'll camp for the night. Very early tomorrow morning, we'll have less than a thousand feet to go before reaching the summit.

It's already late, and if I want to wash myself, I should do it before it gets too nippy. There's no electricity and nary a shower in sight. No matter, just a few steps from the camp is a small pond, which will serve me well. To the amazement of my skeptical hiking buddies, I dive in wholeheartedly—sheer enjoyment to my heart's content. The rocks have retained the heat from the day's sun, so the water is quite warm as a result. It's all very relaxing. With the mist blanketing the valley just below me, I feel like I'm taking a bath up in the clouds.

The tranquility is suddenly disturbed by a violent crack of lightning. The sky roils in anger. The weather changes completely, and rain pours down as though the sky was filled with hundreds of fire hoses spraying down on us. The rain blots out everything in sight. We're cut off from the rest of the world. A waterfall starts to tumble down the mountainside and threatens to wash away our shelter. Without thinking of the danger, we whip out our cameras.

As the drenching deluge gradually subsides, the sky bursts through in a thousand colors. We can now see the mountain's craggy peak, framed by a beautiful rainbow. At sunset, we boil up a pot of noodles, which we quickly demolish before collapsing into our beds, truly exhausted.

It's still deep into the night when the alarm clock goes off. Already 3:30 AM—time to get moving. We have to get to the top as early as we can to catch the sunrise. Before we're even fully awake, we swap tales about the previous night. One guy says he heard some creature snacking on our food. Since he didn't want to risk squashing a rat, he stayed in his bed. Another felt something crawling over his covers before disappearing into the walls. And I thought it was all a dream. It's now clear; our hut is not only a refuge for weary climbers but also a welcome dormitory and dining hall that services an entire menagerie of rodents. These yarns don't do much to whet our appetites. In any case, all we have left is a few packets of stale noodles, and even the rats turned their noses up at those. . . .

After an hour of climbing in the dark, following a white line painted on the rocks and clinging onto a rope on the side of the trail, we reach the summit. The sun, however, couldn't make it out today. Worse still, a thick fog surrounds us. We can't see any further than three feet ahead. If it weren't for the signpost at the summit, I wouldn't have the slightest clue that we are currently sitting on top of the highest mountain in Southeast Asia. We all look at each other, not knowing how to react. Should we be popping champagne now that we've made it to the summit or crying in our beer because we missed out on the sunrise? The fog is as thick as ever, and there's no sign that it'll let up anytime soon. Pea soup for breakfast, anyone?

We decide to turn back. But then, only 300 feet down the path, the first sunrays begin to poke shyly through the haze. It's a spectacular sight. We look up to that strip of rock that we were standing on just a few minutes ago. Meanwhile, as far as the eye can see, the entire valley is radiating under the sun's glory. This image will remain permanently engraved on my mind like an epitaph on a gravestone.

We now have to retrace our steps back down the mountain. It seems easy enough, but we quickly realize that coming down is worse than climbing up. It's like scrambling down a 600-story building on a jagged series of steps interlaced with tangled tree roots and jutting rocks. Although I'm in top shape, I find these endless jolts unbearably annoying.

The 1.5-million-year–old Mount Kinabalu is the world's youngest granite mountain. Keeping in mind that the Earth is about 5 billion years old, Kinabalu is practically a newborn baby. But, careful now, it's still growing at the astonishing rate of two inches per year. To all those interested in climbing it, here's some advice: you better hurry up before this baby gets too big for its boots.

* * *

Chapter 20

....

A Nightmare to Forget

DAY 460, 7:30 AM
Tawau, Borneo—October 17, 1995

The sky has just fallen on our heads. I'm completely dumbfounded. I need all my willpower just to face the situation. Everything is gone—stolen from under our noses. All that's left are the shirts on our backs. At least we still have our health.

The nightmare
Tawau, Borneo—October 17-31, 1995

We're in the border town of Tawau, in northern Malaysia. From here, you can only get to the to the nearest port, Tarakan, in Indonesia, by boat. There are no roads in this part of the country and—to further complicate matters—the ferry crosses just twice a month. We can't afford to miss it. As mentioned previously, Borneo is the third-largest island in the world. The northern part is Malaysian, and the southern part is Indonesian. Oil-rich Brunei also makes up part of the island.

We had a few days of R & R in Malaysia before starting the next leg to yet another unknown country: Indonesia. And then . . . poof! Yesterday morning, the day before our departure, everything a traveler holds most dear—passport, visas, cash, credit cards, traveler's cheques, address book— vanish into thin air. A total disaster!

DAY 1. Caro wakes me, yelling frantically. Our precious money belt has gone missing. I jolt out of my slumber. In a panic, I dump the rucksack contents onto the bed. I'm just going through the motions, because something tells to me that our valuables have gone for good. I'm too wide-awake to hope it's all just a bad dream. If only someone would knock at the door and hand back our stuff with a few words of friendly advice: "Next time, be more careful!" We took turns wearing the belt, which contained our passports and all the credit cards, documents, and money we had. Lately, Caro had been suggesting that we should go back to the way we initially carried our valuables, namely, for each to wear their own belt with their own passports and such. That was the smart thing to do, but we didn't get around to it. I feel nauseous. We haven't got a single penny left, not even a coin for a phone call.

Caro sits at the end of the bed, devastated. I can't face this debacle alone. I'm worried that her sheer despair will push me over the edge. I sit down next to her. "We're going to need each other to get through this one. We've got no choice but to face the music and hope for the best. How? I don't know yet, but I'll need your help!"

First things first . . . we need to scrounge up some minimum cash. Immediately, we think of a nice Chinese guy we met yesterday, who might be able to help us out. He studied in Toronto and started a conversation with us about Canada. Sometimes, the most casual encounters can take on a new weight and point to unexpected directions. We go to the address where his store is located. He's away for the moment, but we're told that his wife is in charge and that he drops by from time to time. He works fourteen miles from here. No luck. However, the cashier believes that he'll be back later this evening. We leave him a written note.

Now we have to go to the police station to report the theft. A young Indian detective agrees to help us. In the meantime, I'll try to reach Visa to cancel our credit cards. While Caro tells our troubles to the officer, I go looking for a bank to resolve the credit-card problem. When the bank clerk sees how crestfallen I am, he calls over the manager straight away. Despite his good intentions and a lot of long-distance calls on his own coin, it proves impossible to get hold of anyone who can actually help us. About ninety minutes later, I stumble out of his office, well and truly shell-shocked.

Meanwhile, Caro and the cops go back to search the hotel. As I arrive, they're in the room of the young Malay who works behind the reception desk, turning it upside down. The poor guy looks on in dismay as the cops wreak havoc on his room. This no-holds-barred search makes me feel sick.

We still haven't eaten anything, and we don't really expect to before we catch up with our Chinese friend.

Just as the police are leaving this mess empty-handed, the owner of the hotel comes hurtling in. Incredulous, he's quick to point out that this is the first theft that has ever occurred on his premises. He's Hindu and prides himself on being a devout man, lighting incense every morning. He assures us that there was nothing suspicious or unusual about this morning. He doesn't get it. He seems dazed, startled, totally appalled. He gives us some cash so we can eat. This charitable tidbit comes just at the right time— it's 2 PM and we're starving.

On a full stomach, we can now think a little more clearly. It's imperative that we cancel our credit cards. From here, it's impossible, but our parents should have no trouble doing it. We have never had problems with the pay phones before, but today, of all days, and irony of ironies, when we need it most, nothing works. To make a call, we must go to the central telephone exchange on the other side of the city. Plus, we're in the tropics, on the fifth parallel, having fun rushing around at 95°F and 95 percent humidity.

After three fruitless calls to our families, I finally reach my sister, in the middle of the night, who assures me that she'll cancel everything.

Now for the traveler's cheques. American Express is unreachable. Their wretched toll-free number, anywhere in the world, is just for show, a marketing ploy. For Asia, we have to call Singapore, at own our expense. Yeah, that's a lot of help, especially when you're completely broke. I go back to see the bank manager, who, this time around, has come through. If everything pans out, our traveler's cheques should be reimbursed within the next three days. But to pick them up, we have to go to Kota Kinabalu, a fourteen-hour bus ride from here.

We keep checking in at our Chinese friend's store. Intrigued, his wife eventually asks us what we want exactly. We go into great detail about our plight, and, obviously inspired by a genius idea, she has a suggestion: "Go see the police!"

No doubt our message never got through to her husband, because if it did, I'm sure that he would have been sympathetic to our cause. Luck leaves us in the lurch yet again. Meanwhile, the little money we were given at noon is rapidly running out, although we're doing our best to make it last.

While we nibble at some dry rice outside the hotel's restaurant, the owner comes over to tell us that we can sleep and eat free of charge at his establishment during the days to come. It's his way of helping us. He also offers to pay our bus ticket for Kota Kinabalu when it best suits us.

DAY 2. As soon as it opens, we're at the Malaysian Airlines office, hoping to get a flight from Kota Kinabalu to the capital, Kuala Lumpur, as soon as possible. In KL, the plan is to pick up our new passports. It's the school holidays, and all economy-class flights (the only ones we could afford with our refunded traveler's cheques) are booked solid for the next couple of weeks. Standby? Not a chance. There has to be another solution . . . we're sure of that. Then Caro has a stroke of genius: "If all the regular flights are filled, why not fly first class, but on the red-eye? Red-eye flights are less popular, so maybe the seats will be cheaper, too." Bingo. There are three seats left. However, we must purchase our tickets at least twenty-four hours before the flight leaves; otherwise, they'll be automatically cancelled and resold. But we get our refund only nineteen hours before the departure. We can't let this chance slip by, so we use every shred of diplomacy we can muster to convince the travel agent that there has to be a way around the twenty-four–hour regulation. After a number of long-distance calls to the head office in Kuala Lumpur, a booking code is finally issued that will authorize payment only nineteen hours before the flight.

DAY 3. We take the bus to Kota Kinabalu. Fourteen hours later, we're back at the same hotel we stayed in ten days earlier. For the time being, we're penniless paupers, but the hotel manager, himself a traveler, generously offers us free accommodation. An English couple, sympathetic to our miserable tale, invites us out for supper.

DAY 4. Today is critical. First, we must pick up our new traveler's cheques at American Express, then go to the bank to convert them to the local currency, pay the airline company for our tickets, and finally get our proof of citizenship from the immigration office, which will allow us to leave the island legally. All this seems like child's play, but in a foreign country, without any ID, everything is more complicated. Although they try, major global companies can't offer the same level of service as they do in Western countries. I went through the same thing in India trying to telex Grindlays Bank, the Indian branch of a big Australian bank. On that occasion, it took five hours to withdraw the money using my Visa card—hard cash I absolutely needed at the time. Even then, the manager had to work overtime to sort it out. Of course, this could happen anywhere, but today, it feels as though we've got to get through every single screw up possible. Now we're being jerked around at the May Bank, Malaysia's largest financial institution. Having patiently waited until it opened its doors, we're told to come back in two hours, when the official exchange rate will be up. While Caro runs back and forth between the bank and the airline company to implore them to give us an extra two-hour reprieve, I duck over to the immigration office to get our precious citizenship documents.

In Tawau, a policeman accompanied us to the local immigration office to get this crucial certificate. Despite the cop's presence, we wasted ninety minutes with little more to show than a worthless scrap of paper, that I then had to present to one of his superiors who would then supposedly facilitate our request. Utter crap! The official name on this sheet is that of the big boss . . . the one who has the fanciest office and works the least by passing the buck every chance he gets. He has me hang about for another half an hour before deigning to tell me to go back and see the clerk whom I dealt with when I first came in. Again, I dictate the whole sorry saga, in plain English. He taps away with a single finger on a quaint typewriter pre-dating the war . . . World War I, that is. I'm in a sweat that he'll give up on me, so I give him my undivided attention, not leaving his side for a second.

What follows next is the rare privilege of witnessing bleeding-edge, pre-industrial technological prowess at its finest. When entering the Malay Peninsula, we filled in an immigration form, then another one when we landed on Borneo Island (eastern Malaysia) . . . in Kuching in the State of Sarawak, to be exact. And when we left to enter the State of Sabah (where we are now), there was nobody at customs to record our entry and register us. So we just slipped through, sight unseen, in ignorant bliss. I'm now told that Sabah's computer is not connected to that of Sarawak, or to Peninsular Malaysia's computer, for that matter. They can get a record of our travels the good old-fashioned way: by sending a telex to Kuching (in Sarawak) to confirm the date of our entry. "If everything goes well, you'll have your papers by tomorrow." Without the damned paper, we can't get through customs, thereby missing our flight, with a fifteen-day wait for the next one. Worse still, Caro has probably already paid for our tickets, which are nonrefundable. Our flight leaves at 5:40 AM tomorrow. I feel like I'm juggling a time bomb, so many dynamite sticks ready to blow up in my face. I take a deep breath, cross my fingers under the table, and try the impossible: with every ounce of diplomacy I can muster, I finally get my hands on the crucial document. It took three-and-a-half hours and just half an hour before the office closed, but I did it. The key to success is knowing how to navigate through the murky waters of "bureaucratic diplomacy"—a major life skill. Roughly, that simply means brownnosing a total incompetent and asking him, with the most ingratiating smile possible, if he can work at the speed of a tortoise rather than that of a slug. Obviously, you also have to convince him to get the job done without handing the file over to his office mate, who's sleeping by his side.

Exhausted but satisfied, I catch up with Caro. She's been worried sick waiting for me. Without further delay, we head straight for the airport, where we'll spend the night, lying on the ground. We're so scared of missing our plane that we don't dare close our eyes . . . even for a moment.

DAY 5. After all the frenzied legwork, we get out of Borneo on time, over a radiant sunrise. Ensconced in our executive seats, a glass of champagne in hand, we bid a final farewell to a majestic State of Sabah, as personified by the giant Mt. Kinabalu, slowly disappearing beneath us.

DAYS 6 to 14. In Kuala Lumpur since yesterday, another race against the clock begins. Our certificate stipulates that we must leave Malaysia within fourteen days, otherwise we'll be considered illegal immigrants. Over the next few days, we recoup our credit cards, our temporary passports (valid for one year), and our new Australian visas. Sad to say, but I must admit that the bureaucracy at the Western embassies is not exactly exemplary either.

DAY 14. After a nightmarish fourteen days, we leave Malaysia and enter Singapore, just one day before our special pass expires.

The more we think about what happened to us, the more questions are left unanswered. Our door was locked. How did the thief get in? How did he know where to find the good stuff? The money belt was under our clothes, at the bottom of our backpack, which we kept next to our heads as we slept. How did he steal it without waking us up? How did he know that our money and our papers were all in the same spot?

Lesson learned. Now that it's over, all that's left is to put the whole sordid affair behind us.

DAY 475
Singapore—November 1, 1995

Today, it's decision time. We must plan a new itinerary that takes into account our current situation. Tapped out of energy, I'm now on emergency reserve. I have a zero tolerance for any more surprises. And, oh yes, the heat . . . stick a fork in me, I'm done.

Our original plan called for us to visit the Riau Islands, south of Singapore. Then, go check out Java, Bali, and Timor by boat. From Timor, we would grab a flight to Darwin, in northern Australia. After that, the plan was to bike to Brisbane, our final destination. But our cash is running low. In fact, our finances are deep in the red.

The Singapore> Bali> Brisbane flight offered by Garuda (the Indonesian airline) is the cheapest way to go. We'll take full advantage of the Bali stopover to enjoy the vegetative tranquility of island life. Here, we'll revitalize and pamper ourselves before arriving in Australia, where our top priority (and job number one) will be to find a job.

DAY 477

Singapore—November 3, 1995

What can you say about Singapore? It would be unfair not to mention the incredible technological advancement of this Asian city. Its telecommunication and public-transportation systems are quite remarkable. At the same time, it's very modernity has deprived it of the old-world charm of its immediate neighbors. The time when a bargain could be had is long gone. Singapore has become so expensive. Even the price of a beer along the "waterfront," as they call it here, is beyond the pale.

Having experienced the wonders of Asia, a three-day stint in this city is enough for us. Public markets are rare, but, fortunately, those that remain have retained their own unique flavor. The Chinatown district is particularly vibrant, but I was mildly disappointed to find the markets in Little India not as hot as those in India itself.

At first glance, it seems to me that this modern city-state is not designed to be lived in but, rather, only geared toward work and productivity. The government tries by all means possible to mold a perfect society. The best example is how they "manipulate" the birthrate. Previously, wary of over-population, the government offered a $10,000 bonus to every woman who agreed to be sterilized. The program was so successful that they must do the exact opposite today. Faced with uneven demographics, the authorities now offer a $10,000 bonus to every professional woman who gives birth. The hope is that this measure will rectify the situation, but there doesn't seem to be any place for stay-at-home moms in the system.

The populace has to conform to very strict laws. For example, it's verboten to chew gum in public places or to jaywalk. It's illegal not to flush the toilet in public restrooms. Cameras were recently installed to nab these criminal non-flushers. Smoking in your own car was once forbidden, but this law was abolished because it was so difficult to enforce. The draconian anti-long-hair campaign of the 80s meant that hirsute hippies bobbing up at the border had a hard time getting in. Drug possession and trafficking are still punishable by capital punishment; two Australian rugby players have been hanged, despite intense diplomatic pressure.

The government's initiative to improve the quality of life is praiseworthy, and the booming economy has exceeded all expectations. Although their laws would make our own human-rights defenders squirm, their triumphant economic success is still admirable. While we're all trying to achieve viable economies in our own countries, maybe we can take home a few clues from Singapore.

DAY 479 and following
Bali—November 5, 1995

Is it any coincidence that our bags have been so poorly handled, given how cheap our tickets were? Just collected my bike, with the back wheel badly bashed in; the wheel rim is bent back and pushed inward, in opposite directions. What on earth did they chuck on top of it to do the damage? An elephant, maybe? Nothing surprises me anymore. Biting my tongue, I patiently wait to fill in all the mind-numbing paperwork needed to lodge a complaint and make a claim. Coming to Bali, this isn't the type of break I had in mind. . . .

Bali is one of 200,000 islands of the Indonesian archipelago, a seaside outpost where tourists are greeted with a warm, if a little overwhelming, welcome. We visit the paddy fields, explore volcanoes, swim with the dolphins, and soak up sun and sea.

We're staying at the Bamboo Losmen, a small, restful, and very friendly guesthouse, spending many hours quietly reading on our balcony, which looks directly onto an atrium full of tropical plants and chirping birds of every kind. It's hot out, but a maritime-sea breeze blowing in the salty, misty air cools us down.

My lopsided wheel aside, in the end, we have come to terms with our misfortune cheerfully enough. Now, we can enjoy three magnificent weeks before setting out for Australia.

* * *

Chapter 21

....

Australia:
A Tough
Transition

DAYS 501 to 542
Brisbane, Australia—November 27 to January 7, 1996

We touch down on a new land today: welcome to Australia, home of the kangaroo and the koala. I'm at the end of the world and I know it—so far from my roots, I can feel it. From my seat in the sky, everything seems so small. But in my head, it all seems so big. I have to get a job right away, because I'm stony-broke. I peer down on the city as though I were sizing up the enemy. It's a jungle out there. I don't feel up to the challenge. My strength is waning. To tell the truth, at this exact moment, I'd rather be heading home than putting in any more effort. But then again, I'm not ready to end the adventure and even less inclined to give up on my world travels.

As soon as we clear customs, Caroline immediately gets on the payphone and systematically contacts all the youth hostels listed in our guide until one of them agrees to pick us up at the airport with all our gear. My bike is still in no condition to ride, and hailing a cab is out of the question. After Asia, everything seems so expensive that we're even thinking of camping out in parks to avoid shelling out the $36 a day for our accommodation.

Brisbane is a city of about a million people. The fresh air of morning gradually gives way to the biting heat of the tropical sun. December marks the beginning of summer. During this sun-filled season, you won't hear even a whisper of the word "cloud" cross anyone's lips.

Sitting on a bench outside a supermarket, Caroline and I enjoy some coffee-flavored yogurt, a favorite treat that I've missed for more than a year. Since we only got in two hours ago, we're still in slow motion. People of all ages stroll around the supermarket barefoot, just like the surfers that flock to the fab beaches on the Gold Coast. Our glances wander absentmindedly on the action around us. As we casually chat about this and that, I get the sudden impression we're in a Tower of Babel. Everybody rushes back and forth. While some customers dash toward the least busy checkout lines, others briskly pack up their groceries before scurrying away. It looks like someone's yelled "Fire!" in a crowded theater. At first, I thought that this wild whirlwind would settle down, but, to my dismay, all the people around are feverishly joining the mad rush. No one escapes it. Caroline reminds me that people are simply carrying on exactly as they would back in Quebec. This fleeting remark makes me realize that I've left the slower pace of Asia. There, I had stopped rushing about. In this world—my world—everything is done so fast, too fast. I would like to be somewhere else . . . where life goes by more slowly. But I have to face reality and learn how to live like this again.

But first, there's survival. We're at the start of the summer holidays, and summer jobs are snapped up fast. We have no employment résumés, and we're certainly not dressed to impress in our shabby clothes. Furthermore, our visas don't allow us to hold professional posts within a company. Worse still, we can't hold the same job for more than three consecutive months.

With such restrictions, searching for a job is no picnic. Meeting rejection upon rejection, day after day, we're ready to accept just about anything.

Convinced that she's hit the jackpot, Caroline is excited to tell me that she'll be a mobile saleswoman. Armed with a small basket of flowers, she'll visit all the posh restaurants around town, accompanied by a driver. If everything goes well (according to her new boss), she'll be raking in about $150 for just four short working hours, from 8 PM to midnight.

When her big night comes, her "small" basket turns out to be a huge wicker hamper, filled with a dozen varieties of flowers and with tiny teddy bears, straight out of a flea market. Her load is so heavy that she can barely balance it on her shoulder. Her hapless outing doesn't stop there. The supposed "chic" downtown restaurants are more like rundown bars in the suburbs, where she has to defend herself against groping patrons, with both arms busy holding the basket.

She finally gets back home at 5 AM, exhausted, disgusted, and in tears. Having paid for the driver, the gas, and the flowers (even the pinched ones), she earns $50 for 12 miserable hours of work. If you deduct the price of the cheap skirt and shoes she had to buy, that leaves her with $30, a basketful of shame, and blisters on her feet.

"Wanted: assistant cook with short-order experience. Flexible hours up to 20 hours a week. Call Mike at *Jaw's Fish & Chips,* at 663-8713." This is the job for me. Plus it's only a few steps from where we're staying.

I meet Mike from Jaws and lay out my extensive (and highly embellished) résumé—not just the bike ride—but the whole kit and kaboodle. I get the job on the spot. Now comes the tricky part: keeping it. I have never done this kind of work in my life, so I have to watch my step and hide how inexperienced I am. I don't have too much trouble serving customers, doing the dishes, and keeping the fridges full. When it comes time to do what I was hired to do . . . that's another story. I sign my own death warrant when I'm asked to fry up my first batch of fish and chips. Like a true neophyte, I take the fry basket from one counter to the next, oblivious to the hot oil dripping everywhere. Big drips, big lies . . . I'm a pretty tall teller of tall tales who won't make it in this business for very long. Well, at least I ended my day (and my fry-cook career) with my earnings plus my 4 percent holiday pay!

Through Rory, an Aussie that Caroline met in Scotland, we meet Keiko, a Japanese girl, and Mike, another Aussie. With these two students, we share a big house in the 'burbs. Our new situation makes life easier, especially since we've cut down on our housing costs. Zipping around on our bikes, we criss-cross the city from morning till night looking for a job.

Two weeks pass by with no jobs in sight. My attitude has changed. First, I thought it was because of fatigue or still not being able to find a job, but, if I'm really honest, it has more to do with returning to regular life, the boring same old, same old.

I'm not immune to the stress of cultural and lifestyle changes. I thought that this would happen only when I got back home. No way mate! As soon as you're back to the Western flow of things, that's when it hits you. I reconcile myself with this new way of life and try to get rid of the depression that has crept up inside me.

On December 15, three weeks after our arrival, Caroline finally lands a dream job. No, really, this time it's fair dinkum, as they say here. She's hired to work in a gourmet delicatessen, specializing in cheeses, charcuterie, and fine foods. Her boss, Andreas, a well-to-do Indonesian with a heart of gold, takes to her right from the start, and in fact, she quickly becomes his favorite employee. He'll even turn a blind eye to the temporary-job law and keep her on after three months.

He regularly invites us to have supper at his place, and we end up being good friends. On the weekends, while Caroline minds the store, Andreas and I play tennis together at a members-only club in a toney part of town. Not that much older than we are, Andreas becomes a kind of big brother to us.

Since I'm still looking for a job, Caroline passed along a job listing she saw at the university-employment exchange: "Wanted: civil engineering student for a crushed rock recycling project." Having contacted the secretary, I meet Mr. Dugald Gray, CEO of Nucrush Inc. Pty. Ltd. I'll be in charge of a research-and-development project that seems very interesting but whose monetary compensation (and that which interests me the most) will depend on how good the results are as well as how in-depth my study will be. I have confidence in my skills, but I'm not going to falsify the data in order to be better paid. Even if the job site is fifty miles from where we live and with all the transportation problems that entails, I accept immediately . . . without even asking about the base salary.

I have mixed feelings right now. Christmas is coming up, and I'm more homesick than ever. I've got the blues, and I'm not trying to hide it. If I look at the situation rationally, I haven't got much reason to feel sorry for myself, but the mood lingers. It looks like I've lost the sacred fire—the burning light of adventure is flickering out. I went through a difficult-but-enriching experience, and I now have to return to sedentary life, without losing any of my good humor and *joie de vivre*. I'll get there, it's just a matter of making a few adjustments.

I get my first paycheck. Not counting my ten-hour weekly commute, I was rewarded a whopping $200 for fifty hours of work. An hourly rate of four bucks . . . whoopie whoop! It doesn't make sense considering I earned $10 an hour at the local fish & chip shop. Not to mention Caro, who's making $14 an hour slicing cheese. Why does learning hard lessons cost so much?

Seeing that we're alone for Christmas, Elizabeth, one of Caroline's regular customers, invites us to her place. I'm also the birthday boy today, and I score a small cake with a solitary candle that we can't seem to light. The fan whirs away at top speed, it's hot and humid, and we swelter in a sticky sweat. The house is decked out in holly, and Christmas carols play in the background as we talk. Oddly enough, I'm not feeling the holiday spirit. Frankly, I miss the cold, the snow, and my family.

My melancholy finally dissipates on this second Thursday of the new year, a full six weeks after our arrival. For the first time, I finally feel at home. At work, everything is bopping along as I had hoped. Tonight, some friends are dropping by, and there's also a letter from Quebec waiting for me. It's pouring rain, and I'm completely drenched by the time I get home, but inside my head, I'm spinning in perfect happiness. So what happened?

I was a bit shaky when I first got here. I thought I could take cover and handle the malaise that strikes all travelers at one point or another. I met a few who have never been able to return to normal life. Some choose travel as an escape, a means to avoid reality. On the contrary, I travel to embrace this reality. I'm not saying I know and understand everything, but I sure am glad of the path that I took. Finally, I realize that happiness is extremely difficult to cultivate if it is not sown in fertile soil.

At work, a day laborer workmate stands out from the rest. With his gentle manner and friendly smile, he's a role model for me. His nickname is Potsy, and when he smiles, he reveals his heart. He's teaching me about life without knowing it. He's poor, but instead of complaining, his heart is rich in human kindness. Saint-Exupéry writes, in *Wind, Sand and Stars*: "By striving for material gain alone, we build a prison for ourselves. We lock ourselves up, in solitary confinement, with our lifeless savings which buy us nothing worth living for." By his kindness, my friend Potsy shines on all those who surround him.

His influence elevates me from my slump. And I've come to accept a fundamental truth: I can't change the world, so I must accept society as it is, because happiness depends, first and foremost, upon your ability to live in harmony with your immediate surroundings.

DAY 556
Brisbane, Australia—January 21, 1996

Caroline worked nonstop during the entire holiday period. She not only slogged through a seventy-hour workweek, but she also worked on the official holidays, which earned her a fat bonus. For my part, I get up at 4:30 every morning, bike for an hour, then meet up with a colleague for a one-hour car ride to work. At the end of the day, I go to bed, dead tired, even before Caro comes back from her work.

Today is our first day off in a long time. We spend the day at the Lone Pine Koala Sanctuary, the biggest species-protection center in Australia. Because of hunting and the loss of eucalyptus tree habitat where they live, these adorable marsupials almost went completely extinct. However, constructive measures were taken to restore their population, and sanctuaries were set up to protect them and better understand their survival mechanisms. These efforts have paid off. For a small sum, you can cradle this aromatic ball of fluff that clings to you like a child. The koala is as soft and still as a teddy bear.

Koalas feed only on leaves from certain types of gum trees, which permeate them with a unique eucalyptus aroma. Thanks to a specially adapted digestive system, it is the only animal to be able to survive on this toxic food, poor in nutritional elements. With a distinct lack of energy, it's definitely the stay-at-home type—sleeping from seventeen to eighteen hours a day and eating for three or four. That leaves just two or three hours to kick back and have some fun. Although toxic, the eucalyptus leaves contain all the water the koala needs to survive. "Koala" is thought to mean "no drink" in the Aboriginal language, although there are many different languages spoken by Aboriginal people throughout the country. The name for koala appears in diverse forms in the written accounts of early settlers as cullewine, koolewong, colo, colah, koolah, kaola, koala, karbor, boorabee, and goribun.

DAY 564
Brisbane, Australia—January 29, 1996

Brisbane is a subtropical city situated just below the Tropic of Capricorn. It rarely rains in the summer. I'm watching the Ford Australian Open tennis final, held in unbearable heat and humidity. While Becker is making mincemeat of his opponent, a warning message crawls across the screen: "Storm approaching!" They must be joking, because there's not a cloud in the sky. The air is so thick, we can hardly breathe. But in the time it takes to say it, the blue sky turns grey, then black. A full-fledged hailstorm clatters down. I actually wanted to hang about and enjoy this forgotten phenomenon, but in spite of my fervor, I could only manage one or two seconds under a barrage of ice-cold missiles, some the size of golfballs. As fast as it darkened, the sky clears and immediately becomes blue again. Becker won, and we all wait for the night to bring us some relief and a bit of cool air again.

DAY 573
Brisbane, Australia—February 8, 1996

I'm still working at Nucrush, a mining company that produces mineral aggregates for concrete manufacturers and road builders. When you crush rocks, you get waste tailings. This residue is simply small-mineral fragments covered with a fine, powdery rock dust. I was hired as an intern to conduct a study on the possibility of recycling these tons of residue so that they could be integrated into already-existing product.

The main idea is to include some of the residue in the formula used to make the concrete. As expected, I face strong opposition from the manufacturers, and my first objective is to make a list of all the pros and cons of using the residue. So I dedicate my first week to visiting existing customers and evaluating their needs. The second, I spend reading scientific articles on this subject. Starting the third week, my actual experimentation will begin.

Results obtained at the end of the first two months are conclusive. Although there are limitations, benefits are significant for both the company and its customers. Better yet, a first customer agrees to try out the new formula that includes the residue waste.

I've been working for two weeks and have yet to receive a penny. Everybody gets their pay envelope while my hands stay empty. It's as hot as hell outside, and on the spur of the moment, I hand in my notice to the secretary. I don't want to work for people who don't know how to respect an agreement. "The file I've been working on is all yours. Everything is there, so you can forget about me!"

I've got a mind to bellyache. I'm only a tourist without any legal recourse. They not only chiseled me out of $400 but also deprived me of all the satisfaction that I got from this project. I'd rather do dishes in a restaurant—at least I'll get paid.

I arrive home relieved but bitterly disappointed by this cruel turn of events. Caro congratulates me on having the courage to leave. "If they don't know how to appreciate your true value, then they're the losers. You'll find another job, and you'll be glad you took a stand." That's reassuring, but I'm still thinking about it. Maybe I did act too fast.

While I'm taking a shower, mulling it over, Caro barges in.

She's quite agitated: "Your boss, Mr. Gray, is on the phone, and he wants to speak to you."

Worried, I pick up the phone.

"Pierre-Yves, I'm really sorry! You're not an employee like the others, and the person responsible for paying you completely forgot. I've worked overseas too, and I know how difficult it is to ask for your due. I promise you I'll fix the situation if you'll come back to work."

As if my bitterness could not be erased by mere excuses, I stay mum. Caro is eavesdropping. I look at her blankly without missing a single word from Gray. "The work you're doing is excellent, and we greatly appreciate it." The ball is now in my court, and I seize my chance.

"You know, when I first met you, you told me the contract would last only eight weeks. So I was ready to sacrifice a better salary to gain some working experience in my field. But I need money now. Or else I won't be able to pay my return ticket and even visit the rest of your beautiful country. It's the fruit season soon, and I was thinking of offering my services to the local farms where workers are well paid."

On the spot, he offers me an immediate pay raise and gives me until the end of the week to think about it. Much to my delight, the phone call ends on a friendly and sincere note. I look at Caroline, who is smiling like a Cheshire cat. She's really impressed. Me too!

On Monday, my pay jumps from $200 to $500 a week.

The following months proved to be a real professional adventure. All of the mineral residue is 100 percent recycled and resold, and I'm given carte blanche to manage three other projects: rate production-line efficiency, set up a quality-control lab, and train the relevant staff.

Like my big brother always says, "The important thing is to put your finger in the door of the company, then your foot, then finally your whole being."

Soon we'll have saved $10,000 between the two of us. Caroline wants to return to Quebec before the end of summer, and I want to get back before winter. We've succeeded in remaking our lives and in finding a certain balance on this new continent. On May 17 of this year, we'll leave everything and start afresh.

Travel means discovery, but it also is means moving on from your discoveries and leaving behind what you've built.

DAY 529

Brisbane, Australia—April 15, 1996

A time for scrimping and saving!

In spite of Caro's reluctance, I want to get a car to go around Australia. She says that my persistence is a pain in the neck, and I'm tearing my hair out convincing her. Exasperated by my obsession, she begrudgingly agrees to kick in her part but flatly refuses to help me spend time looking for a good deal, especially during any of her rare spare time.

With my mate, Lucas, the Nucrush mechanic, I spend hours peeling the used car ads in the classifieds: $1,400 for a '61 Ford Falcon station wagon. In spite of its thirty-five years, it shows no sign of rust and has had just one owner. Lucas assures me that it's in excellent condition, plus it will be easy to resell before we leave the country. I fall in love with the car or, rather, with that killer metal falcon adorning the hood. We're aware that the vehicle will need some work before hitting the long road ahead, but Lucas offers to help for a few bucks . . . plus a few beers while he's working on HRH the Princess, our new ride. Sold!

Three weeks have gone by, with every minute of my spare time dedicated to patching up Princess. But this morning, having just bought four new tires to royally shoe our Cinderella, she comes to an abrupt halt . . . just as we're about to cross the bridge spanning the Brisbane River. Lucas gets out of the car and checks under the hood. The engine is extremely hot. Without tools, he can't get her to restart. With his head hanging sheepishly, he says that the cylinder head gasket is probably shot. That's a $400 repair at the garage, but give him $25 and one working day, and Lucas will fix it himself, "like new." Poor sap that I am, I glance at Caro. For three weeks I've been singing the praises of the excellent car we've got our hands on. Right now, I would be ready to give this junker to the first passerby who wanted it. And God knows there would be plenty of takers here! We're at the entry of the main bridge leading into downtown Brisbane, and our old, wizened Princess is causing quite the slow down. Caro relied on me. The Falcon is ready for the scrap heap. Same goes for the vacant larrikin who bought it. And I bet that Caro would be ready to pay good money to get rid of them both.

My first mistake was to buy a car. The second, to buy a '61 used car. The third mistake would be to keep this *vrai bijou* (as we say in Quebec) a single day longer. I lost my money, I wasted my time, but worst of all, I've lost my passion for Princess. No way do I want to waltz through the desert with this ugly stepsister. I should have listened to my real Princess.

As soon as the engine cranks up again, I'll sell the former Royal. But I'm wondering . . . is there anyone out there, another sucker anywhere in the Land of Oz, who would take it?

As Caro knows too well, Gilles Vigneault sings, "Qu'il est difficile d'aimer . . ." (Lovin' don't come easy). My song ought to be, "Learnin' don't come easy." Having moved heaven and earth, we sell our now disgraced and dethroned Princess to a friend of Lucas for $1,650. That puts us $500 in the hole. Think positive, Pierre-Yves; you learned a valuable lesson. Most of all, I learned that I have a girlfriend who loves me enough to forgive my wacky whims. Fanning the sale cash like a rainbow on the bed, we feel rich again.

Having cancelled the visit to India because of a bad flu, my mother finally confirms that she will come to join me in Malaysia for a three-week stay. How long I've I waited for this moment! This trip would not have been complete if I had not been able to share a small part of it with her. She would so love to experience for herself all the adventures I write about in my journal. In fact, she's been dutifully transcribing my journal since the very beginning of my trip and knows it better than I do myself.

It's a done deal: our plane tickets are bought, and, with our minds at ease, we can take a leisurely three-month bus tour around Australia. Caro will return home on August 4, while I'll leave for Malaysia on August 13. Contrary to all expectations, we have just received the famous parcel posted to Agri. Lost in Turkey, it made its way to our mailbox twenty months after first being posted. Plastered with stamps and stickers of all shapes, sizes, and colors, it has probably circumnavigated the globe a couple of times, at least. A lucky package indeed!

* * *

Fair Dinkum Wildlife Down Under

Chapter 22

....

A Fun Hop Through Kangaroo Country

DAY 685

Sydney, Australia—May 29, 1996

Confident our savings will be enough, we hit the road. We've just spent ten days living in the bush at the summer place of our landlord, Tony. And now we're checking out the bustling metropolis of Sydney. Sydney Harbour extends right to the heart of the city center, and the quays there serve as transit points for ferries that commute to populous suburbs, including those situated along the Paramatta River. The whole area really comes alive at rush hour. Spanning the port rises the iconic Sydney Harbour Bridge, known locally as the "coathanger" and for a long time the world's largest single-arch bridge.

This spectacular structure is the perfect foil to Sydney's other major landmark and younger sibling, the Sydney Opera House. Opened in 1973, it instantly became a national symbol. This futuristic, other-worldly wonder is striking from whatever angle you look at it.

As the sun goes down over the bridge, with the Opera House's billowing roof sails changing from off-white to orange-colored pink and its glass facade glittering under the day's last sunbeams, it's easy to see why Sydney is considered one of the five most beautiful cities in the world.

It is also a cosmopolitan city where all manner of culture and creed live side by side. In the Haymarket district, Paddy's Market is abuzz on weekends, while Asian aromas fill Chinatown all week long. But it's on the front lines of King's Cross and Oxford Street where you can witness gender-bending at its best. In fact, this is the home of the world's largest annual gathering of gays and lesbians. Each year during Sydney's Gay and Lesbian Mardi Gras, drag queens strut their stuff in the most eccentric and elaborate carnival costumes imaginable.

DAY 703
Port Campbell, Australia—June 16, 1996

After a wasted four days in Canberra, possibly the world's most boring capital city (outside of Ottawa?), we spent a week in seductive Melbourne, a gastronomical mecca. Now we're in Port Campbell, a small, seaside town along the Great Ocean Road, a spectacular route that follows the southernmost coast of mainland Australia. For about 200 miles, this stretch hugs the seaside, sometimes at sea level, sometimes curving along the flat of the coastline cliffs. Wherever you are, it never disappoints. Queenscliff, one of Australia's oldest settlements, features typically Victorian architecture. We're blown away by the tremendous waves crashing down on Bell's Beach, which, each year, hosts a world-class surfing competition, the Surf Classic. In Lorne, nestled between the mountains and the sea, we enjoy the hiking trails, lined with rivers, billabongs, and waterfalls. Cape Otway is situated at the southern tip, where the Southern Ocean meets Bass Strait. Much of the area is included in the Great Otway National Park, with rainforests, streams, and exceptional flora, where a rugged coastline meets with pockets of sandy beaches. Amid this natural beauty, it's here, in the small fishing village of Port Campbell, that we discover the prized jewel of the Great Ocean Road. With this stop as our base, we marvel at one resplendent sight after another: the Twelve Apostles, giant limestone stacks rising up from the sea, lined up like orderly sentinels; a nineteenth-century English boat wreck at the bottom of Loch Ard Gorge; the Island Arch, which bears an uncanny resemblance to our own Rocher Percé on Quebec's Gaspé Peninsula; a flock of determined mutton-birds returning to roost after flying 9,000 miles; and, finally, giant waves crashing up against the cliffs.

At six o'clock in the morning, I'm sitting pretty on a rocky outpost jutting out into the sea. A thick fog rolls down the cliff to meld with the sea foam formed by the breaking waves. The rising sun flashes on the horizon and colors the sky a bluish pink. The salt air is fresh and cool. I've seen sunrises on the Turkish coast, on the highest Himalayan Mountains, and on the sands of the Iranian desert, but catching this view stands out as one of the greatest moments of my trip. Caroline is stunned.

DAY 712
Coober Pedy, Australia—June 25, 1996

There's more than just sand in the Stuart Desert. There are also plenty of opals, which is the only reason to be in this bleak and barren place where it's so hot that the townfolk even dig their homes underground. The name "Coober Pedy" derives from the Aboriginal "*kupa*" meaning "white man" and "*piti*" meaning "hole" . . . "white fellow's hole in the ground." Here, water is scarce, and the cost of fuel, exorbitant. There's no greenery in sight. A stifling dust regularly blows in, covering everything in its path, including a smattering of rusted-out car wrecks. An apocalyptic setting indeed and one that recalls scenes from the movie, *Mad Max III*, which was actually filmed at this "end of the world."

The local economy has been been booming since Willie Hutchison, a gold prospector, discovered opal deposits here in 1915. Since that time, more than a quarter of a million mines have been dug out in the area. Each has left a huge cone of excavated rock and earth as a telltale sign on the flat surface. To ensure the town center doesn't look like a cluster of giant ant hills, too, no opal prospecting is permitted inside the town limits. Those who find veins of opals when building their homes bypass the law by claiming they're simply enlarging their place of residence—often by excavating right up to the property lines of their immediate neighbors. As they say here, "It pays to renovate!"

Tonight's our turn to venture underground—we're staying in a subterranean youth hostel. It's cool, and when the lights go out, it's pitch black. And after a sixteen-hour, 700-mile bus ride on a desolate dirt road, you don't need a lullaby to fall asleep.

DAY 719
Uluru, Australia—July 2, 1996

We're in the middle of nowhere, the dead center of the Australian continent, dubbed the "Red Center" because of the distinct red color of the ground. Except for the odd pale-green shrub, some tufts of straw-colored weeds, and the clear-blue sky, no other hues can compete with the predominant signature-red earth. It may be a stark landscape, but the indigenous people have lived here for 22,000 years and counting! Drinking from artesian-fed waterholes and surviving on a diet of kangaroos, witchetty grubs, and seasonal berries, the Aboriginal peoples, predominantly the Anangu, have made this unforgiving land their own.

We are in Uluru National Park, cradle of this amazing civilization. This park is also the famous site of the biggest monolith in the world: Uluru. Sitting on the bottom of a sea that has long since disappeared, Uluru now appears astonishingly in the middle of a desert. It's like someone plunked down a huge rock, 1,000 feet high by 5,000 feet long, into a giant 1,000-square–mile sandbox. For the Pitjantjatjara, the owners and occupants of these sacred places, this rock was formed during the Tjukurpa Period, when all physical objects and beings were created to give us the landscape we see today. You really need to see the desert yourself, home to these people for millenia, to better understand how they have come up with such legends.

Regrettably, their rich traditions are jealously guarded, and only a small fraction of their folklore is known to outsiders.

Having attended a traditional music and dance corroboree (the Pitjantjatjara word for "meeting"), our main focus is to climb this monolith in the predawn hours, so we can arrive at the top before sunrise. Equipped with ropes for the steeper parts of the climb, we make our way in almost-total darkness. The ascent itself took about an hour and a half. Neither fear nor fatigue delayed us. The only thing that counts is getting to the top. Here, Mother Nature truly surpasses herself.

Cairns, Australia—July 1996

It's been two months since we've gone walkabout in Australia, and here we are in Cairns, a gem of a town and one of the most popular holiday destinations on the continent. Bungee jumping, skydiving, scuba diving, and snorkelling on the Great Barrier Reef, rafting, rock climbing, hang gliding, rainforest hikes, Jeep excursions—it's all available, and many other diversions as well, on the Cape York Peninsula, the northernmost extremity of Australia. Whatever you want, they've got it! Tourism is king here. The locals are so good at roping you in to whichever activity they're offering; come to think of it, I bet they could even sell a dogsled ride to a Yukonite.

With Idel and Geraldine, two Irish girls we met at Uluru, we end up at a hotel where we can stay free of charge in exchange for two hours of work every day. Thanks to our lucky stars, Caro and I get to trim the cedar hedge around the swimming pool, while our two less fortunate friends are assigned housecleaning duties and communal-toilet detail. After a couple of days, our circle of friends widens, and, every night, after a day of fun in the sun, lolling about, or catching a few rays, we all meet up in the Wool Shed, where we wear ourselves out dancing the night away.

We take advantage of this final month of holidays to take a scuba diving course in the best locale possible—the renowned Great Barrier Reef. After two days of theory and practice in a swimming pool, here we are, heading out to sea. A high-powered speedboat zips us forty nautical miles off the coast, where we meet up with a thirty-eight-foot sailboat that will be our home for the next three days. My heart was set on this adventure, but as I watch the distant Australian mountain ranges melt away into the ocean, as I look around this menacing expanse concealing a world unbeknownst to me, as the clouds turn the turquoise water a sinister black, so does my fear of water—my greatest fear—rise to the surface once again.

I'm knocked out, underwater. Disoriented, I'm unable to find my feet. With my arms crossed and my face pushed to the bottom, all I see is a cloud of sand swept up by the wave crashing down on me. I'm weightless. I can only feel the saltwater tingling my lips and burning my eyes. My jaw is stiff. Seawater is filling my nostrils. I feel each second stretch out until time stops completely. A hand from above grabs me forcefully by the hair and drags me out of there. I'm four years old. We're at Wells Beach, in Maine, and my father has just saved me from drowning.

Here in the crystal-clear waters of the Coral Sea, I overcome my fears. Marine life of a thousand and one colors, huge turtles, harmless sharks, countless schools of fish calmly flit through bright bands of sunshine, like silk threads shimmering in the deeps. Flying fish spread their fins as they get ready to take flight. Clown fish, sporting vibrant, orange stripes nose at the tips of sea anemones, which answer by gently waving back. Looking for a feed, parrotfish, just like woodpeckers, nip away at the coral reef. Above the surface, turtles gulp in air before torpedoing to the depths, far below. The sharks, sovereigns of the sea, casually investigate their realm as their powerful fins whip through the water. Here, in this marine Garden of Eden, we have only one right and privilege: to watch and wonder.

DAY 749
Cairns, Australia—August 4, 1996

Caroline leaves for North America today. She's sad . . . not so much about going back home but, rather, that we will be apart over the next four months. She hasn't caught up with family and friends for twenty months, and soon they'll be anxiously awaiting her arrival at Montreal's Dorval Airport. She feels like she's ready to leave, but leaving a life of your dreams is never easy. She'll now have to follow a new timetable, one that's not based on good times and sunny temperatures—a time to trade in her slacker life for work and all the stress that comes with it.

As planned, I join my mother in a week in Kuala Lumpur. We'll spend more than three weeks together. After that, I fly to Los Angeles. And then? Home to Chicoutimi.

* * *

Chapter 23

....

Lili: Mom Extraordinaire

DAY 758
Kuala Lumpur, Malaysia—August 13, 1996

Selamat datang ke Malaysia! What a great feeling to be home again! Back in this wonderful country, the only words out of my mouth are, "I love Malaysia!" I want to tell all Malaysians how enjoyable life is in their country—the land of colorful and bountiful outdoor markets and gastronomic delights. It's all about the smiling people, always engaged in lively discussion on the streets, although they also work hard to earn a living. It's the continuous cacophony of buses, cars, mopeds, but it is also the quiet puposefulness of the street vendor going about his business. Behind the apparent anarchy are a people that follow a subtle order. Malaysia strikes a fascinating balance between modernity and tradition, with sometimes ramshackle results. The Malaysian people are making great progress while still keeping things simple and staying young at heart. It's what makes this place so charming.

DAY 759
Kuala Lumpur, Malaysia—August 14, 1996

Now that I'm back in Asia, I've rediscovered my passion for adventure. Extreme situations inspire me. Today's visit to the Canadian consulate puts me through another kind of extreme: extreme incompetence, that is. The carelessness of the staff is exasperating. I phoned this morning inquiring about what I have to do to extend my temporary passport, but I soon realize that it's a waste of time. A better idea is to jump on a minibus and nip over to Jalang Ampang Street. It's also the site of the newly completed Petronas Twin Towers, currently the tallest twin buildings in the world.

It had slipped my mind that desk clerks have the same dour, disinterested demeanor as some Canadian customs officers I've come across. All seem to think that they have to look that way to be taken seriously. Through thick glass, with a hole so small that I had to shout to be heard, I bellowed out my requests. Without even deigning to look at me, the receptionist picks up the phone and seems to be speaking to a supervisor. Having received no acknowledgement whatsoever, I plop myself back down in the waiting room. I'm trying to keep my "consulate cool," an attitude I try to adopt each time I step into the diplomatic arena.

After two hours of inertia, I go back and see the receptionist and ask what's going on. She coolly tells me, straight up, that she just plain forgot me. Was I stupid to have waited so long? After two years traveling the world, I've learned at my own expense that when it comes to embassies, clocks don't have second hands. Here, waiting times are measured in hours, not minutes.

After yet another hour of waiting, I'm facing the embassy clerk who issued our temporary passports after our Borneo fiasco last year. Knowing at the time that I was headed for Australia and probably wanting to get rid of me, she was adamant that I would obtain a six-month renewal, no problem at all. Today, it seems the rules have changed; making up all sorts of excuses, she now tells me, no dice. I take a deep breath, knowing full well that throwing a tantrum or raising my voice would only result in more pointless delays. When I think that bureaucracy back home is just as bad, it sends shivers down my spine. And to also think I once wanted to become an ambassador . . . I ought to have been committed!

DAY 761
Kuala Lumpur, Malaysia—August 16, 1996

It's 9:10 PM, and my mother's plane is about to land. To the very day, twenty-five months ago, I left Quebec.

In Islamabad, Pakistan, while waiting for my bike wheel to get in from London by British Airways, I bided my time watching those reuniting with their friends and family. With tears welling up, I imagined how it would feel to see Caroline or my mother coming out of the crowd toward me.

Today, it's my turn. I still have a lump in my throat, but this time, I'm not wistful or sad. Can't a son cry for joy when he sees his own mother for the first time in twenty-five months? I'm thrilled finally to share my happiness with the very person who has supported and encouraged me throughout my entire life. I can't wait to travel with her, not to mention show her the fun discoveries that new adventures will surely bring us.

And there she is, her head held high above the crowd, sticking out like a weather vane. With open arms and grinning from ear to ear, she rushes to embrace me. She introduces me to friends she met on the plane: Canadian government officials who have come to Kuala Lumpur for a congress. Naturally, she's told them all about my little adventure. She's already taken care of my PR image. She hasn't changed. Not one iota. It's as if I had never left.

In a hurry to show her everything, I whisk her over to the downtown shuttle bus. She doesn't even have time to catch her breath. She taught me how to read and write and recite La Fontaine's fables. Now it's my turn to show her a thing or two. I know she'll be a star student. Having left the nursing profession to raise us, she later became a travel agent. She's already been all around the world, so she knows a thing or two about the best places to stay. However, her past adventures are nothing like what I've got up my sleeve. No, there won't be any grand hotels, no red carpet unfurling from our air-conditioned charter bus. But she's up to it. I'm glad to see that she packed only the items I told her to bring, following my instructions to a T . . . well, actually two T-shirts, dark bermuda shorts, a single pair of socks, a pair of sandals, a swimsuit, a hat, and some sunscreen. No make-up, certainly none of the bewildering array of bottles, sprays, creams, and lotions that she usually schleps around. Just one red lipstick. That's it. Her packsack is so small, you would think it was a handbag.

After a twenty-two-hour flight, and stopovers in Vancouver and Taipei, she feels as fresh as a daisy—but a good night's sleep wouldn't hurt either. Walking through the Chinese quarter, we weave through stalls selling clothes, jewelry, shoes, and watches set up in the street every night, toward the backpacker hostel in which I've booked a room. She turns toward me, aghast, thinking it must be some kind of a joke. The front door looks like the entrance to a brothel. To get inside, we have to step around giant, steaming pots and a bunch of late-night eaters, their noses deep into rice bowls. It's getting late, so the merchants are starting to take down their stalls to make way for the cars tomorrow morning.

She has already visited several Chinese districts in Asia, but spending the night here will be a first. For $15, we get four concrete walls, no windows. That, plus a bed covered in a single sheet and access to the communal toilet, which we share with ten other guests.

I hardly have time to settle down comfortably on the bed when she comes back, discouraged. Apparently, there's not a shower to be found in the hotel. I forgot to tell her that the cold water hose dangling from the wall (and just a step away from the toilet hole) is the shower. Also, I should've warned her that there's no soapdish, much less a mirror. Dark circles on the stained, cracked floor makes her want to look up, not down. At least up there, she can watch geckos, the cute, little tropical lizards, skitter along the rusty pipes like tightrope walkers. She comes back, this time having decided she doesn't really need a shower . . . for a day or two, anyway. Trooper that she is, she flatly refuses to move to the other side of the street, where luxury suites can be had for $140 dollars per night. I didn't look after her too well this first night, but hearing her snore away, my guess is that she'll get over it pretty soon. She likes to keep things simple, at least when she's traveling.

It would be great if my dad was here, too, but as he says it so well, "Someone has to work so that someone else can take a holiday!" He's quietly going about his business at home. He often teases my mom by saying that being home alone is practically a holiday in itself. A sports nut, he plays hockey and tennis and skis whenever he gets a chance. And that's not counting the endless hours he puts in doing odd jobs for my sister Maryse and my brother François. He's a jack of all trades. For more than twenty years, summer and winter alike, rain or shine, he's been riding to work on his prehistoric bicycle. That's why they call him the "biking dentist." At sixty-four, he'll soon retire, after forty years of practice. No way will he stop working, but he'll continue to do what he likes to do most: playing his favorite sports and, especially, doing good deeds for others.

DAY 762 and following
Kuala Lumpur, Malaysia—August 17, 1996

What we like to do most is spend entire days walking and poking around the narrow streets in the coastal towns and fishing villages along the eastern and western parts of the Malaysian peninsula. It's hot, humid, and sticky, but Lili, despite being sixty years young, takes it all in stride and keeps up with my hectic pace, no problem at all. We soak it all up: the local cuisine, the beautiful beaches, the exotic finds at a cornucopia of night markets . . . plus some leisurely hikes through the jungle. Then there's the enriching conversations with characters from everywhere, locals and travelers alike.

As the days go by and my mom relaxes into the easy rhythms of her new life, we venture far and wide. Now we eat in smaller, more obscure places, where we not only discover ever-more delicious food but also get to closely interact with the locals, too. Lili gets so used to our rustic-chic, dinky accommodations, intended for younger, not-so-fussy backpackers, that she deems our first, real hotel to be a royal palace, even if it isn't air-conditioned. Instead, we get a fan that makes such a racket we fear the roof may fly off. Of course, there's no toilet in the room either and no cold-water hose dangling from the wall, for that matter. Instead, we get a metal drum filled with rusty water to wash up with. A box with wooden slats serves as a bed. We sleep under a stuffy mosquito net. And it's a good thing, too, because the bugs are swarming through the screenless window. She came here to eat what the locals eat (and the way they eat it), to drink what they drink, and to get around the same way they do, even if this means hopping on some pretty iffy transportation. She wants to see it all, without passing judgment or comparing it to what she's used to. She wanted to live like the locals do, familiarize herself with their customs, and learn to appreciate the differences between their culture and her own.

We often get together with young backpackers, who share our interests and values, and Lili fits in just like the others. Some are amazed to learn that she's my mother. Far from being a burden, she knows how to hold her own with her easygoing cheerfulness and biting wit. She doesn't come across as someone entering her golden years. Although she has a line or two on her face (which she wouldn't mind getting rid of), she always seems to wrangle unexpected favors and has even won us a few special privileges using her charm and tact. If I inherited my love of cycling from my father, I must have learned my persuasive craftiness from my mother.

Lili is fascinated to see the way people receive us. We went to Seremban to visit the parents of my friend Pui-Leng Lee, the same place Caroline and I visited for a few weeks last year. After a warm welcome, Mrs. Lee asks my mother if she would like to take a shower to freshen up. Taken aback, Lili at first gracefully declines but quickly decides otherwise when I tell her, in French, that it's customary to do so.

Other friends, who are happy to see me again and curious to meet my mother, drop by the small, modest apartment of our hosts. In Chinese culture, family bonds are very strong, and news travels fast. We're served traditional herbal tea, and they insist we stay overnight. My mother takes this opportunity to ask the many questions I haven't been able to answer. Everyone has an opinion, and each is quick to put in their own two cents worth. My mother was won over by this "cultural melting pot" from the start. Our conversation flowed for many hours under the deafening roar of the ventilator and over the clamorous background blare of the TV, always tuned into the Chinese channel. Generosity abounds as Mr. Lee hands us a ceramic vase ("Take it, please!") simply because my mother mentioned that she found it very attractive. His daughter later tells us that the vase was made in Borneo in 1956. Regretting having accepted this present, mom will try everything to give it back, but in vain. This gracious host knows our friendship is worth more to him than mere objects, and if we're happy, so is he.

Mr. Lee is keenly interested in introducing my mother to the wonders of Chinese cuisine. We spend whole evenings enjoying the different delicacies of the night market's food stalls. In Malaysia, the national fad is food and the eating thereof. Never a lot in one sitting but, still, a little nibble at any hour of the day or night. Snacking on a small bowl of noodles along a street is our equivalent of sipping a cold beer on an outdoor terrace on Montreal's *Rue Saint-Denis*.

DAY 785
Kuala Lumpur, Malaysia—September 9, 1996

For this final night, we sleep in the Swiss Inn, the luxury hotel Lili had refused to move to on her first night in town. They have a shuttle service to the airport, and they've promised to get her there on time for her 5 AM flight tomorrow.

All our belongings are spread out on the room's huge, immaculate, white bed. I pass along all the equipment that I will no longer need to my mother. She tries to convince me to keep some warm clothes, but I want to carry the least possible, and I'm already packing over one hundred pounds. In any case, I will be home before it gets really cold. She insists. Now, she's not my travel buddy anymore—she's back to being my mother, a mother worried for her son. She gazes over my gear, deep in thought . . . it's suddenly dawning on her that she's about to let me go again.

Now's the time to pour our hearts out. Lili tells me how much younger she feels. This trip has given her new wings. She's proven to herself that she could go beyond her limits, too. It's never too late. She also better understands where my traveling fervor comes from. She's experienced the same kind of freedom for herself. This feeling, however, makes you forget that life still goes on at home, and that your normal routine is waiting for you just around the corner. She also now knows how good it feels to travel light and how nice it is not to worry about what you're going to wear the next day, how your make-up looks, and whether or not your hair is a mess.

I congratulate her for being such a great traveler, and I tell her how proud I am of my mom extraordinaire.

It's getting late. She turns out the light. This trip ends here, but she's not about to give up her passion for adventure. She's already looking forward to our next journey together . . . India, maybe? But first, she's looking forward to seeing me return home, safe and sound.

I have only 3,725 miles of biking to go, from California to Chicoutimi. I know that I'll make it, but I'll be tired when I get home. Tired from all that I've accomplished, but perhaps also daunted by what I have yet to accomplish. I don't know anymore; I don't know.

* * *

Chapter 24

....

So Near, Yet
So Far

DAY 793

Los Angeles, California, USA—September 14, 1996

After traveling for exactly two years and two months, I get ready to jump on my bike again for the last stage of my world tour—crossing the United States. I'm a little worked up. My guts are about to explode, and it feels as though my body, heart, and soul are at war with each other. I'm like a bull about to be let loose in the ring. I know I'll get there, but I'm wary of the pain and suffering. This is the cost that comes with success.

Little more than a straight line (a long one, admittedly) separates me from fulfilling my dream. I'm 3,800 miles from Chicoutimi, my final destination, marking the end of all that I've endured. Suddenly, I picture myself spread out on the bed in the Dijon youth hostel, praying desperately for a second chance. The mere thought of it gives me steely reserve. I think of my family and friends waiting for my return as I push down on my first pedal strokes . . . Chicoutimi, here I come.

DAY 797
Mojave Desert, California—September 18, 1996

After riding for a few days, I wake up stiff and sore. Last night, my right shoulder hurt so bad that I couldn't sleep. Hunching over the handlebars eight hours a day eventually takes its toll, tiring the muscles and leading to tendonitis if I'm not careful.

Who said that the prevailing winds always comes from the west? I've been riding into a headwind for the last three days. The temperature hovers around 95°F, and the sun hits me like a sledgehammer. I'm in the Mojave Desert, and if you think that deserts are flat, featureless landscapes, the Mohave is the perfect place to discover otherwise! I cross a series of false-flat areas interspersed with a motley collection of mountains. Into this headwind it feels like the road is much steeper than it really is. Anxiety gets the upper hand as the day's fatigue kicks in, and there's still nothing on the horizon. The empty desert is like a vast sea. However, though the undulating sea might bring you peace of mind, the desert is sure to drive you out of your mind.

DAY 798
The Needles, California—September 19, 1996

These last couple of days have been very difficult. I decide to stop here in the Needles, on the Colorado River, right on the Arizona border . . . I need a day off.

I talked myself into thinking that it was all going to be all too easy, and here I am—a victim of my lack of mental preparation. I've come crashing down to earth and hit the ground hard. I've reached a crucial phase. When I look at the length of the road ahead, I get the feeling I'm digging my own grave. In such a hurry to get home, every mile weighs heavily. Perhaps I'm just a half-bike, half-man machine—nothing more than a cycling Centaur. Abroad, I found ways to energize myself by learning about new cultures, new cuisine, new religions, and new customs. Now, that's all over. The landscape no longer recharges me, and because I'm riding in the middle of a desert, my "batteries" are draining fast.

DAY 800
Kingman, Arizona—September 21, 1996

It's 5:40 AM, and I'm already on the road and in a hurry to get home. I leave the lush Colorado Valley to cross into Arizona, the Grand Canyon State. Right from the get-go, I have to tackle a 3,500-foot mountain pass. My bike weighs a ton. I get used to the idea that I'm nothing more than a pack animal. A mile or so from the summit, I get a sweeping view of the entire valley below. Further along, I stop in Oatman, a town built in 1906 during the Gold Rush. It's now a ghost town, with a 600-yard main street and a row of dilapidated, timber buildings bearing signs like Tavern, Bank, Barber Shop, and Hotel. It's exactly how I imagined a Wild West town would look. There are even tumbleweeds (right on cue) rolling through the empty street. All that's missing are the swinging saloon doors, creaking away, paying homage to bygone ghosts.

After the climb to the top, a ten-mile descent brings me onto another sun-baked plain. While I'm melting, an oasis comes into view: a roadside gas station and diner. They are few and far between but always a welcome sight. I still have this nagging pain in my right shoulder. After a night of rest, it goes away, but the more the day goes by, the more painful it gets.

Near the end of the day's ride, as I change speeds going up a slope, my chain slips off and wraps itself around the gears. There's never a good time for this sort of thing to happen. The sun will soon set, and I've still got about ten miles to go before arriving at the only rest stop in this part of the desert. In a panic, I try to pry loose the chain by forcing it . . . not a great idea, because if it breaks, I'll be in a pickle, not a jam. I take a few minutes to gather myself, and after a few deep breaths, I fix the problem. Within ten minutes, I'm on my wheels again.

Just like a semitrailer, I pull off the highway and into the truck stop. Huddled tight next to each other and lined up for hundreds of yards, these road monsters, their engines no longer roaring, stop for the night. I greatly appreciate these desert rest stops, because not only can you get a good feed here, you can also use the water line to take a shower. Wearing just my skintight cycling shorts, I lather up like a madman to get rid of the thin film of the day's accumulation of grime, dust, and sunscreen. Puzzled truckers look at me, shaking their heads, wondering who this nutter is, unabashedly scrubbing away.

After a copious meal, I pitch my tent in the middle of this asphalt parking lot where there isn't a single square inch of lawn. I've put in seventy miles, climbing nearly 5,000 feet in the process. I'm exhausted. As I get ready to settle down under my tent, a truck driver, thinking he's being helpful, gives me some advice, "You better watch out. There are rattlesnakes everywhere 'round here."

I ruefully reply, "Thanks for the tip, but my tent zipper is kaput."

Hopefully they're polite rattlesnakes, knocking first, before they come in. And if one of them ends up knocking me off first . . . so be it!

DAY 806
Winslow, Arizona—September 27, 1996

Yesterday, I visited the Grand Canyon, which lives up to its deepest, best reputation. To top it all off, the sunset, casting its fiery hues over the staggering rock faces, was followed by a total lunar eclipse later that night. Hidden from the sun by the earth, the moon was transformed into a milky halo before emerging again as a shining spoon in the middle of an infinite cupboard full of stars.

My day began somewhat less poetically. A strong north wind drove the temperature below freezing last night. The cold gets to me. Not even my thermal underwear can stop it. I resort to my good old newspaper trick. The stuffed newspapers put an end to my wimpy shivering.

I've already planned out my itinerary: Arizona, New Mexico, Texas, Oklahoma, Missouri, Illinois, Indiana, Ohio, Pennsylvania, New York, Ontario, Quebec, and then, finally, home sweet home.

DAY 808
Chambers, Arizona—September 29, 1996

A punishing, equal opportunity desert: you get to freeze at night and roast during the day. Rolling merrily along for eighty miles, I've only got twenty-five to go before I hit the border of New Mexico. Constantly calculating the distances encourages me. I'm itching to get home more and more each day. I've got to tone it down, or I could blow a gasket. How I yearn to close my eyes and open them again, only a few miles from home.

DAY 809
Mesita, New Mexico—September 30, 1996

My gut feeling has served me well so far, but today it went missing. Arriving in Laguna, at the end of the day after a seventy-five-mile ride, something urges me to keep going. Logically, I should stop here. Although I'm tired, I continue riding to the next town, Mesita, a few miles down the road.

Mesita is an Native American reservation, and posted on the entry sign are not your typical words of welcome: "Staying on the reserve without permission is strictly forbidden. Trespassers will be fined." I have no idea of the severity of the penalty, and I'd much rather just pretend I didn't read the warning. But on second thought, I needed water to cook supper. I might as well ask someone if I can stay for the night and if I can use their hose to wash up at the same time.

As if I was playing a gameshow to pick the winningest house in the town, I spend about ten minutes checking out each house on the street before trying my luck. After the usual exchange, the homeowner gives me some water. My standard where-I've-come-from-where-I'm-going chit-chat arouses no empathy, and I give up on the idea of the shower. Still, I ask permission to pitch my tent somewhere, anywhere.

"You have to ask the guy in charge."

I'm tired, hungry, and impatient, and I just want to go to bed. I'm not in the mood for the Native American reservation version of bureaucracy. "He lives in the white house behind the big tree."

Without knowing exactly why I should be worried about this pedantic regulation, I knock at the door of the small, white house, only to be told by a little old Native American woman that she is not the guy I want.

After a quick phone call, she tells me where to find my guy: "Take this road, which leads into town and talk to Philap Camaja. His place is just in front of the church."

I jump back on my bike, heading along the gravel road where their tribe leader presides. No wucking furries, mate. I spent six weeks on mainly unpaved roads in the Kashmir . . . this dinky 800-yard stretch I could ride backwards.

But this time, an evil spirit is lying in wait—my tire bursts. I should have known. Flat tires only happen at the end of the day, when I'm exhausted or when its pouring rain. No worries. I know that I was born under a lucky star, and each setback usually has its reward. I slowly walk my bike the last 400 yards or so, confident that the tribe leader will welcome me with open arms, as if I were a European explorer with whiskey and guns in tow.

I knock at the door. A woman answers. She mumbles something toward the back of the room. Philap Camaja is not there. I decide to wait for the tribe leader, the real one.

I remove all my saddlebags, dismantle the wheel, and take off the inner tube. There are holes everywhere. Three, just at a quick first glance. As I'm starting to repair the inner tube, a cramp shoots through my stomach like an electrical current. I drank about half a gallon of water in one big gulp before I got to town, and I've got to piss so bad, it's cutting me in two. I'd rather die on the spot than ask for any more help from that cold shrew looking at me through her window.

I receive the final blow when the tribe leader arrives. These two are so alike; they must love each other to bits. "You can put up your tent on the baseball field, but that's it."

I have no idea how I finally got done repairing my tire and putting back my saddlebags. The torture ended when I hit the ball out of the park, finding a great spot on the baseball field—right at home plate. Despite the tornado-like wind pummeling down on me, I somehow manage to pitch my tent, quick as a flash.

I've got neither the strength nor the inclination to prepare supper. To tell the truth, I'm not even hungry. I change states tomorrow—my only consolation.

I found out later that Camaja wasn't even the band leader.

DAY 810

Albuquerque, New Mexico—October 1, 1996

Nipping around the world is easier said than done. Fate has not finished with me yet. It was just letting me get a good night's sleep!

I've got a glorious day in store for me. I go find my bike, locked to the fence, to make sure that the repairs I made to the back wheel last night are holding up.

No. It can't be true! Another flat tire, but this time, it's the front wheel. I'm as hungry as a horse, but I can't get anything to eat until I get this crap tire fixed so I can leave this awful town.

I'm all out of spare tubes, so I'll have to repair the one already on the wheel. It's riddled with tiny pinholes, and all I've got left is this old glue I've been carrying around since Iran. Woe is me! New holes pop up whenever I reinflate my tire. I have to start from scratch. This vicious circle goes on for two-and-a-half hours. I pack my bags fast. I'm so afraid of touching the tires to the gravel that I lug the bike over my shoulder until I reach the paved road on the outskirts of town. Then, I shuttle back and forth between the baseball field and the edge of the road to off-load all of my gear. Those walking by might be asking themselves what use is a bike if you have to carry it on your back. It's all good. I'm finally ready to leave.

You guessed it. The back tire, which I hadn't been worried about, is now slowly deflating. I pump it up again hoping that it will hold out. If I have to, I'll pump it up again every couple of miles. With fingers crossed, I beseech my guardian angel to watch over me for the next few hours or just enough time to get to the next city, Albuquerque.

Forty miles later, eyes peeled on my wheels, I reach the outskirts of the city. I stop at the first restaurant in sight. The special of the day is meatloaf. I'm so hungry that I could eat roadkill.

I'm really into my meal when a native woman approaches and says, "I'm from Mesita, I saw you on the road this morning . . . I think you're very brave!"

I tell her briefly about my travels, and before leaving, she says to me, out of the blue, "Don't worry about your meal, it's on me!"

Surprised, I wave back at her, but she's already out the door.

I go into the city to get some glue and, most importantly, three new inner tubes. The bikeshop guy bursts out laughing when I tell him my flatly disappointing experiences. "Welcome to New Mexico: Flat Tire Heaven." He takes down a small bag, pinned to the wall, full of tiny thorns that look like long, thin needles. "Here's the cause of your problems! They stick to your wheels and follow you everywhere you go. That's why we call them 'hitchhikers.' They come from a shrub native to the desert and mostly grow alongside gravel roads." To avoid more flats, he recommends that I buy a super-tough inner tube, specially made for the desert states. Now that I've got rubber as thick as a gorilla's condom, I should be safe.

I ride twenty miles before I begin leaving the outer suburbs. After a refreshing shower directly from a hose at a gas station, I choose a small park close to the road and wait until dark before settling down. That way I avoid problems with anyone hanging about, or the cops for that matter.

Here I am thinking that my mountain days were over. I've just heard that it's a fifteen-mile uphill ride just outside of the city, and then the road goes down again until you reach the Mississippi. Is this some kind of a joke? The Mississippi is a full 750 miles away. I don't get it. How do you manage to go downhill so long without ending up ten thousand leagues under the sea?!

DAY 811
Moriarty, New Mexico—October 2, 1996

In the middle of the night, I start to feel a hard rain fall, and fall, and fall, so hard that I can't sleep. Ten minutes into it, water has seeped into my tent, soaking through my ground mat. In no time, the tent turns into a wading pool. My sleeping bag and my saddlebags, filled with clothes, are bobbing about in the water. It's pouring in from all sides, from high and low. What's even weirder is that, from the sound of it, the trucks don't seem to be driving on a wet road. I poke my head outside to get to the bottom of it. I can't believe my eyes. I've pitched my tent right in the middle of five watering hoses, and not those that go "chicka-chicka-chicka" endlessly through the night. Rather, these are the silent kind, which release a whole fire truck's worth of water up into the air. Because they're concealed in the grass, I didn't see them when I set up my tent. That's hi-tech for you. What's most frustrating is that they're located in the exact spot where I decided to pitch my tent and nowhere else. And I was worried about things that go bump in the night and local cops.

DAY 812
Santa Rosa, New Mexico—October 3, 1996

I'm up and about a good two hours before sunrise. I slept like a baby, but I'm hungry. Once I've demolished six eggs, baked beans, bread, peanut butter, two pints of water, a banana, an apple, a protein shake, and two chocolate bars, I get back on the bike feeling like a brand new man. Nature battles on, and so do I. I'm biking through the morning fog, rising so high that I wonder if I'm not also ascending to the heavens. Wait, I thought I was going down . . . down to the Mississippi, that is.

I'm ready for battle. Seventy-five miles in the bitter cold. Tomorrow, I attack Tucumcari and then breach the border of Texas. This evening, the night air seems particularly cold, certainly the chilliest I've felt for a long time.

DAY 813
San Juan, New Mexico—October 4, 1996

Finally, an ideal day for riding. There is a light wind at my back as I leave the mountains, light traffic, and delightful weather. In spite of two flats, I make the most of this gorgeous day to whizz through the last ninety miles in New Mexico.

Tomorrow, I will change time zones, leaving the Southwestern states and entering Texas. It's a tangible sign that I'm making real progress.

DAY 814
Vega, Texas—October 5, 1996

Some days, it feels like nothing can stop me. Other days, I want to scream, "Oh Mama, can this really be the end? Get me outta here!" A thunderstorm is passing through tonight, and my tent is completely drenched. It's raining feral cats and prairie dogs. I'm soaked. Everything is soaked. I've just heard that downtown Albuquerque is completely flooded, and the bridge over the river is closed. Since I was there three days ago, it has rained nonstop. We're getting the tail end of the storm here. If I wait for it to clear up, I'll be home sometime by the year 2000.

Decked out in a plastic garbage bag reinforced with duct tape, I charge onto the golden plains of Texas. Strangely enough, the sun comes out as I cross into Texas, as if the big, black cloud that promised to make my life difficult was intercepted at the border.

I meet a cyclist who has biked over 30,000 miles all over the United States. He insists that I'll never get to Montreal with the weather we're meant to get from now until November. "Go south for winter, you'll never make it north. You'll get stuck in the snow before you know it! I hope you have winter camping gear, because it's going to be cold, very cold!"

He's from Austin, Texas, and I imagine he might be a little more sensitive to the cold than I am. At least, I hope so. His advice just encourages me to go on, and, curiously enough, it helps me mentally prepare for the worst. I'm going to keep his advice in mind, and then bike north before Tennessee to bypass the Appalachian Mountains. I should also get warmer clothes, because I'm only carrying those leftover from Asia. I biked across Canada in thirty days, so I didn't expect to move at such a slow pace down here. The days are getting shorter, and I no longer have the spirit or the energy to push my machine as far as it will go. No doubt, I'll get home a month later than I had planned to, that is, mid-November—the start of winter.

The Texas landscape reminds me of the Canadian Prairies, which I've already biked across. Everything is as flat as a tack. Grain silos dot the horizon, here and there. On these vast plains, distance and time become elastic, where miles, yards, hours, and minutes are all interchangeable. I don't feel as though I've ridden anywhere, even after fifty-five miles. I stop. I'm knackered. I need to take a day off, but I'm not going to waste it on this hole of a town, where only a few no-hopers remain, clinging to memories of a more prosperous time.

DAY 815
Groome, Texas—October 6, 1996

My bike chain breaks and ends up forcing me to keep going after sunset. In fact, the end of each day is becoming ever-more painful and laborious. A friend gave some money so that I could spend the night in a hotel, but at $55 a night, I'm saving this luxury for my days off only. Tonight, I will pitch my tent behind the town's abandoned gas station, but tomorrow, at the break of dawn, I will check into a hotel. A hotel room is like an oasis for me, a creature comfort that breaks up the myriad miles of deserted desert I have to cross. There, I can stretch out on a real bed and listen to music as I study my maps.

I'm surprised to find that the water hose still works at this old gas station. My body has surely not forgotten its Nordic metabolism to be able to endure such a glacial shower, fully exposed to the howling wind.

* * *

Chapter 25

....

Not All Angels Have Wings

DAY 818
Clinton, Oklahoma—October 9, 1996

Goodbye Texas and howdy Oklahoma. No more fields as far as the eye can see. The landscape is hilly and strewn with trees. I'm in a pensive mood as I watch the sun set, and I keep thinking about the road I've traveled these last two years, two months, and twenty-five days to be exact. I'm at peace with myself, and I can see that my efforts have come to a head. I know I'll get there, but the price to pay is increasingly high. Yesterday went by without a hitch, but today, I took on a tornado. These days drain me completely. It's utterly demoralizing to be constantly battling against the cruel wind, my invisible enemy. When the wind unleashes its fury, no one can defeat it, not even the most stubborn of cyclists.

DAY 821
Chanders, Oklahoma—October 12, 1996

I'm in a world of pain. The wind is out to get me. They say it's always blustery out here. Judging by the wind turbines that line the roadsides, I believe it. This morning, for the first time, I just want to sleep in. My flame is flickering low.

The following days weigh on me, as if I had to climb the Himalayas . . . on a unicycle.

I wish that I would get more revved up the closer I get to home, but it's the exact opposite. When I think of my imminent return, I get a boost. But when I face up to reality, I feel listless.

DAY 823
Vinita, Oklahoma—October 14, 1996

I've got a lump in my throat. Again, I question whether I can see this through and come full circle. I'm at the end of my tether. The gulf that separates me from my goal might grow deeper as I ride on. I was thinking of taking a rest in two days time, but I can't go on. I have to stop here, right now. I'll book into the nearest hotel. Later, we'll see how it pans out. Home seems so far away.

DAY 825
Vinita, Oklahoma—October 16, 1996

I'm still in Vinita. After two days of total rest, my head swirls with unanswered questions. I'll cut my daily ride from seventy to fifty miles. For sure, I'm done with the 100-mile days. And no more campsite meals—I simply don't have the appetite or the energy to prepare them. I have to carefully manage all my resources, even financial. Plus, I'm going to triple my vitamin intake.

Before we separated in Tehran, my Nietzchean friend, Jean-Pierre, reminded me, "Courage, Pierre-Yves. What doesn't kill you makes you stronger."

Tomorrow, I'm getting back on the road, first thing.

DAY 826

Neosho, Missouri—October 17, 1996

I'm kind of panic-stricken. It's unbearable . . . I called Caroline, but she wasn't home.

Even though I left Vinita on a beautiful, sunny day, it's now freezing cold out. The temperature dipped from 80°F to 40°F. This cold spell was forecast, but I didn't expect the change to be so brutal.

It's pure insanity to put my body and mind through this. I implore my angel to show me the way: "If you're with me, let me know, and I'll keep going. Otherwise, I'll throw in the towel. I can't finish this trip under my own steam. Please, send a sign."

I look for a vacant lot to pitch my tent. The sun is setting, and it looks like tonight is going to be a cold one. My choice spot is at the back of a convenience store. The store manager gives me the OK to camp there, although he doesn't quite understand why I'm keen on camping on his back lot. The lumpy ground is more like a potato plot, but I don't care. I want to sleep and forget about everything, forget all the effort that I've put in since the first pedal push, all the effort that I'll never see come to fruition. I'm giving up.

My tent is fluttering under this savage, northern wind. My soul deadened, I unload my bike like a zombie. I don't bother to acknowledge the curious bystanders. All I could tell them is that my trip ends here. My head slouches down anytime anyone smiles at me. Leave me alone! I want to endure this pain all by myself. Surely, there's no one who could understand what I'm going through.

"You can stay at my place if you want!"

A tear in my eye, I rudely turn down his offer.

He insists: "It's gonna be a cold one tonight!" A moment or so passes before he adds, "You'll get a hot meal, plus you can take a shower and sleep in a nice, warm bed. If you like, I can help you to put your gear in the car, and you can follow me by bike to the house."

Sold, I toss all my stuff in the trunk of his car, and I am all his.

DAY 827
Neosho, Missouri—October 18, 1996

Here I am, rescued from the darkness. My angel has come through for me once again.

After a hot shower, a delicious supper, and a restful night, I wake up to the sound of music and the tantalizing smell of bacon—all due to the boundless hospitality of this generous couple. It's 6 AM, and we're already starting where we left off last night. I tell them everything. They are diehard cyclists, too, so they're interested in my whole story, including all my misfortunes. They understand what I'm going through and find the words to get me back on track. The atmosphere is sublime. It's been months since I've felt this good.

My host, Kelly, can't stop telling me how glad he is to have met me. He asks Laurie, his wife, to take a snap of us together, so he can prove to his friends that he took in a cyclist on a round-the-world tour. As if their welcome wasn't more than enough already, they come back with a pile of clothes: a GORE-TEX® cycling outfit, ski gloves, and a woolen balaclava. Everything to face the winter. I can't believe my eyes. I look at Laurie, dumbfounded. She tells me plainly that her husband has put on weight, and this stuff doesn't fit him anymore. Besides, he seems so happy to give them to me that I've got little choice but to accept them gratefully. No matter that the size isn't perfect, I'm in seventh heaven. I look like a kid who has just received a Tonka truck for his birthday.

"We're happy to contribute to your reaching your dream," they say. With heartfelt warmth, they hug me in their arms as if I were their own son.

Kelly bikes with me to the outskirts of town. I give him one last hug. Deeply moved, I say to him, "If I ever finish this journey, it'll be thanks to you guys!" I kept on saying thanks, but he interrupts me. "All the pleasure was ours." And since he's very religious, he adds, "Please, take good care of yourself, and may God bless you."

There is frost everywhere on this chilly fall morning. I get back on the road again. Yesterday, I was alone. Today, I'm not alone anymore.

DAY 829

Rolla, Missouri—October 20, 1996

If the only thing you think about is moving forward, you'll never get there. I'm my own worst enemy, just like in Iran. Upon leaving Neosho, I made a resolution to stop checking the map to see where I am, to stop calculating the distance left, and to stop looking at my watch for at least ten days. Moreover, I'm not allowed to daydream about my return home. I'll eat when I'm hungry and stop when I'm tired, no matter what time of day it is. It's not going to be easy to follow these new rules, as daydreaming has been such an important part of my daily routine since the beginning. I've made it through three consecutive days without breaking the rules, and I only have seven to go. In fact, that's the only thing I'm allowed to count: how many days I've managed to stick to my resolution.

DAY 831

St. Louis, Missouri—October 22, 1996

After such a flurry of lightning last night that I wondered whether I was going to end up electrocuted, I forget my helmet in a restaurant. I was so wrapped up in thought and plastic bags that it took me twenty miles down the track before I even noticed my helmet was actually missing. Fortunately, a Good Samaritan (and fellow Canadian), whom I met at the gas station where I realized the error, gave me a roundtrip lift to the restaurant to retrieve it. Forty-five minutes later, I'm on my way again, this time with a well-protected head but under driving rain, with poor visibility and the road flooded with water. I suddenly come upon the scene of an accident. A car is in the ditch . . . then another, and still another one. In all, I count eight wrecked cars! The road is blocked. Two injured passengers are lifted out of the ditch, whereas a third lies covered with a sheet. "He was only fifteen years old," says the ambulance driver, adding that it all happened barely forty-five minutes ago. I could have been right there in the ditch with them.

This stark image hits me hard, and I can't take my eyes off it. All of a sudden, two cops yell at me: "Get off the road, you're going to get yourself killed!" Their grim faces relax a bit once I tell them that I'm Canadian and that I'm just looking for the best route to follow. They have a quick discussion between themselves and tell me that the secondary road is in a very bad state with no shoulder. It's certainly not any safer, so they give me permission to continue on the highway. "Do your best to keep out of the way. At fifty miles an hour, all it takes is an inch of water for a car to hydroplane and hit you!" I look at the bottom of that ditch one more time before hitting the road again.

Chastened by what I've seen and exhausted by riding sixty miles in pouring rain and tree-destroying winds, I finally arrive at the home of Kelly's friends, who are waiting for me with open arms. What a great feeling to find myself once again with a real family. And with terrible weather forecast for the next few days, it couldn't have worked out better. I've regained my confidence, and I have a lot of faith that I'll make it. But there are still five whole days left until I'm allowed to daydream again.

I'll set my watch back one last time when I cross the Mississippi, just outside of St. Louis. I think I'm around 1,550 miles from home. Oops! I've already forgotten all about my resolution. Bravo, anyway!

DAY 841
Fayette, Illinois—November 1, 1996

I camp in a truck stop. Two strange men start rattling my tent, telling me that I'm not allowed to camp there. I get dressed quickly, hoping to settle this misunderstanding amicably. But these two lackeys tell me it's not up to them and that I should take it to the boss.

Calmly, as per usual and like I've done so many times before, I give him a short rundown on my travels and mention that I've been using these truck stops since the very beginning of my journey, without ever having been bothered. In fact, that's why I've never asked permission. After all, what difference does a little itty-bitty tent make when the whole parking lot is filled with trucks, anyway? Even before I end my pitch, he starts yelling that his precious truck lot is not a friggin' campground. I ask him to make an exception for just this one night, and I swear to him I'll be leaving very early tomorrow morning. He doesn't want to know. Worse still, he does not even want to listen to me. He keeps repeating it's not his problem and orders me to pack up sticks. It's freezing cold; all my gear is laid out for the night. I'm completely zonked, and I don't have a clue where I'm going to go. It's so late now. I feel my anger well up. I try again to get him on my side, but it's no use. I feel ridiculous that I've had to stoop to this troglodyte's level. If I'm being kicked out, I might as well get up on my soapbox, so I tell him what I really think. I don't hold back, and he ends up calling the cops.

I go back to the tent to pack everything up. As I'm about to leave, a patrol car arrives on the scene and intercepts me. After a brief discussion with the owner, the cops return and tell me the truck stop manager is entitled to refuse because it's his property. "I knew that, but he could have been more understanding and less narrow-minded," I say. My stomach is like a bowling pin.

I leave with my luggage piled willy-nilly on the bike. I look like a hobo, but I pique the interest of a young guy. I give him the abridged version of my situation, and he gets me permission to camp at a McDonald's managed by his friend. There, they treat me to a second dinner in exchange for a more elaborate version of my tale. Breakfast will be on them, too. I love it when my angel is at his post. He's the Employee of the Month, every month. . . .

DAY 843
Lafayette, Ohio—November 3, 1996

I might have overdone it today to get here, but it was worth it. I'm at the only bar in town, and the barmaid is hanging on my every word as I tell her my story. Meanwhile, the barflies, their elbows firmly planted on the bar, are deep into the football match. When she tells me that I'm her hero, the men look away from the screen for a moment. Soon after, they're just as impressed by my feats. They all have their own story to tell, but these are mere trifles compared to mine, or so they say. Many of them have ridden over the same roads throughout the United States as I have, but on a motorbike, and even then, the road seemed long for them. I would have never expected to be Mr. Popular in some small town in Ohio, and I'm flattered. Without having ordered it, a giant meal is set down in front of me.

Before I burst with a full stomach, a doggy bag comes to the rescue. When I finish my meal, I go back into the kitchen to thank the cooks. I feel right at home. After the cooks stuffed my pockets full of goodies, I leave the steaming hot kitchen and ultimately the warm company of my new bar buddies to be alone in my bitterly cold tent.

Back at my tent, the sky crashes down on my head. I forgot my bag of freshly laundered clothes in the bar and now everybody's left. In a frenzy, I pace around in circles, like a dog in a cage. Each half-day counts. If I wait for the bar to open at eleven tomorrow morning, I'll never reach Cleveland by tomorrow night. I run to the gas station across the street to ask them if they know the owner of the bar. His name is "Jeff," apparently. "Jeff who?" Nobody knows. I can't believe that in a town of 150 people, no one knows Jeff's last name. Everyone I ask starts to back away. Do I look like a hobo? (With my clean clothes still in the bar, I probably do.) I go to the police station, but the door is locked. A woman is hanging out her laundry, so I rush over to ask a few questions. She doesn't know Jeff, either. But maybe her husband knows him. Without hesitating for a moment, I walk into the house to talk to her husband. I explain to him why it's so important for me to get into touch with Jeff. The man sees how unnerved I am.

After three phone calls, we finally reach him. "Go back to the bar, and he'll open it for you within the half hour."

The Jeff I'm looking for turns up twenty minutes later. I'm so sorry to have bothered him at this time of the night. I go to bed numb with cold. No doubt about it, this one was all my fault. . . .

DAY 844
Mentor, Ohio—November 4, 1996

This morning, my clothes are so stiff that they can stand up by them-selves. I yelp as my nylon pants first touch my thighs. I dart outside the tent and jump up and down in an effort to get warm. There's no getting used to this.

Monday morning's reckless drivers are giving me the heebie-jeebies. There's no getting used to them, either. I'm riding toward Medina, where there are plenty of restaurants. I eat my breakfast with a nice, retired gentle-man. He picks up the tab. Breakfast also came with a side order of thick billows of Craven A smoke. Nothing's perfect.

Here I am, back on my bike. I'm riding on a roller coaster of a country road, rising and falling and rising and falling, on and on with no end in sight. Suddenly, I see the highway. It's beautiful—there's a shoulder, and the wind will be at my back. Although it's illegal to bike on a highway, I can't resist the temptation. I'm ecstatic, but not for long. After just a few moments on the highway, a police officer pulls me over. I've ridden on several other highways in the Midwest without being caught. This time, the traps have got me.

It's no use telling him that the secondary routes are a thousand times more dangerous than the highway. I guess I'll keep going my merry way, zigzagging across Cleveland's potholed streets. Although I get lost more than once, I finally make it across Cleveland, a city of 1 million people. My only comfort is that I'll be sleeping in a hotel tonight, and that I'll get the day off tomorrow. The one night cost me $45, all gone up in smoke—a good reason to camp out as often as I can.

DAY 845
Mentor, Ohio—November 5, 1996

"It's Election Day!" That means a day off for me. I think Clinton is going to win this one.

But a "day off" is never really a day off when you're on a bike tour. There's always something to do. I had to bike ten miles just to get to the laundromat.

The weather is beautiful, but they're predicting snow this weekend. I leave Ohio tomorrow and valiantly ride into my last American state: New York. I'm practically home, yet there's still 930 miles to go.

This just in: Clinton is reelected.

DAY 847
Silver Creek, New York—November 7, 1996

I'm too eager to get home. I biked seventy-five miles today. That's too much. I'm starting to understand what this vicious cycle is all about: the bigger day I put in, the more tired I am. The more tired I am, the less I feel up for another big day, and the further I feel from home. Yet I'm amazed how forgiving the human body is. I feel much better after a good night's sleep. At least, that's done the trick up to this point.

DAY 848
Elden, New York—November 8, 1996

If I weren't lying in my tent with my bags all to one side, it would just fly off like a kite. Later on, it's the rain's turn to do damage. Bundled up in plastic bags, I manage to doze off a little until dawn . . . I can finally pack up camp.

The daytime is no more promising than my night of unrest. There's a low-pressure front wreaking havoc through Pennsylvania, and it's about to hit the Finger Lakes area soon. Rivers are gushing along the badly damaged roads. The temperature hovers around the freezing mark, and the rain is fiercely cold. After several hours on the road, I take refuge in a laundromat. I eat and I dry off a little, but I soon hop on my bike again. I have no idea what's keeping me going.

I camp out illegally in a park, as far I can get from the path. The police seem to be on constant patrol. I'm regaining my spirits, little by little. The last twenty-four hours put me to the test, so much so that I can barely manage to hold my pen. I've dedicated this day to my grandfather, who is in the hospital. I'm sure that he was the one who kept me going.

DAY 852
Adams, New York—November 12, 1996

I've prayed so hard for the rain to stop, and my wish has been granted: it's snowing now. I can't see heaven or earth. There are already six inches of dense snow on the ground. The roads are impossible to drive on, and traffic is gridlocked. The restaurants are closed. In my snowman disguise, I push my bike to the gas station. The attendant greets me and offers up a few words of consolation. Somewhat. "Ten inches fell up north, but don't worry, it'll all be melted before noon." He's right.

What a day, and it's not even over yet! I head to the hotel where I planned to stay the night, but it closed its doors years ago. The owner was assassinated. I've been drenched in water for the last fifty miles, but I have no other choice but to pitch my tent over a blanket of snow. The temperature drops to 17°F, and, according to the forecast, this cold snap will be over only by Friday, November 15—the day I'm scheduled to reach Montreal.

DAY 853
Toward Cornwall, Canada—November 13, 1996

I wake up in the middle of a snowstorm. Six miles down the road, I manage to escape the whiteout completely, as if I've jumped into a whole new world. I'm dry as a bone for the rest of the day.

DAY 854
Cornwall, Canada—November 14, 1996

"Welcome to Canada. Do you have anything to declare?" I'm tempted to parrot Oscar Wilde's "I've nothing to declare but my genius" but settle for, "I'm happy to be back home." I feel like yelling out for joy, but the customs official's indifference renders me speechless. Like he probably does a hundred times a day, he stamps my passport and listlessly signals for me to move forward.

It's been two years and four months.

I race through Cornwall, so I can get as close to Montreal as possible. Tomorrow, a team of journalists from Radio-Canada will greet me in the city. I have only eighty miles left.

DAY 855
Toward Montreal—November 15, 1996

It's 8°F (that's -13°C back in Canada). With the windchill, it's actually 2°F (-17°C). I spent last night encamped on a vacant lot on the banks of the St. Lawrence River. It's still dark when I leave this morning. There's no way I could have endured another day like this if it weren't my last before reaching Montreal.

* * *

Chapter 26

·····································

Indeed, the Earth is Not Flat

DAY 862

L'Étape, Quebec, Canada—Parc des Laurentides—November 22, 1996

For four days now, I've been watching the mile after mile endlessly scroll by.

After a series of radio and TV interviews, people have been recognizing me everywhere I go. A few will even rush over to congratulate me. Their constant encouragement gives me wings.

"Let's go, man, you're getting near the end!"

"Go Pierre-Yves! Go Chicoutimi!"

"Step on it, not far to go now!"

"Keep it up, you're almost there!"

Little by little, I'm starting to realize what I've achieved. Many other people might also have had this dream. I've pulled it off thanks to everyone who has helped make this trip possible. I'm feeling a whole mix of emotions. I've been gone for such a long period. This whole time, I've been dreaming of making it across the world, and soon this great adventure will end. I'm in a state of shock. The last few weeks have been so challenging that it's hard to believe the end is approaching. I would have liked to express how I feel, but something holds me back. I learned so much during my travels. And I suffered a lot as well. I cannot cry for joy without my tears betraying me. I'm like a survivor who's expected to be delighted to be coming home. Each time I catch myself smiling, I remind myself of how much it cost me to get to this point. My body is totally worn out, but my heart, my very core, is keeping me going. I don't have the strength left to dream. I can only hope that tomorrow will unfold smoothly. My last day on the road.

Tonight, the hotel manager of L'Étape lets me stay in his room for the night. It's a heavenly gift, served up on a silver platter. Quebeckers are an extraordinary people. The other day, someone from Grondines kindly offered me accommodation for the night. In Louiseville, another guy pulled over to give me $50 to spend on a hotel room. There's nothing that can top receiving such heartfelt words of encouragement in your own language. Everywhere I go in this beautiful province, I feel totally at home. Even so, tomorrow's my real homecoming.

DAY 863: MY LAST DAY
Quebec, Canada—Saturday, November 23, 1996

After a restless night, I leave more determined than ever. The road ahead is clear. It didn't snow, and Mother Nature is on my side. Throughout this journey, she's given me the occasional rough ride, regularly subjecting me to her supreme might. Today, she gracefully accepts my victory. She's turned the page, and soon enough, I will too.

Perched on my bike seat, I feel gloriously triumphant. In a trance, I watch the inches flash past under my front wheel. I feel like I'm cruising on an ocean of asphalt as my spirit sails over a sea of tranquility. There's not a single car on the road. Blissfully, I savor these last moments of intense happiness.

Perhaps too much good feeling can't last long, which was confirmed by an abrupt change in the weather. The odd snowflakes floating in the sky now become full-blown flurries, carpeting the whole area white. After only six miles, there are several inches of snow on the ground. I can't see any car tracks to follow. I go downhill, straddling the bike frame, with my feet sliding on the ground on each side to keep my balance. I'm carrying so much weight, and my narrow tires provide little traction. I need to concentrate hard to prevent myself from toppling over. Trying to ride in these conditions is nearly suicidal.

A muffled roar behind me snaps me out of my bubble. I look back to see a billowing white cloud from which emerges an ominous rumbling. I didn't go round the world, only to be cleaned up by this snowplow, now bearing down on me! I get over to the side fast and frantically wave so the driver can see me. This evil monster slows down somewhat but passes so close to me that a wave of plowed snow pins me to the ground. I'm stuck on the side of the road in a snow bank up to my thighs, with a cascade of snow rolling down my neck and back.

With the snow falling heavily, the increasing traffic gives me more worries. Since I stick to the car tracks in the middle of the road, I have to stay aware of the danger posed by passing cars. When it comes to trucks, I make a bee line for the shoulder snowbank, at the risk of injuring myself. Although I'm dead set on increasing my speed, the miles I have yet to ride seem never ending. Pushing on is just plain idiocy. I am playing a game of Russian roulette, and I won't put the gun down. I just can't give up; this need to go on is getting the better of me.

A cop shows up to escort me. He's received a plethora of profanity-filled calls from irate truck drivers who claim to have seen a madman riding a bike on this very road. I escort the police cruiser (he drives behind me) for about ten miles.

My brother François arrives on the scene to take over the escort. He thanks the police officer then looks at me with pride. His beaming smile says it all. I'm so happy to see him again, but I've also got the last stretch of road on my mind. Even though I don't have far to go, I'm worried that my luck will run out before I get there. My guardian angel surely is exhausted, too, and I'm worried that he'll let me fall into the devil's clutches.

Under normal circumstances, I would stop for the night, but today, I've decided to gamble my life against this folly.

Chicoutimi—Twenty-one kilometers. Numb from such a stressful final stretch, it takes a few minutes for it all to sink in. I have to keep reminding myself that I've finally done it. I went round the entire world under my own steam. If I had let myself cry all my repressed tears contained in this moment, the area would have experienced another torrential downpour and more devastating floods like it did the previous summer. Fortunately, I'm more in a mood to celebrate than to cry. I have reached the end of my dream. Thank heavens to all those who sent me positive energy and good vibes, I'm returning home safe and sound.

1:30 PM. I arrive at the Chicoutimi golf club, six miles from the city center. Family and friends line the road. The press is out in force, too—radio, TV, newspaper reporters—everyone is there. I did not expect such a warm reception. I'm touched to see all my family and friends again. Curiously, nobody dares to approach. I'm the center of attention—surrounded by a throng who watches my every move. I feel like I'm in an invisible cage. Silence reigns. Each person wants to experience my moment of triumph. I am blessed. It would only take a single word to break the magic of this instant, even if it were the best word anyone could possibly say.

Snowflakes drift down from the sky like softly falling stars. I am covered with snow, and sweat is freezing up on my skin, but I wish that this moment could be forever suspended in time. Caroline, Lili, and Élizabeth, a childhood friend, finally break the ice and sweep me into their arms. My father stands back, visibly proud of his son. Soon, they all come over to me one by one, as if they were offering their condolences.

After monopolizing the first few moments of my return, the mass of reporters and photographers leave, and it's time to hop back on the bike. With my friend Jean-François riding beside me and with a honking, tooting cavalcade of supporters, I ride the last mile or so to the Town Hall, where an official reception has been organized in my honor.

On my bike, I feel invincible. Nothing can stop me. With no hint of their imminent retirement, my legs pump with effortless ease. As tough as it has been, all my gargantuan efforts come down to only a few inches, here and there, on a giant map of the world. All those inches have finally added up to today, and so now I have proof positive that the world is not flat. Indeed, it's beautifully round.

It's four o'clock in the morning. I partied all night with my friends. I'm lying in my own bed. For the first time, I'm not pondering on what I want to achieve, but rather, I'm musing about what I have just accomplished. My eyelids are heavy, but behind them lie images that can never fade: the shining faces of the Tibetan kids, the sweaty smell of a salt-of-the-earth Kashmiri worker, the rich aromas of Malaysian cuisine, the cold hand of the poor Kurdish beggar, the solitary anguish of a freezing cold night in the middle of the Iranian desert, the peace I found on the highest mountain passes in the world.

It was a crazy, fabulous dream. Now forged into precious, indelible memories.

And an invaluable launching pad for future dreams.